Accosting the
Golden Spire

Throughout the usual work of accountants, there is the constant pressure to follow the principles of GAAP. Audit procedures are prescribed and due adherence to the rules will produce statements of historical results and current fiscal condition, which meet all the criteria.

—Melvin I. Shapiro, CPA

Accosting the Golden Spire

A Financial Accounting Action Adventure

Fourth Edition

D. Larry Crumbley

Christine Betts

Stacy A. Mastrolia

Robert "Zeke" Sarikas

CAROLINA ACADEMIC PRESS

Durham, North Carolina

Library of Congress Cataloging-in-Publication Data

Names: Crumbley, D. Larry, author. | Betts, Christine. | Mastrolia, Stacy, author. | Sarikas, Robert.
Title: Accosting the golden spire : a financial accounting action adventure / by D. Larry Crumbley, Christine Betts, Stacy Mastrolia, and Robert Sarikas.
Description: Fourth edition. | Durham, North Carolina : Carolina Academic Press, LLC, [2019] | Includes bibliographical references and index.
Identifiers: LCCN 2018059100 | ISBN 9781531012649 (alk. paper)
Subjects: LCSH: Taxation--United States--Fiction.
Classification: LCC PS3553.R77 A33 2019 | DDC 813/.54--dc23
LC record available at https://lccn.loc.gov/2018059100
e-ISBN 978-1-5310-1265-6

CAROLINA ACADEMIC PRESS, LLC
700 Kent Street
Durham, North Carolina 27701
Telephone (919) 489-7486
Fax (919) 493-5668
www.cap-press.com

Printed in the United States of America

Dedicated to our families

Contents

Preface

This supplementary text may be used near the end of a principles of accounting course, at the beginning of an intermediate accounting course, or in an accounting ethics course. The educational novel would be ideal for an MBA program which has a light coverage of accounting or could also be used in CPA firms' in-house training programs.

Accosting the Golden Spire: A Financial Accounting Action Adventure mixes financial fraud, crime, ethics, and accounting together to provide a better way of learning the accounting process. If used as a supplement to an accounting course or a principles of finance course, this gripping and at times humorous novel provides a painless way of learning many accounting and finance principles. This suspenseful novel put accounting concepts into words a novice can understand and enjoy. Since much of the plot is in foreign countries, the book could be used in an introductory international accounting or finance course.

Lenny Cramer, a professor at the Wharton School, operates a small forensic accounting firm. He teaches, testifies before Congress, and appears as an expert witness in a court battle. The real action occurs when he investigates financial fraud in a friend's jade shop. This investigative accountant uncovers a plot to steal treasures from a remote Asian country in political turmoil.

Featuring a sleuth who handles balance sheets and income statements the way most detectives handle guns, the humorous characters put accounting and business concepts into real-life individual and business decisions. Along the way business practices and political controversies, contemporary individual and corporate planning, forensic accounting, tax fraud and avoidance, and the dynamic and exciting life of CPAs and financial consultants are elucidated in a way both students and instructors will find gripping as well as informative.

The novel approach is an excellent substitution for a dull practice set and is a flexible teaching tool to overcome boredom in the classroom. The concepts and attitudes a novel teach last long after the dull facts in a textbook are forgotten. We suggest that you do not spoon-feed your students. Add some excitement and adventure.

Classroom tests of the third edition and the previous two published editions have demonstrated repeatedly that students enjoy reading instructional thrillers, and they learn the accounting concepts more readily than through traditional texts. Some testimonials are listed below:

> "Proves that the phrase 'suspenseful accounting' is not necessarily an oxymoron."
>
> — *Wall Street Journal*

> "Master of the teaching novel, a new form of instruction designed to explain to students what CPAs really do."
>
> — *Accounting News*

> "He focuses on protagonists like the forensic accountant—the investigator of ledgers—allowing the otherwise dry material to take on the aura of mystery. The dramatic intrigue, in turn, helps the student-reader to retain the principles."
>
> — Administrator

> "I had never read an accounting novel before. It is a 'novel' idea which helped me to want to read more. Usually accounting books are rather dry. Making the topic more interesting and adding drama and humor is important in teaching. It keeps the learner engaged. I enjoyed reading *Golden Spire* very much."
>
> — *Accounting Major,*
> *California State University, Northridge*

Discussion, true/false, and multiple-choice questions are available to adopters.

D. Larry Crumbley, Ph.D., CPA, CFF, MAFF, CRFAC, FCPA,
Louisiana State University

Christine Betts, CPA, MST, EA,
Franklin Pierce University

Stacy A. Mastrolia, Ph.D., CPA, CGMA,
Bucknell University

Robert "Zeke" Sarikas, Ph.D., CPA,
Eastern Washington University

Accosting the
Golden
Spire

One

I'm not sure I'm the fall guy in the sense of the word. As far as spears in the breast are concerned, I don't mind spears in the breast. It's knives in the back that concern me.
—Donald T. Regan

Frank Harrison liked to dress in white clothes. To him, white clothes went best with his dark features, and at the same time, conveyed a sense of freshness and an aura of serenity. As he looked at himself in the mirror, he was pleased by the appearance of his white linen, double-breasted suit with no vents and double-pleated full slacks. He would feel cooler in the sweltering heat outside.

White clothing has a subtle appeal of luxury and worldliness which dates to the days when dry cleaning was inaccessible to the masses. Frank liked this feeling of superiority. He also felt that wearing white gave him an edge over those individuals who met him for the first time.

"That woman had better be ready," he muttered to himself. Frank hated being late and hated being kept waiting even more. He glanced at his watch. 7:42. Plenty of time to get to Angela's by 8:10 and Mellini's at 9:00 for his dinner reservation.

Frank loved seafood risotto—especially the way Mellini's prepared it. They used genuine Arborio short-grain Italian rice from the Po Valley of Italy. This type of rice plumped up and became creamy when cooked in chicken broth, but the rice must be stirred constantly with a wooden spoon over consistent medium heat. Otherwise, the

3

rice will stick. Mellini's prepared it just right and served it with clams, mussels, and shrimp.

"There," he said, placing a red boutonniere in his lapel. Another glance at his watch. 7:46. "Time to leave," he thought to himself, picking up his keys before he went out the door of his Center City townhouse.

"Rats! I'll kill the mutt!" he said as he stepped in some dog excrement outside his house. He began dragging his right white leather shoe along the sidewalk. Frank spotted a little patch of green grass across Front Street and began to wipe his shoe on the grass.

"Good-for-nothing dog," he muttered as he walked to his car. It was now 7:49 and Frank knew it took only fifteen minutes to get to Angela's place. He started to relax.

As Frank began to cross the street to go to his car, he suddenly heard a splash. Too late to jump away, he was sprayed with dirty water when a passing van drove through a puddle of water in the street.

"No!" he raged as he pounded his right fist on the hood of a parked light blue Chevrolet that was also dripping with dirty water from the splash. Frank stared down at his trousers and saw the effects of the splash. His jacket was stained as well as his shirt. Only his red boutonniere escaped unscathed.

Furious, Frank walked back to his house to change. He knew that he would undoubtedly be late for his date with Angela, and that fact just infuriated him more.

As he approached his house he saw a brown cocker spaniel beginning to raise its leg against his door. Frank became incensed.

"You. You're the cause for all this," he thought to himself. "I'll fix you," he muttered.

With an insincere smile, Frank approached the dog slowly, being careful where he stepped to avoid a repeat of his previous predicament. In a sweet tone he said to the dog, "Hi, fella. How're you doing? You're a good dog."

The dog looked up at Frank with big brown eyes and began to wag its tail as Frank approached. "That's a good dog. Would you like to come inside with your friend, Frank?" he asked. The dog tilted its head to the side, tail still wagging, looking at him.

"Come on, come on, fella. Come on in, fella. It's okay. Frank's got something nice for you. There you go. It's okay," Frank said, opening the door.

After staring for what seemed the longest time, the cocker spaniel went into Frank's home, carefully sniffing the floor as it entered.

Frank immediately walked to the kitchen. "I've got something special for you," he said, opening his refrigerator door. He pulled out a little piece of ground beef and said, "Here you are, fella. It's okay."

Frank laid the beef on the floor near the dog. The dog began to sniff at the beef. Then it carefully licked a little bit of the meat to decide if it was desirable. Finding it appealing, the dog soon ate it and began to wag its tail quickly.

"Good boy!" exclaimed Frank. "Do you want some more? Here you are." This time the dog ate it out of Frank's hand. It was clear that the dog was beginning to both like and trust Frank.

"How would you like to take a nice warm bath? That's a good boy! Come on! Come on, fella," Frank said, walking up the stairs.

The cocker spaniel, confident that it had found a new friend and possible master, dutifully followed Frank up the stairs.

As he looked at himself again in the mirror, Frank began to calm down. He was about six-foot-one and one hundred seventy-five pounds with dark hair. He was certainly not the type of man who was physically imposing, but he had a sleek look about him. He also believed he had a certain smoothness about him that made him irresistible to women.

Frank began to turn his attention to Angela. He checked his watch. 8:20. He decided to call her on the phone and let her know that he was going to be late.

"Angela? This is Frank. I got a little tied up with something here, but I am leaving in about five minutes. I should be there around twenty of nine."

"Okay, Frank," said Angela. "What time is our dinner reservation?"

"Nine o'clock. We might have to rush a little, but we should make it."

"Okay, see you in a few minutes, Frank. Bye."

"Bye."

Frank again placed the red boutonniere in his white lapel. "It isn't as nice as my other white suit," he thought to himself, looking in the mirror, "but it'll do. Besides, I'm late."

Frank quickly headed for the door. As he left his house he glanced at his watch. 8:25. He should be able to get to Angela's by 8:40 if nothing went wrong.

This time Frank made it to his white Nissan 370Z without incident. Traffic was rather light for this time of night in Philadelphia, and Frank began to make good time in driving to Angela's South Philadelphia row house. In Philadelphia, many of the downtown streets are one-way and often closed to vehicular traffic. Since it was after eight at night Frank decided to proceed west on Walnut from his Front Street address. As he approached Fifth and Walnut, he glanced to his right and could see police barricades two blocks north around Fifth and Market. Independence Hall, the Liberty Bell, and many other historical sites were being decorated in anticipation of the arrival of a number of tourists for Philadelphia's annual Fourth of July celebration in a few weeks. He was glad that he would be back from his trip to the Far East in time for the festivities.

Frank knew that the traffic lights were timed on both Chestnut and Walnut Streets, so he drove between 25 and 30 miles per hour. Hopefully, he would not have to stop for a red light the entire way. Frank was making excellent time since most of the businesses in Center City Philadelphia closed at night except for restaurants, movies, and theaters. He continued to drive past many closed stores on the largely barren streets that were well lit by the bright street lights shaped like old-fashioned gas lamps. Suddenly, Frank decided to turn north on 10th Street to pass by the jade shop of which he was part owner.

The shop was located on Sansom Street, which is a small side street between the major arteries of Chestnut and Walnut Street. This section of Sansom Street was known as "Jeweler's Row" because of the large number of jewelry shops located in this area. Prior to the construction of suburban shopping malls, anyone buying jewelry in the metropolitan Philadelphia area either shopped at Jeweler's

Row or bought jewelry at an excellent discount because of "the low overhead" from the trunk of an automobile from a guy named Lefty who was known around the neighborhood as a dealer of hot merchandise. While business was not quite as good as it had been in its heyday, many Philadelphians still came to Sansom Street to shop because the huge selection of jewelry stores in a concentrated area allowed most customers to find whatever they were seeking.

Even though jade was a sideline for Frank, his knowledge of jade was highly regarded among those in the profession. Frank's main line of business was his consulting firm, Kuaker City Consulting, Inc. His firm did a great deal of consulting for many prominent businesses in the city. He competed with many national and regional CPA firms. Since Kuaker City Consulting was one of the largest consulting firms in Philadelphia, Frank had many contacts throughout the city.

Frank was a little concerned when he formed the partnership with Dana Scott. Through a mutual friend they discovered that they were both bidding to buy the same jade shop. Frank called Dana and told her, "We should be in partnership together. A partnership's income is taxed only once as part of the owner's share in the business. A corporation's income is taxed twice—once at the corporate level as part of corporate income, and again at the stockholder level as a tax on dividend income." He was able to talk Dana into a partnership, Frank suspected, because Dana was short of working capital.

Frank wanted to make sure that Dana Scott was a responsible person before he entered into a partnership agreement. Frank knew that in a partnership, mutual agency exists, which means that if one partner signs an agreement involving the partnership, the other partner is just as responsible for the agreement as the partner who physically signs it. He did not know if Dana realized it, but a partnership with an irresponsible individual could lead to financial disaster. Unlike in a corporation where there is limited liability to the owners (and stockholders can only lose their original investment in most cases), a partnership provides unlimited liability to the owners.

Frank's investigation of Dana Scott convinced him that she was an intelligent, responsible businessperson with whom he could deal. To be on the safe side, however, Frank placed many of his personal assets in the name of Kuaker City Consultants to limit his liability should something unforeseen occur with the partnership. This strategy would protect these assets from seizure to satisfy creditors of the partnership. He knew that Dana was unaware of his actions.

All was peaceful around his jade shop as he drove by and saw the metal cage around the front window. Almost all retailers in this area had such cages in front of their windows to guard against theft and vandalism after closing. The jade shop also saved some money on insurance premiums due to this additional security.

His thoughts were interrupted as he turned back onto Walnut and continued west until he turned on Broad. Broad Street was Frank's favorite in Philadelphia. His consulting firm was located just a block north of here at Broad and Chestnut. City Hall was one block north of his firm at Broad and Market. Broad Street should be 14th Street [in Philadelphia the numbered streets run north and south], but the number fourteen had been skipped. But without question, Broad is the major street in Philadelphia. Broad runs the entire length of the city in an almost complete straight line with City Hall directly in the middle at Broad and Market Streets. Market Street is the dividing line between north and south in the city.

With City Hall as large as life in his rearview mirror, Frank saw that Broad Street was already decorated for Independence Day. Flags were hanging from wires above the street, and red, white, and blue bunting was wrapped around the light poles. Soon, on his right, he saw the imposing image of the Union League at Broad and Spruce. The Union League was an organization that was exclusively male until the mid-1980s and was headquartered in an old red stone building shaped like a castle, with various flags hanging outside its windows. Just about every important Philadelphia businessperson and politician were members. Frank was, and he saw many business decisions and political deals made on its premises.

"Watch it, jerk!" he yelled as a yellow taxi with an advertisement for an Atlantic City casino on its roof swerved in front of him.

Frank continued south on Broad and began to enter some more residential areas. Trees became more visible as Frank began to pass row house after row house much like the blue-collar area where he had grown up in Southwest Philadelphia. Frank began to think about Angela. This would be his first date with her. Angela was the type of girl he liked: 24 and a high school graduate. Frank liked girls who were not too bright, because he felt they were easier to intimidate.

Frank was not interested in a serious relationship with any woman. He had been married for six months—fifteen years ago. He was distrustful of women ever since his mother left his father when Frank was only twelve. He preferred instead to win over any pretty face he saw just for the night and not worry about tomorrow. He saw women as sexual objects with the ability to handle some domestic work. But Frank Harrison was smart enough to keep his opinion of women as private as possible, and as a good executive he made exceptions. After all, he did have a woman as a business partner.

As he parked his car in front of Angela's house, Frank was pleased. Normally, it is very difficult to find a place to park in many of the residential neighborhoods of Philadelphia. Not only was Frank able to find a place to park, but it was right in front of Angela's house. He felt the night just might turn out to be successful after all. It was 8:37 and they had an excellent chance to make their dinner reservation. He could taste the seafood risotto.

Frank walked up the steps to Angela's row home and rang the bell. Like thousands of other row homes in Philadelphia, one had to walk up three steps to reach the doorway of the three-story brick structure. As was typical of many South Philadelphia neighborhoods, some people were sitting out on the steps in front of their homes talking to their neighbors or watching what was going on along the street.

"Hi, Angela, you ready?"

"Hi, Frank. No, not yet. Why don't you come in and wait?"

"All right."

Frank was immediately seething. "How could she not be ready?" he said to himself. "Do you think you'll be much longer?" Frank asked, looking at his Rolex, which now indicated that it was 8:42.

"About five more minutes. There's beer in the refrigerator if you're thirsty."

"You know we have a reservation at 9:00 at Mellini's."

"I shouldn't be much longer."

Frank began to pace. "That idiot," he thought to himself, growing more impatient by the minute. "She's not attractive enough to take this long."

It was now 8:45. Frank estimated that it took 20 to 25 minutes to get to Mellini's from Angela's house. He grunted.

"Maybe I should call the restaurant and tell them we are going to be late."

"Whatever you think is best, Frank. I'm going to be only a few more minutes."

Frank picked up the phone and called Mellini's.

"Good evening, Mellini's Restaurant. This is Vito. May I help you?"

"Yes, my name is Harrison. I have a reservation for two at 9:00, and we're running a little late. Will there be a problem with my reservation?"

"Well, sir, our policy is to hold our reservations for ten minutes before we open up your table. We are particularly busy tonight, so I do not think we will be able to hold your table beyond 9:10."

Frank looked at his watch. 8:49. "Is it possible to change my reservation to a later seating?"

"I am very sorry, sir, but our only other seating this evening is 9:45 and we are booked solid at that time."

"Surely you can do something for me! I am one of your best customers."

"Believe me, Mr. Harrison, I would like to help you out, but I cannot. We are booked solid. There is nothing I can do."

Frank began to get angry. Frank liked to think of himself as a big shot. He did not like people when they did not try to give him special privileges. He also felt that he could intimidate Vito.

"I don't think you understand. I'm Frank Harrison. I have dinner at your restaurant three or four times a month. Do you expect me to believe that there is nothing you can do for me?"

"Sorry, Mr. Harrison. If you would like, I can get our manager, Mr. Orsini, to talk with you."

"Yes, get him," Frank almost shouted.

Frank looked at his watch. It was now 8:52 and Angela was still upstairs. "What in the world could be taking her so long?" he wondered. Before he had any more time to get angry with Angela, a voice came on the phone.

"Hello, this is Ray Orsini. May I help you?"

"I'm Frank Harrison, and I have a reservation for 9:00 that I would like to have held for me or changed to 9:45."

"Mr. Harrison, the best I can do for you is to hold your reservation until 9:10. We have a large crowd this evening, and I cannot possibly hold your reservation beyond that time."

"I have dinner at your restaurant at least three or four times a month. Is this how you treat loyal customers?"

"I would like to help you, Mr. Harrison, but it's not possible. I am sorry."

"You are no better than your lackey Vito. How can you treat good customers this way? Didn't you ever hear of goodwill?"

"I know all about goodwill, sir, that is why—"

"You don't know a single thing about goodwill. Goodwill is the value of establishing a good name. In accounting, goodwill is an intangible asset that equals the excess of the purchase price of an entity over the sum of the fair values of all its identifiable assets less its liabilities. You people seem to be trying to create negative goodwill by creating a reputation that you show no favoritism for your good customers." Although Frank knew a company was not permitted to capitalize internally-generated goodwill on its balance sheet, he was determined to make his point anyway.

"I'm sorry you feel that way, Mr. Harrison. We appreciate your patronage, but there is nothing I can do tonight. Would you like to make a reservation for another night?"

"Fine." With that Frank slammed down the phone and began muttering to himself, "I'll fix those haughty blue bloods."

Frank was very sensitive about his blue-collar background. Frank's father was an electrician in a General Electric plant in Southwest Philadelphia where Frank was born and raised, and unlike many of his clients and business associates, Frank had to work his way through school at Temple University. Many people he dealt with professionally respected Frank for his business capabilities, but it took time for him to prove himself. Early in his career, he had been passed over by potential clients who had gone to Ivy League schools—like the University of Pennsylvania's Wharton School or other prominent private schools like Villanova University located in Philadelphia's exclusive Main Line—because they felt that Frank's bachelor's degree from Temple and MBA from Drexel University did not qualify him to do high-level consulting. Frank felt that he had to work harder than others to establish himself as a well-respected consultant.

Although he was now very successful, snide comments were still made about both his alma mater and his socioeconomic background. Frank knew that many of his clients felt that he did not have the so-called "proper breeding," and try as he might to ignore it, he was still bothered by it. Frank did find some solace in knowing that many of those rich snobs paid him good money for his Temple University knowledge, rather than hiring another firm composed entirely of Wharton graduates. Nonetheless, Frank always remained suspicious of those who considered themselves among the upper crust of society.

"Hi."

Frank turned around. Finally, Angela was ready. She was smiling. The expression in her dark brown eyes indicated that she was oblivious to everything else in the world except what Frank thought of her appearance. She wanted to be complimented. "They all do," he thought, but Frank was not in the mood for paying compliments.

"Well, I hope you're happy. Because you are so late we missed our dinner reservation. Now what are we going to do for dinner?"

"I'm sorry, Frank, but I didn't know."

"What do you mean you didn't know? I told you we had a dinner reservation at 9:00."

"I forgot, but you were the one who was late. You even called."

"Listen, idiot, I know I was late, but when I got here you still were not ready."

Frank was extremely angry now. How dare she try to blame him for being late? He took a deep breath and looked at her. She obviously was astonished at being spoken to in the tone of voice Frank used.

It was clear she did not like being called an idiot. At this point, Frank did not care. She was not as attractive as he had thought she was when he first met her at a Center City bar the previous night. The darkness of the bar and the drinks he'd had must have made her more appealing to him than she was here in the bright light. But he did have to admit that she had a nice figure. *What was that country/western song? "The Girls Get Prettier at Closing Time."*

"I won't have some old man talk to me like that," said Angela in a trembling voice. "Get out and take your nasty attitude with you."

Angela had struck a nerve. Frank was thirty-eight years old, but he felt that he looked ten years younger. He worked hard at maintaining a youthful appearance by working out daily at the gym and using a tanning machine. He loved to boast to people that he had the same size waist he had had in ninth grade. To have Angela call him old was more than he could tolerate.

"Who are you calling old, moron?"

Angela, in a combination of screaming and crying, shrieked, "Get out! Get out now!"

"Fine! You want me to leave? No problem. I'm out of here, baby, but no one talks to Frank Harrison like that and gets away with it." Frank preferred to use his own name whenever possible as a form of self-promotion.

As Frank went towards the front door, he noticed a small glass vase sitting on a fragile looking end table by the door. As he went out the door Frank slammed it hard enough to hear the windows vibrate and a crashing sound of the vase hitting the floor above the sound of Angela's screaming voice.

"No!" Angela shouted as she began to sob uncontrollably. As Frank got into his car he could hear two elderly women out on their step talking.

"I wonder if this one beat up poor Angela."

"He looks like the type who would like to hit women, Rita. You can never trust men with white suits unless they look like Antonio Banderas."

Frank pivoted toward the women quickly and in an angry voice said, "For your information, ladies, I didn't touch her, but sometimes I get a kick out of slapping old busybodies around."

The women recoiled and quickly went inside the house. They watched Frank through the mini-blinds as he drove away.

———————

Halfway through his drive home Frank calmed down enough to think about his upcoming trip to Myanmar. Before he left, he wanted to study about the government of the country formerly known as Burma. He decided that he would stop at his consulting office to pick up his iPad, so he could spend some time reading about Myanmar on the Internet. Hopefully something useful would come out of this lousy night.

———————

"What?" mumbled Armando Mellini. Then he recognized it was the telephone. It was two-fifteen in the morning. "Who could be calling at this time? I hope everything is all right," he thought to himself.

"Hello, Mr. Mellini," said the voice on the other end of the phone. "This is ABD Security Systems. The alarm has gone off in your restaurant. We have already notified the Philadelphia police. They said they would send a car around immediately."

"Thank you. I'll be there right away."

"Who was that? Is Uncle Giuseppe okay?"

"It was the security company. They said that the burglar alarm went off in the restaurant," Mellini said to his wife as he began to get dressed. "I'm going over there and see what happened."

"You be careful, Armando."

"Don't worry, my dear. The police are on their way. You go back to sleep now. Love you."

As Mellini got into his car he thought how glad he was that he had listened to his accountant's advice and signed a contract with the security company.

"The cost of having a good security system is an operating expense just like the salary expense you have for your employees, the cost of utilities, the depreciation deduction on your restaurant kitchen appliances and dining room tables, and the amortization of your food and liquor licenses," his accountant had told him.

"They are all necessary expenses your business incurs in its day-to-day operations," the accountant continued. "They are not like the accounting classification of personal expenses which are not associated with your restaurant business and, under the business entity concept, cannot be recorded as expenses of the company when calculating net income. Neither are they like non-recurring items which result from unusual, non-recurring, material events, such as loss from the condemnation of a building. The expense of paying each month to have a good burglar alarm system in operation is something I would not hesitate to incur."

Mellini was not one to hesitate. He had followed up on his accountant's recommendation that same day, securing a sizeable discount by prepaying his security service quarterly. At the end of each month, the accountant would record the security expense for the period by making an adjusting entry to the prepaid asset account.

Mellini's accountant had helped him with other things as well. He helped establish a good internal control system by separating duties which made it more difficult for employees to steal from Mellini. One such control was to have the servers bring the bill to a cashier who rang up the bill on the cash register and gave any change back to the servers. The cashier then kept all the lunch and dinner checks and credit/debit card copies to give to the accountant.

The prenumbered customer orders had to be reviewed by three people: the chef, to indicate that the order was received; the servers, to indicate that the order was paid for; and the cashier, to indicate that the bill was rung up. Each customer order had four copies: one for the customer; one to be controlled by the chef in the kitchen; one to be kept by the servers; and one to be retained by the cashier.

At the end of the day, the manager would reconcile the three sets of customer orders with the day's cash receipts to help insure that cash was not being stolen from Mellini and that meals were not being given away without proper authorization. Since the establishment of this system of internal control, cash receipts had increased by five percent and inventory shrinkage had decreased by eight percent.

The implementation of a petty cash system by the helpful accountant had worked also. A petty cash system is a record keeping process for small cash disbursements typically associated with an office. Some items, such as postage, have to be paid immediately in cash. In a typical petty cash system, a small amount of cash, say $200, is placed in a locked cash box. Each time cash is needed for small expenditures such as postage, cab fare, or emergency supplies, the individual authorized to control the petty cash box writes a voucher explaining what the cash is to be used for. This voucher is later supplemented by a receipt for the purchase of the item or service. When the cash is replenished, the documents are typically reconciled to determine if all the cash is accounted for. Once this process is completed, the transactions that used up the petty cash, such as postage and taxi fares, are recorded as expenses in the general journal and the petty cash box is replenished.

The petty cash fund helped Mellini know how some of his cash was being spent for things around the office. This system worked a lot better than his old method where the staff would come to him asking for twelve dollars to pay UPS and then he would not have any record of the expenditure later. In the old system, many expenses went unrecognized, causing income to be overstated and income taxes paid to be higher. Using the petty cash system, every minor two-dollar expense did not have to be separately recorded when it occurred, either. Instead, the lump sum of petty cash expenditures could be recorded in the aggregate when petty cash was replenished. In the past, Mellini suspected that some people might have asked him for cash that was greater than the amount of the expense. By having a formalized system of keeping track of the petty cash, Mellini was spared the responsibility of having to remember to make a note of the expense. Overall, Mellini was pleased with the work his accountant had done for him.

Mellini did not have any problem parking his car on Passyunk Avenue at that time of night and was relieved to see that the police were already there. He had heard stories about how long it sometimes took for the Philadelphia police to respond to calls, but they were already at the South Philadelphia restaurant close to the Philadelphia Sports Complex.

"Excuse me, officer, but I'm Armando Mellini. I own this restaurant."

"Could I see some identification, Mr. Mellini?"

Mellini pulled out his wallet and took out his driver's license. The police officer looked at the name on the license, then the picture. The picture was a reasonable likeness considering that it was a driver's license photo. Mellini was 44 and had a round face with dark eyes and a swarthy complexion. His dark bushy hair was beginning to recede. His nose and ears were disproportionately large for his face. What the picture failed to reveal was the four-inch scar Mellini had behind his ear because of an accident he suffered while in the Air Force, and his rotund diminutive stature. At a quick glance he could look like the actor Danny DeVito, except that Mellini was taller at five feet eight inches.

The officer looked at Mellini and returned the license to him. "There you are, Mr. Mellini. I'm Officer Mulroney. It looks like an act of vandalism. Your front window was broken, but nothing appears to have been taken. Officer Hawkins and I inspected the interior, and everything seems to be in order, but you ought to have a look for yourself before we file a report."

After spending fifteen minutes looking through the restaurant, Mellini was satisfied that nothing was taken. All the tables with their respective red and white checkered tablecloths were in place. The cash register was neither damaged nor open. Mellini's accountant had instituted a system whereby the evening's cash receipts were always dropped off in an overnight depository at the bank to limit the likelihood of theft. The kitchen and barroom areas were untouched. The autographed pictures in the lobby of Frank Sinatra, George Clooney, Rihanna, Justin Bieber, Jimmy Rollins, Sandra Bullock, Drake, and some sports figures were not damaged either. The only damage was the broken front window, which needed to be replaced. Glass also needed to be swept up. Overall, the expense was not great and would be covered by the business insurance policy.

"I do not understand why someone would do something like this," Mellini said to Mulroney. "This is generally a safe neighborhood. My father started this restaurant forty-seven years ago. People come here—they eat, they enjoy. They come before the Phillies games, they come after the Phillies games. Now this!

In all the time my family's been here, there has never been anything like this. Why now? It serves no point."

"Normally, it's just kids who are looking for trouble, although the ones who did this to your window must be real sick," the officer stated.

"Why do you say that?"

"Normally," Mulroney said, "broken windows like this are caused by someone throwing a brick or a stone or a beer bottle. Something along those lines. But in all my eight years on the force, I've never seen anyone use what was used to break your window tonight: a brick tied to a dead cocker spaniel."

"You mean a dog?" inquired the astonished Mellini.

"Yeah, do you know anyone who would do this to you? A disgruntled employee or someone you fired recently?"

"No one," replied Mellini pensively.

"I hope you don't take offense at this question, Mr. Mellini, but have you had any problems with the Mafia? Could they be threatening you?" inquired Mulroney.

"No! Absolutely not!"

"Throwing a dead cocker spaniel through a window is not the way the mob generally operates," conceded Mulroney. "Most likely it was just some kids. Murphy have someone take that dog to CSU. Maybe the Crime Scene Unit can tell us how that dog died. We might be able to find something out about the perp this way. Mr. Mellini, I'm going to have you fill out a couple of forms and then you can get to the task of covering up your window and return home to bed."

"I still can't get over it," Mellini said. "A dead cocker spaniel. Who would do such a thing? Even Hitler liked animals."

Two

─────

The requirement that inventory be recorded at its historical cost is modified in one situation. When the market value of the inventory falls below cost, the inventory should be written down to its market value and the corresponding loss should be included in the income statement.
—Nikolai, Bazley, and Stallman

A Thai plane descended through clear skies, crossing the Gulf of Martaban and the Bay of Bengal in route to landing in several minutes at Yangon, Myanmar. This landing could not be as frightening as landing in Hong Kong, thought Lenny as he awoke when the woman seated next to him touched his arm. His two previous flights into Hong Kong had prepared him for anything. The planes bank steeply over high-rise buildings and straighten out just in time to land on a large island at Chek Lap Kok airport.

But Hong Kong, the freckle on the face of Asia, was behind him. He had found the city to be an exuberant mix of high fashion, high finance, deluxe hotels, and traditional Chinese culture. Prior to the transfer of sovereignty from British colonial control to the People's Republic of China in 1997, there was serious speculation that Hong Kong's unique blend of "East Meets West" would disappear. Such fears proved to be unfounded as Hong Kong continued to flourish under the principle of "one country, two systems."

Lenny hurriedly stood up from his aisle seat and retrieved his empty mineral water bottle from the overhead compartment. He walked back to a petite Thai host who exchanged the empty for a new bottle. When he got back to row 18, seat C, Rebecca, his daughter, was engaged in a conversation with the woman sitting in the middle seat.

Safe mineral water was essential for the next four days in the Republic of the Union of Myanmar. He and Rebecca had survived China without getting the dreaded diarrhea or "Delhi Belly" by following several rules: 1) don't drink untreated water, 2) peel all fruit, 3) don't eat or drink dairy products, and 4) eat only cooked vegetables.

What had the guide book said? You will get sick in Asia. The bacteria in Asian water and food is different from that in American food. He and Rebecca had drunk a lot of soft drinks in China.

Their Thai guide who met them in the Bangkok airport earlier certainly had not been encouraging. Prawit Chareonkul casually mentioned that the next four days would be rugged. He handed each of the eleven tourists in his group five or six towelettes. They said "With the Compliments of Diethelm Travel. Your Guide to Unusual Places: 140/1 Wireless Road, Lunpini, Patumwan, Bangkok 10330, Thailand." For some reason the name of the travel agency had made Lenny think again about diarrhea.

"Use these; it will be hot," Prawit calmly spoke. "In some of our travels, hotel rooms may not have air conditioning. You'll have rats running around your room, and roaches may crawl over your face during the night. The plumbing may not work." There were some strange looks on the tour group's faces.

Prawit then suggested, "Go to the shop over there and buy several cartons of cigarettes. You can use them for trading and for tips in Myanmar."

The ageless and likable U.S. tour director, Joan Kelley, shot back, "We've already paid for our tips." She always looked after her "children," which was how she thought of her tour group.

Typical of non-smoking Americans, several of the tour members mumbled that they would not be a party to killing foreigners by giving them cigarettes. Only one-man heeded Prawit's first important advice.

Another male tour member asked, "What is the official exchange rate in Myanmar?"

Prawit responded, "1,600 *kyat* (pronounced 'chat') to 1. There is 100 pya coins per MMK, but pyas are rare. The 1,000 MMK is common. There is still a disparity between the bank rate and the black-market rate, but we do have ATM machines in the major cities."

"Is there a black-market rate?"

"Yes. About 1,700 MMK to $1 if the *kyat* is falling, but the black-market rate can vary significantly."

"Is it safe to exchange money on the black market?"

"No," was Prawit's quick response. "Although the military junta ruling Myanmar dissolved in 2011 following a general election in 2010, under the semi-civilian government the situation is somewhat improved from the 35-year-long prior regime. It's still illegal to exchange money on the black market and a crime for a Myanmar citizen to accept dollars without a license."

The entire dialogue caused Lenny to chuckle to himself as he thought of the impact an economic climate like Myanmar's would have on accounting. Assets, for example, include all costs necessary to make the asset operational. Consequently, the cost of a machine would include not only the purchase price of the machine itself, but also costs such as shipping and installation. Measurement of the cost is relatively easy in the U.S. since everything is usually included on the invoice. In Myanmar, however, a company would have to capitalize the purchase price plus the cost of cigarettes to bribe individuals to deliver the machine. However, Lenny knew that Myanmar did not follow international accounting standards, or any standards, for that matter. Around 166 countries follow IFRS standards, but not the U.S.

"What a nightmare!" he thought to himself as he tried to determine in his own mind if a gain should be recognized on the cartons of cigarettes when they were traded to reflect their increased market value over their original cost. Lenny decided that a gain would be recognized on the disposal of the cigarettes if their market value was determinable. Otherwise, the capitalized cost of the asset would simply equal the asset's acquisition price and the cost of the cigarettes plus the cost of any other items needed to make the asset operational.

Lenny's train of thought was broken by Rebecca's voice. "Earth to Dad! Earth to Dad! Come in, Dad." She reached over the woman in the middle seat, grabbed Lenny's arm and said, "Dana's from

Philadelphia, also. She has a gem shop. Look at her beautiful ruby drop necklace."

Lenny glanced over for the first time and looked at the large ruby worn by the woman between him and his daughter. His eyes moved downward slightly, but he immediately looked up into the blue eyes of Dana Scott. She turned in her seat to take Lenny's hand. He blushed slightly.

"Hello, Dr. Cramer; my name is Dana Scott. Your daughter has told me a lot about you. Did you enjoy your short nap?"

"Well, I'm not sure I went to sleep. Maybe I dozed."

"Rebecca says that you are an accountant. That's certainly not my cup of tea. Do you teach or practice accounting?"

"Both. I teach at Wharton, and I also have a small accounting firm." At that moment the plane touched down at the Yangon International Airport. "Where is your gem shop located?"

"Oh, I bought out another gentleman last year. It's located on Jewelers' Row—Sansom Street. I own two-thirds of it, and my partner owns the remainder. He's sitting up in first class—finagled a free upgrade somehow. With all his finagling, I wish he had come up with a way to improve our cash flows. I just had to contribute another quarter of a million of capital into the shop." Dana looked over at Rebecca who had taken out her smart phone and was putting in her ear buds. "I'm sorry. I must be boring both of you with needless details. Change of subject. Are you with the Joan Kelley tour group?"

"Yes."

"Great, my friend and I"—Dana pointed to a woman in seat D—"joined the tour but just for Myanmar and Bali. This trip is a business expense for the shop, as I am looking to purchase some inventory. Janet also works at the gem shop."

Dana leaned over Lenny and said, "Janet, this is Professor Cramer. He teaches accounting at Wharton's School of Finance. Maybe we should get him to tell us where all of our cash is going."

A sparkle from the ruby drop caught Lenny's eye, and he imagined that it was winking at him. She was so close he could smell her perfume. Lenny turned to his right and saw a smiling, friendly redhead. To both Janet and Dana, he said, "Please, call me Lenny." Janet was wearing a jade necklace and a wide jade bracelet.

For some reason the plane had stopped on the runway. Feeling an overwhelming desire to continue the conversation even though Rebecca had lost interest, Lenny turned back to Dana and said, "So you're having cash flow problems? Tell me about your inventory. How often do you turn over your gem inventory?"

"Whoa! Talk to Janet. She's my bookkeeper. I don't know a debit from a credit. Would you like to get together this evening after we arrive at the Strand Hotel? We could meet at the Grill."

Lenny instinctively looked at his watch. It was 5:15. "You know debits are on the left and credits are on the right. Uh, I don't know. Rebecca needs to get her beauty sleep."

"Oh, come on, Dad. I'm 13 years old. I'm not a kid. We can eat supper with Dana and Janet. You can teach both what a T account is. There's probably nothing on TV. Really, there probably won't even be a TV!"

The plane finally reached the airport entrance, and a few people jumped up before the seat belt light went off. Lenny smiled, "Okay, we'll think about it."

Rebecca looked at Dana and smiled too. "That means yes."

Once inside the Mingaladon airport, which is 10 miles north of central Yangon, the passport game was relatively easy. The eleven-member tour group met the local Burmese guide, who led the group outside where the hassle began. About 50 kids of all ages surrounded the group. First, they begged for the orchids which the women had received on the Thai plane. They wanted the safety pin attached to the back of the orchid. Then they began begging for paper, books, money, or anything they saw in purses or hand-carried luggage. They were all skinny and dirty.

This country is a smorgasbord of more than 130 officially recognized ethnicities, with about 65% Bamars, who migrated from southwest China more than 3,000 years ago. Almost 90% of the country is Buddhist. The military seized power in 1962 and eventually changed its name from Burma to Myanmar. They also changed the name of its capitol from Rangoon to Yangon.

Finally, all eleven pieces of luggage were located and placed on the bus, and everyone climbed aboard. Each person was limited to one piece of luggage. It was still hot at 6:30 p.m. Someone asked that the air conditioner be turned on, but it didn't work.

Lenny was in the back of the bus, and Rebecca was sitting two seats in front of him with Dana. Lenny noticed that there was a distinct lack of high-rise buildings and modern automobiles in Yangon. Apparently, Myanmar had been isolated from the influences of the outside world. No one was rushing around, and there were few neon signs. Surprisingly, the streets were wide and were planned on a properly British colonial grid system.

Lenny's thoughts were interrupted by the voice of the local guide. "Yangon, formerly, Rangoon, was the capital of Myanmar from 1885 to 2006 when the military government relocated the capital to Naypyidaw. Yangon, Myanmar's largest city, is in the fertile delta country in what used to be called south Burma. The city, with a population of about four million, stands at about sea level and is situated on the wide Yangon River. In 1885 the British conquered upper Myanmar, and the Burmese kingdom ended. Let me cover—"

Lenny saw Rebecca talking and gesturing to Dana. Lenny chuckled to himself. Rebecca Lea Cramer. Going into the seventh grade, she was a brunette with blond highlights, slender and athletic looking. She had beaten the boys in physical fitness tests in the fifth grade. Tanned, with a sprinkle of freckles on her nose, she was growing out of her tomboy stage into a young lady. At 13, she was the youngest of his three children, but her self-assurance and grown-up behavior made her appear to be 14 or 15.

Rebecca's mother had died only eleven months ago. A swift but painful death. The after-effects were more painful to Lenny than to Rebecca. He now had a live-in housekeeper, who was only a partial substitute for a mother. The housekeeper was *no* substitute for a wife. This extra stress caused what his doctor called "chronic fatigue syndrome"—a mysterious disease, little understood. Many of its victims were young professionals. Lenny had developed headaches and sensitivity to light. Something was draining his physical strength and mental energy. His doctor suggested a vacation.

He had seen a flier on a campus bulletin board advertising an Asian study tour. The small ad was partly covered by a large brochure advertising a CPA review course. He called Joan Kelley, a marketing professor. Apparently, she had taken about 15 trips throughout the world. He made a reservation for Rebecca and himself, but almost canceled when it came time to pay money. Unlike most of his travel, this trip was not for business which meant the travel expenses would not be tax-deductible for Lenny and Rebecca. The thought of having to pay full price for the vacation almost made him cringe. On top of that, it had not been much of a vacation so far. There was a difference between a vacation and a trip. A trip was much more demanding. "But demanding as it might be," thought Lenny, "it was pleasant to spend some quality time with Rebecca, and more than pleasant to be in the company of an interesting woman like Dana."

The bus stopped at 92 Strand Road in front of the Strand Hotel. Prawit indicated that dinner was scheduled for 7:30 and breakfast the next morning from 7:00 to 8:00. The tour group would leave for Shwedagon Pagoda at 8:00.

Both the hotel and its furniture were surprisingly elegant. The room that Lenny and Rebecca were sharing was large and belied the shabbiness that had been common at the Strand prior to the remodeling in the 1990s. Gone were the visible signs of rats or cockroaches. With the aid of the Government of Myanmar and an international group of investors, the grand lady had been restored to her original charm. Lenny's room sported two-poster beds, polished teak floors, whisper-quiet ceiling fans, and a thoroughly modern tiled bathroom. Burmese lacquered vases adorned the table in the spacious sitting room and in the decorative nooks. There was even a TV with satellite reception. Lenny looked out of the window to the street below. Most of Yangon was still in disrepair. He could see moss growing through the peeling stucco of the old English Raj mansions nearby. The muddy Yangon River about a block away drifted lazily toward the Gulf of Martaban. Still, Lenny was glad he and Rebecca had opted for the scenic view.

Lenny and Rebecca were at the Strand Grill five minutes early. Several minutes later Dana, Janet, and another gentleman—Dana's partner—arrived at the old-world dining room. Dana sat down beside Lenny, which pleased him. She had changed clothes. She was stylishly dressed, hair perfectly coifed, and wearing jade earrings.

Only the black leather money belt around her waist was incongruous, but Lenny knew the money belt was a necessity in some foreign countries. He wore a thin money holder, attached around his neck, which lay under his shirt on his chest. He still had 10 fifty-dollar bills there. He also had some money in his belt and his billfold. Like a Boy Scout, he was always prepared.

"Hi, Lenny. Hello, Rebecca. How is your room?" Dana asked.

Rebecca said, "Big! And there *is* a TV with a gazillion stations but there's no free wireless in our room, so I have to go all the way down to the lobby to check Facebook."

Lenny rolled his eyes. "Yes, you can tell that this was a grand old hotel when the British were here. Our room is spacious." He looked back at Rebecca. "And I think we'll do just fine without the Internet *in our room*." Lenny folded his hands and brought them up to his face to rest his chin. "Dana, tell me more about your cash flow problem."

"You're not going to bill me, are you?" she asked.

"No," Lenny chuckled, "but you know the value of free advice?"

Before Lenny could finish mouthing the punch line "It's worth what you—" Dana joined him to finish the sentence "—pay for it."

Lenny smiled. "You know that one."

Dana nodded.

"Really," Lenny said. "Tell me about your inventory."

"Well, I sell colored stones and some jade. As I said earlier, I bought the shop last summer and I should be making a nice profit by now. I have a high mark-up on my stones, but there seems to be no cash at the end of the month."

"You may have sludge in your inventory," Lenny interjected. "Have you been reducing your inventory? How often does your inventory turn over?"

Dana smiled and said, "What kind of stone is a *sludge*? Whatever it is, I know we don't sell them. And yes, Janet and I have been trying to reduce our inventory. That's a good strategy, isn't it?"

"Reducing inventory levels can be good medicine for a company as long as sales grow, and prices don't fall. Of course, the effect on net income will be different based on your inventory method."

Lenny stopped as if he were turning a page of his lecture notes, then he said, "But about the sludge, think of your inventory of precious stones as a pond with an incoming and outgoing stream. The pond has three layers of water. The top layer of water, or your inventory, is fresh water because it stays in the pond only a short period of time."

At that moment Rebecca interrupted, "Be careful, Dana. Daddy likes to talk shop, and when he does he repeats things twice like he's lecturing to his undergraduate students." Rebecca laughed and turned back to Dana's partner, Frank Harrison, who was talking to Janet.

Lenny winced slightly but kept going, "This first level turns over quickly, possibly resulting in stockouts and dissatisfied customers. A stockout occurs when your customer cannot find a beautiful stone she likes in your inventory and leaves your shop empty-handed."

He continued. "Now the middle level of water in the pond moves more slowly because it is away from the main flow. But some of it is pulled out with the fresh water. The real problem is the third level— the sediment at the bottom of the pond. It's the sludge inventory. This sludge may not move at all, sitting there for years. You thus have high holding costs which create no value to your company." Lenny paused and then seeing Dana's evident interest, started up again.

"The key is to reduce your inventory at the bottom of the pond. Decrease the amount of sludge. I have seen companies where sludge represents as much as one-half of the inventory value, but accounts for only ten percent of sales. Remember, after carrying charges are deducted, these sediment sales produce no profit at all."

Lenny noticed that while he had eaten nothing from his plate, everyone else at the long table was almost finished. He began to eat the beef curry rapidly.

Dana reached over, put her hand on Lenny's arm, and said softly, "You must really enjoy your field! I could learn a lot from you, I think. We should spend some time together."

Lenny had already noticed the gold band and large pear-shaped diamond ring on her finger. "I hope I'm not being too forward. Are you married?" Lenny asked, wanting to hear that she was not; that the rings were family keepsakes.

She said, "Not any more. I was married to Jimmy Friedman, who is the Executive Vice-President for product design at Ascentric in Philly. We married after I earned my marketing MBA from L.S.U."

Lenny plunged ahead with the questioning. He did want to know more about her. "Where did you get your undergraduate degree?"

"Pfeiffer College. That's in North Carolina. I grew up in Somers Point, New Jersey. Jimmy and I didn't have any children. We couldn't find a way to have a successful career and a family. I guess you make choices and you give up things. We managed to have two successful careers."

The waiter took Lenny's plate, and he asked the group if they wanted dessert. Rebecca's hand shot up, but Lenny raised his eyebrows and shook his head no. Rebecca frowned.

Lenny turned back to Dana and said, "What did you do before you bought your colored stone shop?"

"I was Vice-President of Consulting and Information Systems with Hi-Tech Equipment in Boston, Massachusetts. I was HTE's first female corporate vice-president. I spearheaded our company's entry into consulting—a new line of business."

"Why did you leave Hi-Tech?" Lenny asked.

"Oh, a number of reasons," replied Dana. "Ego mostly. The eldest son of the founder and president of the company was promoted over me. Ray Wong is bright and talented, but he has been arrogant and naive on the way up the corporate ladder. Three years ago, the company had a profit of $11 million, but last year it had a loss of $15 million. The company is stumbling."

"Would Wong have the top position if he wasn't related to the founder?"

"Unlikely. Besides, the company faces an uphill battle in the marketplace because of some fierce competition. I believe a woman can go far in business if she's dedicated and serious," Dana smiled, "but she has to try harder than a man."

Dana continued. "My assumption when I started at Hi-Tech was that being a woman would not prevent me from becoming the chief executive officer one day. I had not planned on someone inheriting the job. But that's life. Ray Wong will spend the next 20 years of his business career being compared unfavorably to his father." Dana frowned and said, "That's enough about me. What about you?"

At that moment a waiter entered with eleven cups of ice cream and set a cup in front of each tour member. It looked good. Rebecca and Dana started eating theirs. Lenny nibbled at his ice cream. "What would you like to know about me? I like accounting, particularly forensic accounting. I like teaching and consulting." Lenny took another bite of the ice cream.

"What are your hobbies?"

"Probably work."

"That figures. Besides work, what do you like to do?"

"Oh, I collected stamps as a kid. I like to play tennis. I like roller coasters. One day I would like to sky dive."

"Really? That's too adventurous for me. I like to keep my feet on the ground. Do you golf?" Dana queried.

"Not much. I've tried several times." Without pausing Lenny asked, "What colored stones do you like the best? You have a beautiful diamond there." Lenny pointed to her left hand.

"Yes, that's a 2.3 carat, pear-shaped stone. My ex-husband gave it to me about six years ago. But I really like rubies, too."

After the meal and interesting discussion, Lenny and Rebecca retired to their room. Remodeled or not, mosquitoes were still an issue in Yangon, and in all of Myanmar for that matter. Since there was no mosquito netting around their beds, that night Lenny and Rebecca covered their bodies with bug repellent. Lenny dreamed about being inside a pear-shaped ruby prison.

———

The tour bus's first stop Monday morning was outside a large building covered with sheet metal. A slight rain fell on a brownish sign outside the main entrance to the building:

NOTICE TO ALL TOURISTS

Tourists are kindly requested to observe the following rules regarding mode of dress in the precincts of pagodas as prescribed by the board of trustees of the pagodas.

1. All foot wear (including socks) are strictly prohibited.
2. Shorts should not be worn. Men should wear shirts over their underwear/vests. Women should have brassieres when wearing T-shirts and blouses.

3. The pagodas are places of worship and meditation
   and scanty attire is considered as irreverence in
   Myanmar.

Disregard of these rules is considered as religious irreverence in Myanmar.

Thank you for your co-operation.
Tourist Myanmar

Ted, the medical doctor traveling on the tour, wrapped a towel
around his waist to cover his shorts and walked into the building.
Since most Burmese men wore plaid skirts — called *longyis* —
rather than pants, only his white skin and camera would distinguish
him from a local native — so he said. One tour member stayed on
the bus rather than walk without shoes in the mud created by a
recent rain.

Lenny took his shoes off, and red mud squeezed through his
toes as he walked about 20 feet through the parking lot. Inside the
pagoda was unbelievable. There was a gigantic Buddha lying on its
side. Shwethalyaung, informally referred to as the Reclining Golden
Buddha, is an impressive structure and ranks as both Myanmar's
most beautiful and largest reclining Buddha.

The enormous face of the Buddha was propped up on his right
arm staring at Lenny and Rebecca as they entered the Chauk Htat Gyi
monastery. The Buddha was stretched out around 181 feet to the right
of the entrance, surrounded by a four-foot spiked metal fence. It was
impossible for Lenny to get the entire Buddha focused in his Pentax
SLR digital camera. He liked the camera rather than his cell phone.
The statue had been cut from a massive piece of marble. The robe on
the Buddha was made of gold, trimmed in silver.

The feet at the other end of the Shwethalyaung appeared to be
at least 52 feet tall. The bottom of the toes had red swirls like fingerprints, and there were hundreds of reddish designs carved into
the bottom of the marble feet — fish, tigers, cups, and other religious
symbols. To get his shot, Lenny finally climbed about 10 feet up a
light pole, turned the camera sideways, and photographed as much
of the Buddha as he could.

Rebecca shouted, "Be careful, Dad." Two monks dressed in red robes walked by as Lenny was climbing down. They merely grinned; Lenny imagined they were thinking "dumb tourist."

Back on the bus Lenny read a description from his worn itinerary about the next stop, the Shwedagon Pagoda:

> The most spectacular attraction in Yangon contains 13,153 foot-square of gold, 5,451 diamonds weighing 2,078 carats, and 1,383 of rubies, sapphires, and topaz. This vast collection of riches decorates the Shwedagon Pagoda. The topmost vane with its flag turns with the wind, and the very top of the jeweled vane is tipped with a single 76-carat diamond. This pagoda, the spiritual center of Myanmar, attracts monks, school children, and a steady flow of Buddhist worshipers from all over Asia to its many chapels, satellite pagodas and image houses.

The Shwedagon Pagoda is not in the center of Yangon, but the pagoda is located three kilometers to the north. Yet to Lenny it dominated Yangon. As they approached it in the heat of the morning, the pagoda rose 326 feet above its base, glittering bright gold.

Rather than taking the southern stairway, the tour group took an elevator to reach the hilltop platform. Again, no shoes or socks were allowed. As he looked down at his bare feet, Lenny remembered the pictures he saw in 2012 of then U.S. President Barack Obama, and Secretary of State Hillary Rodham Clinton's visit to the Shwedagon Pagoda. Mrs. Clinton had visited the prior year and had been the first U.S. Secretary of State to tour Burma in half a century.

After the elevator opened, the group saw that not only was there an U.S.$10 admission fee, but there was a U.S.$4 video camera fee. Lenny paid the camera fee to be permitted to carry his camera inside. Lenny thought to himself, "Just another way to tax foreign tourists and generate revenue for the country, since the average Burmese tourist does not have a camera." Lenny knew that the average citizen in Myanmar lived on only $5 to $6 per day.

After exiting the semi-gloom of the elevator, Lenny saw that the mighty pagoda was only one of many structures on the hilltop plat-

form. Many of the structures were large, colorful, and beautiful—
a cacophony of technicolored glitter.

Lenny touched Rebecca on the shoulder and said, "This is the
Disneyland of Myanmar," as he surveyed the beauty with pleasure.
Rebecca turned. "Sure, Dad. Disneyland minus all the rides!
But it is beautiful, like the colorful jagged mountains in Bryce
Canyon, Utah."

Dana touched Lenny's back and said, "I agree. That's an astute
observation. Which way are you going to walk?"

"Why not go left? That's the direction to take at all Buddhist
monuments. Clockwise. We'll have to walk on that bamboo runner.
This marble is hot. Can you imagine how many lives have been lost
trying to defend this magnificent hilltop from capture and looting?"
Lenny noticed that Dana's partner was taking many photos of the
area surrounding the pagoda.

There was a wide inlaid marble-slab walkway around the
Shwedagon pagoda. On both sides of the walkway were hundreds
of other buildings, monuments, temples, religious symbols, bells,
and pagodas. Their splashy colors sparkled in the sunlight.

"Lenny, do you know the legend behind this pagoda?" asked Dana.

"Not really," Lenny replied.

"Apparently, two Mon merchants from Lower Myanmar obtained
from the original Buddha some hair relics and on their return to
Yangon—well, it was called Dagon then. Dagon was changed to
Yangon in 1755. On their return, they enshrined the hair in a small
temple, which later became the kernel over which this large pagoda
is built."

"How do you know this?" Lenny looked quizzically at Dana.

"I read it in one of my books last night. Janet and I couldn't
sleep, so we read. By the way, Yangon means the *end of strife*."

After a short pause, Dana continued, "Do you believe there's a
76-carat diamond on the top of the pagoda?" Dana pointed to the
massive structure in the middle of the hilltop.

Lenny looked intrigued. "You know, I thought about that, too.
It's hard to believe any government regime would allow it to remain
up there in plain sight—if it was ever up there. I read that the pagoda
is covered with more gold than is kept in the Bank of England."

"There is also a very large emerald on the top," Dana responded. "It catches the first rays of sun in the morning and the last rays at sundown." After a long pause she leaned closer to Lenny and asked quietly, "Sometime today, would it be possible for you to touch me?"

Lenny was stunned. "But ... I'm with my daughter."

"I realize I'm being forward," Dana said haltingly, "but being with you has made me smile. You may not have noticed, but several times today I've put my hand on your arm, your shoulder, your hand. I know accountants aren't always viewed as touchy-feely types, but I'm sensing you're different. I like you."

She then turned and strolled down the walkway. Lenny thought she might be blushing. He knew he was.

Lenny felt rattled for some time as he walked around the pagoda.

Rather than taking the elevator, Lenny, Rebecca, Dana, and Janet walked down the long southern steps. There were many small shops for tourists along both sides of the steep rock stairs.

Near the bottom of the stairs Lenny said to no one in particular, "We are walking down the same steps that Rudyard Kipling climbed when he fell deeply and irreversibly in love with a Burmese girl."

Lenny managed to stand behind Dana as they boarded the bus. Gently he brushed the fingertips of his hand down Dana's back, if only for an instant. She hesitated slightly as she stepped forward but said nothing. She was smiling.

Over the next two days Lenny's morose and distracted attitude seemed to disappear, almost in proportion to his contact with Dana. She would listen entranced to Lenny and seemed to be sincerely interested in his professional work. She entertained him with stories, too. A fleeting smile came to his face more often. By unspoken agreement, they did not discuss their prior marriages. For these few days, they were just two people in a strange country getting to know one another. On two other occasions in Yangon, Lenny brushed against Dana in some gentle and discreet way.

From Yangon the tour group flew to Bagan. In the terminal hundreds of birds were chattering from the rafters. Around Bagan, in the scorched wasteland was the most amazing sight to Lenny. As far as the eye could see, stood over 5,000 pagodas, temples, and shrines dating back to the 11th century. Many were decaying. The evening boat ride down the Irrawaddy was even more indicative of the backwardness of Myanmar. Yes, living in the middle ages was an accurate description.

Lenny saw the ox carts, carrying large drums, come down to the river to obtain the household water for the next day. Fishermen were preparing for their all-night search for food. The entire primitive social and economic structure revolved around the river. About three-quarters of the population was concentrated in the Irrawaddy basin in the south.

Mounds of dirt on the bank of the river were there to be sifted for gold and silver. Any found gold was placed on a pagoda for merits. The more merits obtained during life, the better the next life of the giver after rebirth. For centuries the Burmese have been filled with a passion for covering the country with pagodas. Building a pagoda outweighed any wrongful acts a person might do during life.

While the tour group was visiting the Shwedagon Pagoda, Dana approached Lenny and asked, "Have you exchanged any money?"

"Some at the hotels," Lenny responded.

"Have you exchanged any on the black market? The rate of exchange is much better," Dana observed.

"No, I'm afraid. It's a violation of Burmese law to exchange currency at an unauthorized place."

"Well, that guy over there has exchanged money for several of us." She gently turned Lenny around and pointed to a Burmese stranger giving something to Ted. "He's giving 1,680 to $1."

Lenny walked over to the man, and after darting glances from side to side, he asked, "Will you exchange money?"

"What kind?"

"U.S. dollars," Lenny said softly.

"How much?"

"U.S.$20. But can we go behind the wall?" Lenny pointed to his right. Lenny walked cautiously behind the wall, looked around, and handed the young guy a crisp $20 bill.

The Burmese fellow gave Lenny four stacks of multi-colored *kyat* bills. Lenny turned and walked rapidly back to the tour bus. Inside the bus he counted his treasure. He had gotten 1,680 to $1.

Lenny rationalized, "That's much better than 1,600 to 1. I made a 5% return on my investment in 30 seconds." Success can sometimes cause rationalization and quiet fear and conscience.

Lenny had read that illegal commerce was widespread throughout Myanmar. The domestic black market was the main source of consumer goods. In other words, a Burmese citizen could obtain better quality goods from Thailand through the black market. But, to purchase those goods, the citizen of Myanmar had to have a "hard currency" such as U.S. dollars or Japanese yen. Black market exchange provided the needed dollars for a smooth-running underground economy.

"I wonder if this gain is taxable?" Lenny laughed to himself. "If I were a businessperson, how would I treat on financial statements the additional 1,600 *kyats* I received over above the 32,000 that I would have gotten by converting currency at the bank? Maybe as a foreign currency exchange gain?" Because, even illegal and gambling income are taxable, as Al Capone discovered. Internal Revenue Code Section 61 provides that all income from whatever source derived is taxable income.

The tour bus left Bagan at five in the morning to avoid the afternoon heat. Along the narrow road to Mandalay, the small tour bus would head for the left dirt shoulder when it passed another truck. Once at a stop along the road and again at the half-way house at Meiktila, Dana came up behind Lenny and lightly ran her index finger down his back. Both times cold chills ran through his body.

After the bus left the half-way house, Ted asked, "Does anyone know the song 'On the Road to Mandalay'?" But no one could think of the words from the Rudyard Kipling poem set to music and made famous by Frank Sinatra in the late 1950s.

Lenny interjected, "My grandfather talked about the fierce fighting here during World War II. It raged to the end of the war, and Burma suffered enormous losses and major damages."

After a short pause Lenny turned to Dana and asked in a quieter voice, "What type of partnership do you have?"

"Oh, I think it's a limited partnership. I'm the managing partner. Frank has only a limited financial interest."

"I noticed in the Asian edition of the *Wall Street Journal* last week that new limited partnership formations continue to be strong," Lenny said. He sensed that Dana knew that a partnership was an association of two or more persons to carry on as co-owners of a business for profit, but that she wasn't aware of all the nuances involved in modern partnerships.

After shifting his weight in his bus seat, Lenny continued, "Does Frank take part in the control of the business?"

"Sure. He is quite helpful, and I rely on his advice heavily. Why do you ask?"

"Well," Lenny answered uneasily, "if a limited partner takes active part in the control of the business, then he's technically considered a general partner."

"That's interesting." Dana rolled her eyes and asked, "What is missing from your life that you used to get from a person you are no longer around, no longer with, or cannot be with?"

With a perplexed expression, Lenny could only say "Eh, uh, what?"

Dana laughed aloud and then replied, "Oh, that's just one of the questions from this book that I'm reading that's based on the popular Question of the Day App. See!" She handed Lenny her Kindle; there were speech bubbles on the screen.

Lenny read the title: *Question of the Day: Where Truth Is the Dare,* by Al Katkowsky.

Then Dana continued, "Why don't we answer these questions together? You have to tell the truth."

For the remainder of the bus ride, Dana, Lenny, Joan Kelley, and Prawit alternately answered many personal questions from the book as the scenery sped by.

Their evening in dusty Mandalay was uneventful, and Lenny's room at the Mandalay Hotel was marginal. The air conditioner dropped the temperature somewhat, and he saw no roaches or mice, though the mosquitoes were a real problem. The hotel was across the street from the replica of the Royal Palace, the original having been totally devastated by the heavy fighting in World War II. All around were bamboo homes, ox carts, horse carriages, and dirt streets.

The next morning, the tour group went up the Mandalay Hill. The barefoot pilgrimage up the 1,700 cool, stone steps was strenuous. Lenny passed local merchants, beggars, school children, small temples, statues, and benches on the way to the top. The view at the top was worth the climb. The gigantic lions at the bottom of the hill did not look as large from the top. Also, Lenny rested his hand on Dana twice while they were looking into the Royal Palace. She had told him in one of their many conversations that she had come to need this contact with him, that he calmed her as well as made her feel alive. But that was the extent of the physical contact between them. Each felt unspoken constraints.

A twin-turboprop plane with no toilet brought Lenny, Rebecca, and the tour group back to Yangon and the Inya Lake Hotel, surrounded by 27 acres of tropical and verdant gardens. Lenny read the *New Light of Myanmar*, one of the two English newspapers, on the short flight. He mentioned to no one that he remembered hearing that travel by plane had not always been safe in Myanmar. Back in 1987 two Burma Airways planes had crashed within four months of each other, killing all passengers on board. One Fokker Friendship 27 crashed southeast of Bagan, and the other one crashed near their intermediate stop today—Heho. Lenny noticed the 8,200-foot-high mountain after their takeoff from Heho. The first crash had been into that mountain about 280 miles northeast of Yangon. In 1989, another Burma Airways Fokker F-27 crashed on take-off, killing not only everyone on the plane but three people on the ground as well. And in 1998, a Myanmar Airways Fokker-27 smashed into hills near Tachilek airport, killing 34. The five survivors were brutally slaughtered by the neighboring Shan villagers and the crash site plundered.

After arriving safely in Yangon, five members of the tour group went with Prawit to the Bogyoke Market. There were approximately 100 small shops at this market, and Lenny bought some lacquerware for Rebecca. He paid for the merchandise with U.S. dollars, sneaking the bills to the merchant so that the merchant would not be caught accepting hard currency. Even though the *Kyat* is the official currency, by far most merchants preferred payment in U.S. greenbacks or some other hard currency.

Lenny spotted a finely carved old ivory Burmese dancer. The dancer was in costume, sitting in the lotus position. The piece was about five inches long and three inches wide. The first time he asked how much the merchant said 180,000 *kyats*. Lenny had heard that old ivory costs more than a new ivory carving. This phenomenon was the reverse of most merchandising situations. Typically due to inflation, the older the inventory, the lower its price.

"How much in U.S. dollars?" Lenny asked politely.

"$106."

Lenny mentally calculated that the merchant was saving him about 9,600 *kyats*. If he exchanged money at the official rate, the cost of the ivory carving would be about U.S.$112. Lenny turned and left the stall. No wonder most tourists paid for merchandise with U.S. bills.

He returned shortly and found Dana negotiating hard with the same merchant for some jade necklaces and bracelets. The merchant was sitting in the lotus position on a raised platform surrounded by his merchandise. Prawit seemed to be helping. Dana's negotiations lasted over an hour.

At one-point Lenny broke into the conversation and asked the merchant, "What is your lowest price for that ivory carving?" Lenny pointed to the carved Burmese dancer. "And how do I know it's real?"

"We can light a match to it. Plastic will melt. Ivory will not. This is very old ivory. Very expensive. I'll let you have it for U.S.$90." Lenny got Dana's attention and asked her to get him a good price for the carving. She told the merchant, "He'll give you $40."

The merchant acted offended and said, "No! No! Too little."

Dana continued to bargain for the jade. She was trying to trade cash, SD film memory cards, lipstick, a pocket calculator, and other miscellaneous stuff for the jade.

During a lull in the bargaining, Prawit spoke to Dana. "Do you know that the Burmese government holds an annual Jade Emporium every spring? In 1983 the international auction was held at the Inya Lake Hotel where they had a 36-ton jade boulder for sale. No one bought it, however." Dana only frowned in response.

Somehow an agreement was reached, and the merchant gave Dana the jade items. Lenny did not see Dana give the merchant any cash.

Prawit then pleaded, "We have to go. It's time to get back."

Dana spoke loudly to the merchant. "The carving is not worth $50. He'll give you $40. Besides, aren't ivory imports banned in the U.S. because elephants are an endangered species? Can he get it through U.S. customs? Do you offer an export permit with sale?"

"No problem. No problem. He can hide it in a sock inside a shoe in his suitcase." The merchant raised his arms to demonstrate that all was well.

Prawit quickly cut in, "Lenny, we have to go now." Lenny turned to the merchant, smiled, and said, "I'll give you $70."

Shaking his head with a pained expression, the merchant shot back, "No."

Lenny turned to go. Dana picked up her packages, and Prawit began to walk away.

"Okay. $75." The merchant almost shouted.

Lenny was not surprised. He had read in one of his books that you received a merchant's lowest price as you went out his door. After a pause Lenny asked the merchant, "Is $75 in bills okay?"

The merchant leaned over and handed the wrapped old ivory carving to Lenny. He whispered, "Give the $75 to Prawit when you get on the plane. He'll get it back to me."

During the taxi ride back to the hotel Lenny wondered how much commission would be paid to Prawit from the transaction. Had he paid too much? Then he began to worry about customs. He had filled out a Myanmar customs document declaring all his money when he entered Myanmar. He had officially converted only $20 to Burmese currency. Yet he had just spent well over $75 and had no documentation to prove he had legally exchanged funds. Would they lock him up for a currency violation?

His fear about rotting in prison disappeared that evening, at least temporarily. Joan Kelley had arranged for some of the tour group to visit and meet the U.S. Deputy Chief of Mission, Eleanor P. Samson. After the visit Lenny read that other countries with currency black markets were Argentina, Egypt, Iran, and Venezuela. In Russia, the largest black market was for plagiarized dissertations.

Two large Lincoln Town Cars picked the group up at 8:00 at the front of the Inya Lake Hotel and drove for about 35 minutes across

Yangon to the Embassy Compound. Lenny noticed that Dana had a long conversation with Rebecca as their fancy car sped by beggars and poverty.

The Deputy Chief's house was large and modern. She indicated that it had been built with the assistance of elephants for a major trading company a number of years ago.

After the normal pleasantries, Ms. Samson cocked her head and said, "Let me warn you about your travel in Myanmar. Cholera, hepatitis, plague, rabies, typhoid fever, and malaria are endemic in Myanmar."

Ms. Samson paused for a moment and then continued, "Several weeks ago one of our Americans got typhoid fever—probably from the ice cream at the Strand."

Jaws dropped among the tourists. The delicious vanilla ice cream they had eaten at the Strand several nights ago could be lethal.

Dana asked, "How long does it take to catch typhoid fever?"

"The incubation period is about 10 to 14 days," responded Ms. Samson.

Lenny was now truly worried. Not only could he go to prison for currency violations, but he could also die a painful death with typhoid fever. The anxiety inherent in his growing friendship with Dana paled beside these concerns.

Three

_____

*A woman noticed that a particular store always had a
sign on its window indicating that all merchandise was
"sold below cost." She stopped at the store and asked the
merchant how he could stay in business. The merchant
said, "Oh, that's no problem; we always buy below cost."*

—Anonymous

Lenny did *not* have a fever, rose-colored eruptions, or abdominal
pains the next morning. He rationalized that the yellow fever,
typhoid, and cholera shots that he had received before he left on
the trip would protect him. He reminded himself to be sure to take
his two malaria tablets on Saturday.

He had other worries. Customs. Not only had he underestimated
the amount of U.S. dollars he had when he entered Myanmar, but
he had also spent well over $75 while in Myanmar. He had signed
an official currency declaration when he entered the country and
had unofficially converted $20 into *kyats*.

Lenny was standing in front of the mirror in the upstairs
bathroom at the Mingaladon airport in Yangon. He checked the
front pocket on his yellow "Royal Hong Kong Yacht Club" polo
shirt. The Alka-Seltzer cold tablets foil package looked casual to
him. He touched the package, and he could feel the old ivory carving
hidden inside the foil. Would the customs officer ask to see the
package?

Prawit had said earlier, "If he asks to see the carving, place these
two packs of cigarettes on the counter along with the carving. Hope-

41

fully the officer will keep the cigarettes and let you keep the ivory carving." Prawit did not suggest any other alternatives.

Lenny's hazel eyes stared back at him through the photo-tinted gray glasses as he combed his short, brown hair. There were some gray hairs, but he was not yet losing his hair. The foul odor in the bathroom brought him back from his day dreaming, so Lenny walked downstairs just in time to move his baggage into the international flights area.

While waiting for their inspection, Lenny noticed that the customs agents were checking the luggage of some other tourists very closely. Perspiration appeared on Lenny's forehead. He tried to joke with Rebecca.

Joan Kelley came over and stopped in front of Lenny. "Can't you afford to buy shoelaces for your daughter?" She pointed to Rebecca's tennis shoes.

Lenny looked at Rebecca's fashion Keds. There were no shoelaces.

He shook his head in embarrassment and replied, "She probably has ten pairs at home."

"Really, Dad," Rebecca said, winking at Joan. Joan went off laughing.

Lenny fell silent for a while, and then Prawit approached the group and commanded, "Get in line over there." He pointed to a custom's official. Lenny did not wish to be first or last. He got behind Ted, but just as they finished with Ted, Ted's wife broke in line in front of Lenny.

Then it was Lenny's turn. The official merely pretended to check Lenny's and Rebecca's hand luggage. He checked the US$10 departure fee receipt and waved Lenny to the door of the waiting room. Lenny smiled in relief as he made his way to the waiting room. He wondered if something was illegal if you did not get caught.

The flights from Yangon to Bangkok, Thailand, to Jakarta, Indonesia and to Denpasar, Bali, were long. While waiting for luggage to go through customs in Bali, Dana walked over to Lenny and asked in a low, passionate voice, "Could you arrange for us to be alone sometime in Bali? I really wish you would kiss me." She smiled mischievously.

Lenny blinked in surprised reaction and could only respond, "I'll try."

The group stayed at the Bali Hyatt in Sanur, situated on 36 acres at the water's edge of the Badung Strait. Finally, a vacation spot with gleaming white beaches, tropical charm, and live volcanoes. An unspoiled 90-mile-long beauty of lush green terraced fields of rice waited for the tour group.

Ah, volcanoes. Lenny had always wanted to see a live one after frequently mentioning them for teaching purposes in his accounting classes. Lenny would tell his students that any losses or gains that arise from events that are both unusual in nature and infrequent in occurrence are reported separately on the income statement, but are included in net operating income.

Lenny would use the example of a loss resulting from a volcano eruption as being unusual and infrequent. Of course, an exception would be if the volcano erupted on a routine basis. Lenny was excited to finally see his unusual and infrequent volcanoes first hand.

No tours were planned in Bali, so five members of the group rented a van with driver and drove north toward Mt. Batur and the volcanic lake. Along the way they stopped at a wood carving factory, where Rebecca bought a wooden carving of a woman's head. The view of the volcanic lake and surrounding mountains was breathtaking. There was no live volcano, however. Returning southward again, the small van backtracked to Kuta Beach, a popular beach on the Southwest Coast. There, Lenny, Rebecca, Dana, and Janet swam in the Indian Ocean, collected seashells, and walked in the white sand.

That evening Lenny managed to be in the elevator alone with Dana while Rebecca was looking at paintings by the local artists in the lobby. It was his first romantic kiss since the death of his beloved wife.

The kiss was short but not too short. Lenny smiled. "Dana, what's happening here?"

"I don't know," was Dana's response. "I am simply attracted to you. There is a great deal of tension."

"Tension?" Lenny repeated the word.

"Yes. You know that I was just recently divorced."

The elevator started to open, and Lenny quickly said, "Will you call me when you get back to the States?"

"Sure," was Dana's simple response.

Several minutes later Lenny picked up Rebecca in the hotel lobby. She asked, "Dad, why is Dana always near you?"

"Oh, I believe that's just your active imagination."

"Sure, Dad," Rebecca said doubtfully.

Early the next morning, Lenny, Rebecca, and Janet left Bali on Singapore Airlines for Bangkok and Tokyo, in route to Los Angeles and Philadelphia. Lenny and his ivory carving would have to face a U.S. customs agent in Los Angeles.

Dana Scott and her business partner, Frank Harrison, took a noon Thai flight to Bangkok. Thanks to Frank's frequent flyer points, Dana was able to join him in first class. She was just settling into her seat.

"Did you hear that?" Frank asked Dana.

"Hear what?"

"As soon as the fasten seat belt sign goes off, a number of passengers unbuckle their seat belts. I hate that. There should be a stiff fine. If we have state laws requiring passengers to wear seat belts in a car going 65 miles per hour, certainly seat belts are needed in a 600-miles-per-hour bullet going through the air. If there's a sudden jerk, those people will be thrown on top of me."

Dana knew from experience that it was best to try to humor Frank when he began to get moody.

Dana pointed to her belt. "Look, mine is fastened, and you were right about joining a tour group in Myanmar. We were not checked by the Burmese customs agents when we left," smiled Dana.

Frank started to reach for a cigarette out of habit, fidgeted with the pack, swore under his breath about the in-flight no smoking policy, and stuck a piece of nicotine gum in his mouth instead. He had to stop smoking.

"Did you notice that Prawit gave the customs agents two bottles of whiskey?" Dana said. "That's why they didn't check the tour group. If we had gone into Myanmar alone, I can assure you that they would have searched us closely."

Frank lowered his voice and queried, "Did you buy the Buddha head?"

"No, the merchant only wanted cash. He would not accept my travelers' checks." Dana shook her head in frustration. "And I had beat him down to a low price."

"Well, you know we have two customers who wish one." Then he whispered in Dana's ear, "I got one. We'll make 400% mark-up on it in the States."

"Do you think it will have a ruby inside the head?" Dana asked excitedly.

"Who knows? That's why we can sell it for $900 in Philadelphia and make a hefty profit."

Dana reached into her Gucci purse, pulled out a jade necklace, and handed it to Frank. "Now tell me about jade."

Frank took the necklace and slowly observed it, rubbing each stone with his fingers. He took his ballpoint pen and tapped it on several of the stones. Then he said, "Very good. It's jadeite. Jadeite occurs in an attractive, intense green that cannot be found in nephrite."

Frank paused and then said, "Let me back up. There are two types of jade—called jadeite and nephrite. Both are crystalline aggregates, composed of fibrous, intergrown crystals. Jade is tough. No other mineral can match the toughness of jade. Of course, that means jade is never absolutely transparent."

Handing the necklace back to Dana, Frank continued, "Feel the stones. No other stone can be appreciated in so many forms—sight, feel, and sound. You can see the beauty in these stones. Feel the beauty."

Frank turned to Dana and stated, "Ancient gemstone lore attributes many powers to various types of stones. Black jade gives strength and power. White jade quiets intestinal disorders. Green jade ensures high rank and authority."

Frank reached over and put his hand on the necklace in Dana's hand. "Green jade contains the concentrated essence of love, which it passes to the wearer."

Dana ignored the sarcasm and asked, "What powers do rubies have?"

"Many. A ruby ensures love and promotes passion." He smiled broadly. "A ruby ensures beauty and stops bleeding. A ruby aids firm friendship. A Capricorn who has ever worn a ruby will never know trouble."

"You're making that up." She looked inquisitively at Frank. "I'm a Capricorn. No wonder I love rubies."

Frank raised his right hand with three fingers pointing up, "Scout's honor." He then said, "When is your birthday?"

"January 18."

"January 18, what?"

"I'm 29."

"Sure, you are," Frank laughed. His irritable mood lifted somewhat.

For a moment Frank was distracted by the noise and people around him. He shifted his seat and started again. "Empress Dowager of China, around the turn of the century, had twelve sets of jade bells hung in carved wooden frames eight feet high by three feet wide." He closed his eyes. "Can you imagine the sound of those bells?"

Dana asked, "Is this imperial jade?" pointing to her necklace.

"Pretty close. Imperial jade or emerald jade is used to describe an intense emerald-green, semitransparent, chrome-bearing jadeite. But many people believe a medium yellowish green of high intensity is the best jade—called apple green. Your stones are in between these two colors. The finest greens are caused by chromic oxide in the stone. It's the same stuff that's responsible for the color of more expensive emeralds."

"Now what is the difference between jadeite and nephrite?" Dana asked.

"Jadeite is heavier and harder. Jadeite is shinier, and ranges in colors from white to black. There's green, yellow, blue, red, and lavender. Nephrite is a fibrous, waxy stone. A nephrite stone simply does not have the beauty or desirability of jadeite."

"Does most of the jadeite come from Myanmar?"

"About 90 percent. Some can be found in China, North America, and Japan. Wyoming has an attractive grayish-green nephrite."

"So why are we going to Chiang Mai tomorrow if jadeite comes from Myanmar?"

Frank laughed. "Do you really wish the entire story?" He faked a yawn and put his right hand on Dana's knee.

"Frank, you're not going to start that again," Dana exclaimed.

"Look," Frank pleaded, removing his hand. "I thought I could sleep for a while on the plane, we could buy a bottle of wine, and retire to my room this evening for a gemology lesson."

"Frank, no! We're business partners, not playmates."

With a mischievous smile Frank observed, "I saw you leading that Ivy League egghead Cramer around on a leash in Myanmar. I'm sure your boyfriend would like a detailed report of your adventure there."

Dana turned and faced Frank. Her voice cracked as she said, "And I'm sure the next customs agent would like a tip about the Buddha head in your suitcase."

They both sat in silence for several minutes. Then Frank pulled out the in-flight Thai magazine and turned to the Thai route map. "Okay, okay. A truce. I'll be a good guy."

Dana said, "Besides, how do you know what I did? You were too absorbed in Janet. What did you two do—visit all 6,000 of the pagodas in Myanmar?"

"Look, partner, she's not married. And yes, I did give her some jade. No big deal. Besides, I'm not a Buddhist priest—forbidden to touch or be touched by a woman, or to accept anything from the hand of a woman. Women were not even allowed in many of the temples we visited, remember?"

Dana sat looking straight ahead, brooding. "I'm sure you'll be able to get a massage tonight at the hotel," she stated.

Frank took out a pencil and began marking on an in-flight motion discomfort bag. Then he said, "Most of the world's jadeite comes from within an 80-mile radius around Hpakant, Myanmar. It is found in dikes of metamorphosed rocks—don't ask me how to spell it—in the Hpakant Valley." Frank drew a circle around the name Hpakant. "This town is about 200 miles north of Mandalay, near the India border."

"Why didn't we go there?"

"Too dangerous—one of the most inhospitable and malaria in-fested jungles. Plus, the area is controlled by an ethnic armed rebel group called Kachin Independence Organization." Frank wrote down the initials KIO. "The Myanmar government had negotiated a cease-fire with the KIO in 1994, but in late 2010 the ceasefire unraveled when the KIO refused to become part of the Burmese Army controlled Border Guard Force. By December, the KIO had returned to its pre-ceasefire ways of extorting taxes from local companies operating in the Kachin State to pay for its extralegal bureaucracy.

"So, here's how things work in Jade Land. A mine owner obtains a KIO license and hires some miners. The workers either scour a stream bed or work a small quarry. With the aid of a water buffalo or oxen, they will haul out jade boulders weighing from a pound to several tons. The rough jade has an opaque skin somewhat like the shell of a nut."

Frank paused, caught his breath, and continued. "Suppose the miners find a promising boulder—normally in March, April or May. During the rainy season the shafts fill up with water. The mine owner takes the boulder to Hpakant and sells it. Half of the proceeds go to the miners, who divide the proceeds equally. The owner keeps the other half, but he must give a five-percent tax to the KIO. They mark the stone 'taxed.'"

Dana interrupted, "A tax paid to a group of warlords?"

"Apparently so. The boulder moves from Hpakant to a larger town, Mogaung, by bullock cart. Mogaung has been the jade trading center for two centuries.

"Oh, I forgot to tell you. Buying the raw material is like buying a pig in a poke. It's a gamble all the way. Only a small window is cut into the skin of the boulder to reveal the surface color."

Frank leaned closer to Dana and continued. "In Mogaung the rough jade is sold secretly to major traders using hand signals. Let me have your left hand."

"Frank, we've already had this discussion. Business partners …"

Frank interrupted, "I'm just trying to demonstrate jade trading. Here, I'll use my left hand. Totally innocent." Frank reached over and took hold of Dana's left hand with his left hand. "Now, the seller and bidder," he said, "put their hands under a piece of cloth. The bidder will say 'hundred' or 'thousand' aloud. The bidder will then stick out the appropriate number of fingers. For example, if the bidder says hundred and sticks out four fingers, he is offering $400."

Removing her hand, Dana asked, "What if *she* wishes to bid $600, $700, $800, or even $900?"

Frank appeared perplexed. "You know, I don't know. Maybe *she* puts two hands under the cloth."

Dana laughed. "Frank, you're pulling my hand, eh, leg."

Frank raised his Scouts' honor sign again and said, "Truth! Anyway, from Mogaung each boulder goes on a cavalcade of mules over clandestine trails through 400 miles of rugged border country controlled by various warlords. Its destination is Chiang Mai where five syndicates of Chinese Thai handle most of it. Hong Kong bidders come to Chiang Mai and take most of the boulders to Hong Kong where they are cut into jewelry and art objects. Remember Kowloon in Hong Kong. There are almost 500 jade shops and stalls along Canton Road and the nearby Yau Ma Tei Jade Hawker Bazaar."

Dana nodded. "I noticed mostly jewelry when we were on Canton Road. Where do they sell elaborate figurines?"

"Remember jade is very hard, so most jade is cut into faceted jewelry or cabochons. Carving elaborate figurines is time consuming and costly. Starting from a block of jade 16 inches square and 8 inches deep, it may take six months to cut a figurine using diamond drills." Frank illustrated the size of the block with his hands.

"I have some interesting factoids of my own," Dana added. "Did you know that the early Chinese often buried bodies with jade objects? Often they would put a piece of carved jade under the corpse's tongue."

"I see, you've been searching the Internet," Frank said. "Did the article you read say most of the jade is cut in mainland China."

"Yes ..."

"Maybe years ago, but not any longer," Frank said. "After World War II and the Communist revolution in China, many of the traders and carvers migrated to Hong Kong for the free enterprise system."

"Do sellers ever try to pass off other types of stone as jade?"

"Sure," replied Frank. "Quartz, glass, enamel on metal, garnet, serpentine, and feldspar are only some of the substitutes for jade. There are definitely fakes around."

"How do you grade jade?"

"You look at three factors: color, translucency, and evenness of color and texture. Color, of course, is the key factor. The best quality jade has an intense, evenly distributed pure green color and is semitransparent."

Frank thought for a moment and then continued. "Pierced jade is less valuable than unpierced."

"Why?"

"Well, generally, carving is used only to remove inferior material from the rough stone. To reduce labor costs, a jade boulder is cut into a design to fit the shape of the boulder. The cutter wishes to make as few cuts as possible. Jade is harder and tougher than diamonds."

Frank stopped and reached for another piece of nicotine gum. "We have to worry more about jade being dyed to enhance its color. Hong Kong merchants can dye low-quality jade a rich green by heating it slowly to 212 degrees Fahrenheit and soaking it in chromium salts for several hours. This dye penetrates the cracks between the jade crystals and may fool an unsuspecting buyer."

"How can I detect a dye job?" Dana asked.

"It's hard but be careful of a green color that seems to float on the surface of the jade. In that case, the dye did not deeply penetrate the stone."

Frank stopped for a moment and then asked, "Do you know about irradiated stones? Colors of stones may be enhanced by being exposed to radiation, especially celestial blue topaz from a white topaz or a milky white sapphire to a translucent blue."

"Isn't that dangerous?" asked Dana.

"Reputable U.S. firms are trustworthy since the Nuclear Regulatory Commission will not allow any gems released until they have properly cooled down. But you probably need to buy a Geiger counter and carry it with you on gem-buying trips."

"Should I avoid irradiated gems?"

"Probably only the hot ones. Irradiation has become about as acceptable to the gem industry as heat-treated stones. Now the real controversy is with crystal growers."

"You can grow gems?" Dana appeared shocked.

"Absolutely," Frank replied. "There is even an International Organization for Crystal Growth, the IOCG. Natural-gem people label laboratory-grown gem crystals synthetic, but the crystal growers despise this term."

"What gems can be grown?" queried Dana.

"Well, obviously cultured pearls. Then, there are Ramura cultured rubies and Chatham-created emeralds. I remember an ad several years ago. It had a box with a cereal bowl filled with synthetic emeralds. The box said '100% natural ingredients. Chatham-created emeralds. *Chatham-created emeralds, the natural manmade gemstone.*' Obviously, there was an outburst of protest from the natural gem people."

"Can I detect a lab-grown gem?"

"The best growers use a hydrothermal or flux method. Responsible growers will dope their products, so they can be identified as lab-grown. But there are many irresponsible people. Interestingly, a lab-grown emerald is actually a purer form of emerald. The stone can be flawless. Natural emeralds are seldom flawless."

"What's the future for lab-grown gems?" Dana asked.

"Impressive! Proponents argue that an orchid that is grown in a hothouse is still a real orchid—so why is a lab grown gem not a real gem? Remember, crystal growers use the same ingredients as Mother Nature. Of course, the cost of lab-grown gems is significantly less than natural-grown gems, providing the seller—us—with a lower cost of goods sold and higher profits."

Dana thought for a moment. "How long will it be before the Japanese start growing gems and flooding the market? Certainly, increasing the supply of gems can lower profits for everyone in the supply chain."

"Good point," replied Frank. "But worry more about Thailand."

"That reminds me," Dana interjected, "we purchased a new diamond detection machine before I left on this trip. Do we expense it?"

"How much did it cost?"

"About $450."

"Will it last more than a year?"

"Sure," responded Dana. "As long as they don't invent a new kind of fake diamond."

"That's the answer. There's a matching principle in accounting. The costs of generating our revenues must be matched against the revenue in the accounting period when the revenue is earned. We match the cost of equipment with the revenue generated from it by using a depreciation procedure. The $450 cost will be allocated to each accounting period over the useful life of the equipment, or the period until the machine's physical life is exhausted," explained Frank. "Suppose the useful life is ten years. Using the straight-line method, each year for ten years we'll record $45 as depreciation expense. To smooth income for financial statement purposes, we'll probably use the straight-line method."

"What about for tax purposes?"

"We'll use an accelerated method for our tax return—something called MACRS—Modified Accelerated Cost Recovery System. Under MACRS, more depreciation expense will be recorded in the early years of the asset. For equipment like the diamond detector, depreciation is at twice the straight-line rate and is computed using the double-declining balance method. You can logically defend this accelerated method since maintenance probably increases as the depreciation expense decreases over the life of the asset. The idea, here, is that you are smoothing the total expenses over the asset's useful life. In fact, for tax purposes, we can write the detection machine off over a seven-year period. The higher our depreciation expense, the less taxable income, and, therefore, we will have a smaller tax liability."

"What do we do with this difference in tax expense between financial reporting and tax reporting?"

"Any difference between our income tax expense, which is based on our accounting income, and our income tax liability is recorded to an account called deferred taxes. It is treated like a liability." Frank smiled in self-satisfaction.

"I've had enough accounting," Dana said "What's the saying? Old accountants like yourself never die, they just lose their balance. Frank, if you keep talking depreciation this and deferred that, I'm going to become unbalanced myself. Tell me about Thailand, instead."

"Fair enough." Frank spit out his gum and stuffed the gray glob between the pages on the in-flight magazine. "Ah, Thailand," he said. "The crossroads of Southeast Asia. About the size of France, it is the only country in the Far East that was not colonized by the Europeans. Thailand is an enchanting Buddhist kingdom where the past and present mingle in perfect harmony—if you believe the travel brochures. A constitutional monarchy but ruled silently by the military. You'll see more olive-drab military uniforms on the streets than saffron-robed monks. I like Bangkok. It's a shame we're going directly to Chiang Mai. Bangkok's Grand Palace is a spectacular building. Did you see 'Bridge on the River Kwai'?"

"Sure, on Turner Classic Movies" said Dana.

"The 'Death Railway' was built by POWs over the Mae Klong River—known to the rest of the world as the River Kwai. The Thai government capitulated immediately to the Japanese invasion in World War II, and the country suffered no damages. Not like the bloody jungle battles of Upper Myanmar. Did you know that the treacherous Myanmar Road is said to have cost exactly one man per mile?"

Dana shook her head and was silent for a moment. Frank then resumed.

"The official language is Thai, but they understand English in hotels, shops, and restaurants. During my last trip I saw Thai-style boxing at the Lumpinee Stadium. A ritual preceded each bout. There was classical Thai music and the barefooted gladiators roared around attacking each other with fists, elbows, knees, and bare feet. The crowd jeered and shouted as they gambled in the aisles." Frank made a half-flapping gesture with his hands. "The bouts consisted of five three-minute full-contact rounds with two-minute intermissions. You can't see action like that in the States, except maybe at an illegal pit bull fight."

Dana frowned and replied, "Sounds sick. What's the music for?"

"To give the Muay Thai boxers rhythm and encouragement, of course. Maybe we can catch a martial arts movie in Chiang Mai instead."

Frank sat silent for some time as if exhausted, and then he handed Dana the discomfort bag and the in-flight magazine and began reading the *International Herald Tribune*.

Dana almost thanked him for all the information she had been given but was wary of appearing to encourage his personal attention. Instead she opened the magazine and began reading an article on page 36 entitled "Diversions: Bangkok's Chic Street."

Their stay in the ultramodern Suvarnabhumi International Airport in Bangkok was short. Dana did stroll around the airport, after converting US$50 into 1665 bahts. [A baht is little over 3 cents in U.S. currency.] She was drawn to the traditional Thai cultural artwork displayed in several of the terminals, including a golden pagoda set amid an oasis of palm trees.

About 500 air miles later Dana and Frank arrived at the City of Roses. Northwest of Bangkok, Chiang Mai is the cultural capital of the north and the world's largest center of such cottage industries as silk, wood carvings, silverware, charmingly painted umbrellas, temple bells, and pottery. In this small city of about 150,000 people located in a fertile valley, a person can bicycle around its old moat in 30 minutes. A short taxi ride and 40-baht took them to the Chiang Mai Orchid Hotel.

Although the four days and nights in Myanmar were unexpectedly pleasant, the Orchid Hotel was even nicer than the Strand. The decor inside was of Thai-Burmese design, and there were lovely woods, carvings, and weavings throughout the hotel. Dana was so exhausted she fell asleep early.

Dana met Frank at 7:30 the next morning in the three-tiered Maerim coffee shop. Cimi Kiengsiri, their dark-skinned local guide and student at Chiang Mai University, was already eating when Dana arrived. After a hearty breakfast, Frank, Dana and Cimi walked to a four-wheel drive Nissan for their trek to the hill tribe region where Thailand, Myanmar, and Laos touch. Known as the Golden Triangle, the area is the smuggling capital of the Far East—especially for opium.

They took Route No. 108 from the town for about 35 miles, and Cimi turned right on a by-road for another 5 miles. There in front of them was the Mae Klang Waterfall. Cimi spoke reasonable English. "The Mae Klang Waterfall," he said "is the best known waterfall in Thailand. It rushes down from a height of 99.4 feet."

Before leaving the waterfall Cimi took a rifle and shotgun from his trunk. Dana knew that the trip today to Mae Sai could be extremely dangerous. Back on Route No. 108 Cimi pointed out the entrance road to Doi Inthanow, a national park with Thailand's highest mountain. After about two more hours of driving past many temperate fruit fields and elephants working in the teak plantations, Cimi parked the Nissan when the dirt road literally stopped, and they began their hike through an area barely touched by the twenty-first century. Through teak forests and thick jungles, past mist-shrouded mountain scenery, the three traveled for three hours to reach a native village called Mae Sai. They were in the lower extremes of the Himalayan foothills. The greatly increased humidity kept them from enjoying the slightly decreased heat.

The village was composed mostly of huts. At the north end of the village they met a group of men dressed in floppy hats, bush shirts, jeans, and sneakers. They were carrying shotguns and rifles and seemed to be guarding about twenty mules. The mules were carrying pack saddles to which heavy sacks were roped.

Frank spoke to Cimi and pointed to one of the mules. "Take Dana over there and show her some raw materials. I need to talk to the boss of this group." Frank walked over and began talking to a brute of a man.

From the corner of her eye, Dana saw a large rat crawl from beneath one of the small huts toward the underbrush. Right behind the rat was a pale brown snake about three feet long. One of the guards sitting under a tree jumped up and shot at the snake with both barrels of his shotgun. He missed.

Dana turned to Cimi and asked, "Why did he do a foolish thing like that? He could have shot someone!"

Cimi had seen the snake also. He smiled and replied, "That was a Russell's Viper. It's deadlier than a cobra."

"Russell's Viper?" Dana said. "Never heard of it."

"Well, Miss Dana, if that snake bites you, death would occur within minutes. About the only way to survive is to have a doctor with you. That snake can bring down an elephant."

"But it's so pretty," Dana said. "Kind of a deep yellow with three rows of large black rings running the entire length of the body. Cimi, if Russell's are so deadly, why don't they exterminate them?"

"Too many rodents around for them to eat," Cimi offered. "Plus, the harsh human conditions and the warm climate are conducive to a large snake population. One mother snake can have a litter of over two dozen babies."

Cimi directed Dana over to one of the mules as he spoke in Burmese to one of the men sitting under a large teak tree. The man got up from his resting place, ambled over to the mule, and opened one of the sacks. He pointed inside and said, "Chous Seine. Jade."

Dana saw a brown rock about the size of a basketball. She spoke to Cimi, "Ask him if I can see the window."

Apparently, the tribe member understood enough English because he pointed to a small cut in the shell-like rock.

Dana could see the green surface color. She asked the tribe member, "Is this a good piece of jade? Does the green color go throughout the rock?"

The tribe member took an old beat up flashlight from his knapsack and shined it into the cut. He said, "Good color. Good stone. Very valuable."

Cimi laughed and said, "Pure gamble."

From the corner of her eye Dana saw Frank pass a large manila envelope to the caravan leader. The caravan leader fingered the envelope and then nodded. He rejoined his men. Frank walked casually over to Dana and the mule.

"So how is the raw material?" he asked. Before Dana could answer Frank continued. "They'll sell this load to one of the Thai Chinese bosses in Chiang Mai. Most of it will go to Hong Kong. Have you seen enough?"

Perspiration was running down Dana's back and face and her blouse was soaked. "You betcha. Definitely enough," she said as she wiped her right hand over her forehead and flicked the sweat off her face. Thailand from early March to the end of May is uncomfortably hot.

Back on the trail Dana caught up with Frank. "Just curious," she said. "Who were those men?"

"Shan tribe members. Tough characters who are very good at transporting jade across the border from Myanmar," Frank said. "They're probably members of the Kachin Organization."

"What was in the manila envelope, Frank?"

"Oh, a small facilitating payment—"

"You mean bribe?" Dana said.

"I prefer inducement ... bribes are a violation of the Foreign Corrupt Practices Act but let me finish. Yes, there was a small inducement plus my contact info including cell number, but most importantly a letter of introduction from Carson Denig, one of our suppliers. He's offered to help us establish our own source for jade."

Frank slapped a mosquito from his arm, immediately changing the subject. "What did Professor Cramer tell you about our cash flow problem?"

"I'm not sure I really understood. He was talking about inventory methods and something called *sludge*," Dana said, wrinkling her nose as she pronounced the term. "Frank, what inventory method do we use?"

"Specific identification. Most jewelers do. It's simple and straight-forward. Costs are assigned to cost of goods sold and ending inventory by identifying the specific cost incurred for *each* unit sold and *each* unit in ending inventory. For example, if a specific jade carving remains in inventory at the end of the year, the cost of that carving is included in ending inventory at exactly what we paid for it. We don't use averages or more complex methods such as FIFO or LIFO or any of their variants." Frank slapped at another mosquito, this time on his forehead.

"This actual cost flow method is quite appropriate for our jewelry shop," Frank continued, "because we have a small volume of separately identifiable units in our inventory. Even better, because we rely on specific identification for our inventory costing, we can also combine it with a perpetual system for tracking inventory. In other words, the cost of each gem or carving is identified as it is sold which allows us to keep a real-time tally of the merchandise on hand and the cost of goods sold and, therefore, net income."

"What happens if a customer steals one of the jade carvings from the display counter? I can't watch everything that happens in the shop." At that moment a tree limb flew back, smacking Dana in the face. She could taste blood in her mouth and took out a handkerchief to press it against the inside of her lip.

"You ok?" Frank said. A tear trickled down Dana's face to mingle with the sweat above her lip.

"I'll be better when we get back to Philly," she said. "But as that isn't really an option right now, do continue." Dana worked the handkerchief some more.

"Well," Frank said, "as I was saying, even though our perpetual inventory system gives us an inventory figure at the end of the year, we still do a physical count of the inventory. We then compare our physical inventory count at year end with the book figure. Any difference is our *inventory shrinkage*—customer theft, breakage, and so forth. It's just another expense of doing business so we record any shrinkage to cost of goods sold."

"This inventory business sounds more involved than I anticipated. Maybe I should take an accounting course," Dana said.

"No need," replied Frank. "You have Janet and me to handle the numbers. What I would recommend instead is that you take the Gemological Institute of America's Colored Stone course. Most of our business is gems, and you can never know too much about the merchandise."

By sunset Frank, Dana, and Cimi had reached their parked car. Dana was dragging, but Frank had gotten his second wind.

"Dana, do you still want to go to the ruby mines along the border of Cambodia?" Frank corrected himself, "I mean Kampuchea before 1980. Cambodia was officially Kampuchea. The country is just south of Bangkok. Not entirely safe."

"No, thank you. I've had enough walking and enough wilderness adventure. Is there anything else we can do in Bangkok, instead?"

Frank smiled, hesitated, and then decided to forgo a snide remark. Dana noticed the hesitation and silently congratulated Frank on wisely restraining himself.

Frank finally replied, "I could get us into a Thai laboratory which cooks gemstones. They specialize in rubies and sapphires."

"I would like that," Dana said.

On the trip back to Chiang Mai, Frank began drawing on a sheet of paper and then handed it to Dana in the back seat. "Here's a diagram of our inventory process. You may have to use the flashlight to see it. Sun's going down."

Dana reviewed the penciled outline with the help of a flashlight:

Cost of beginning + Cost of jade = Cost of jade
jade inventory   purchased   available for sale

Cost of jade − Cost of ending − Shrinkage = Cost of
available   jade inventory   jade sold
for sale

She then said, "Not bad. I think I can understand this."

At 2:30 the next afternoon, Frank and Dana arrived at Corelab, a high security gem treatment laboratory. Only 20 minutes from Bangkok's downtown jewelry district, the cybernetically controlled laboratory is hidden by shrubbery and patrolled by guard dogs. Inside the lab, Frank introduced Dana to Ken Ho, the computer genius staffing the ten computer-controlled electric ovens.

Mr. Ho pointed to one of the ovens. "A computer controls the temperature of the ovens by taking readings of the treatment process every five seconds. No longer is the gem burning done in an oil drum insulated with coconut rinds."

"What is your success rate for cooked stones?" Dana asked.

"We do carefully select gems that show promise of improvement. Our success rate is about 90 percent," Mr. Ho said.

"How long do you treat rubies and sapphires?" Dana asked.

"As long as necessary. Each parcel of gems may be cooked for a few hours or up to a week."

"The ovens I understand, but what does the computer do?" Frank asked.

"The computer does what a machine operator can do but 1,000 times faster. Basically, the computer monitors the temperature and automatically adjusts the heat and the oven atmosphere to ensure that the duration and intensity of each phase of the gem burning process follows the prescribed sequence."

Mr. Ho pointed to a colored photo on the wall showing two parcels of rubies. "Notice the red rubies on the right. They've received treatment. The pinkish ones on the left were from the same lot before treatment."

"How much do you charge for this treatment?" Dana asked.

"We break each parcel of stones into three lots. The client gets two lots and we take one lot for payment."

"Has the industry accepted heat treatment?" Dana inquired.

"Almost an accepted industry practice today," was Mr. Ho's response.

After bidding good-bye to Mr. Ho, Dana and Frank decided to visit several gem factories before returning to the hotel. Early the next morning they left the Chiang Mai Orchid Hotel en route to the airport for their return trip to the U.S.A.

Four

As a general rule, a witness may only testify to facts and
leave inferences or conclusions to the judge or jury. An expert witness, on the other hand, may testify in the form
of an opinion based not only upon those facts perceived
by the expert, but on facts perceived by others, as well,
and made known to the expert at or before the trial; this
may include the evidence or testimony of others.
—Francis C. Dykeman

Lenny had hoped for a call from Dana Scott when she returned
from her trip. But she did not call, so Lenny finally called her at
the jade shop. They agreed on a meeting at an out-of-the-way
restaurant south of the city the following evening. Lenny arrived
early at the Fish House and ordered a Diet Coke. Five minutes later
Dana sat down at his table.

"Hey, handsome!" Dana said. "How was your day?"

"The usual. Would you like something to drink, a soda maybe?"
Lenny took a sip of his Coke.

"A drink sounds good, but I think I'll have an iced tea."

"So how was your day?" Lenny asked casually.

"Not so usual. This afternoon we had a professional gem switcher
in the shop."

"What happened?" Lenny asked.

"Janet, our bookkeeper, was helping out this afternoon. We were
busy. She was showing a two-carat ruby to a male customer. Ap-

parently, he was a switch artist. Anyway, Janet was distracted, and he ripped us off."

"Ouch! I'm sorry. What was his technique?" Lenny was more interested now.

"Oh, these guys use cigarettes or eyeglasses as props. They get a lot of movement going with their hands, and zap! They switch the stone. We've caught on to their methods so now we use locking tweezers, but the guy today had been in the store before. He asked Janet to see a two-carat ruby, and then switched both the ruby and the tweezers in a single move. He was very smooth."

"What did you do?"

"I called around and apparently this same guy has hit about six other shops on the street. One jeweler told me that this person hit him twice. He vaguely recognized him from an earlier theft. He swore that he never took his eyes off the guy, yet he made the switch undetected. He got a second diamond from him and left a CZ."

"What's a CZ?"

"Cubic zirconia. Looks like a diamond but weighs about twice as much."

Abruptly Dana changed the subject. "I really need to hire you. My cash flow problem is not getting any better. I worry that either Frank or Janet may be taking money from the business somehow. A sleuth like you should be able to solve the mystery."

"Maybe you're just not playing the float game well enough," Lenny suggested.

"Does that have to do with inventory?" She laughed aloud.

"Not completely," replied Lenny. "You need to shorten the elapsed time between the sale of your gems and the actual time the cash is collected and deposited into your bank account, you know, the days in accounts receivable calculation. This process involves your method of billing and your method of bill delivery. There are a whole range of cash management strategies."

"For example, Lenny?"

"Suppose you get a purchase order. The invoice should be prepared from the purchase order and mailed immediately. It doesn't matter if the invoice reaches the customer before the merchandise does. The customer will put the bill into a current payment file, and you'll get paid ahead of other people."

"I'm not sure such a change would make a significant difference in my jade shop. Most of our sales are for cash, debit, or credit."

A disinterested waiter brought the iced tea, and as he left, Dana smiled and said, "I'm interested in your proposition that we spend some time together."

"Great. You've made my day. Why are you interested?"

"Oh, probably because of your pleasant personality and sense of humor."

Lenny spent an enjoyable hour talking with Dana. When they parted, he promised to call her in several days. It would have been nice to spend a little more time with her, he thought. *I wish I didn't have to prepare for my day in court tomorrow.*

"Professor Cramer, for the court's record, please state your full name and current address."

"Paul Leonard Cramer, the third, 1245 Liberty Court, Philadelphia, Pennsylvania."

"Dr. Cramer, we want to thank you for testifying today as an expert witness about certain accounting matters. But first, before we get your testimony, I have several questions for you concerning your background. Where did you obtain your Ph.D.?"

"University of Illinois."

"Where did you receive your MBA?"

"Harvard."

"Where did you receive your bachelor's degree?"

"Amherst College."

"Are you listed in Who's Who in America?"

"Yes."

"What years were you president of the American Accounting Association?"

"That was 2005–2006."

Lenny had rehearsed the answers to most of these questions. He liked the grueling task of preparing beforehand and participating in the courtroom battle over accounting principles. He saw it as a

challenge—anticipating the many trick questions asked by the opposing attorney and then giving a thoughtful, professional response.
Probably the stress was not worth the daily fees he received, but he
loved it. He sometimes imagined the opposing attorney to be a
black clad medieval knight racing toward him on horseback with
a long, sharp lance. Lenny always toppled the vicious knight in his
daydreams.

"Professor Cramer, have you written any accounting books?"

"I have written four accounting books. Two principles of accounting textbooks, a forensic accounting book, plus an accounting
casebook for MBA students."

"Would you please explain what is meant by forensic accounting?"

"Briefly, forensic accounting is a science that deals with the
relation and application of accounting facts to business and social
problems." Lenny smiled and turned toward the jury. "As I tell my
students, a forensic accountant is like the CSI characters on TV,
except a forensic accountant uses accounting records and facts to
uncover fraud, missing assets, insider trading, and other white-
collar crimes." Lenny turned back to the pinstriped lawyer.

"Dr. Cramer, by CSI you mean Crime Scene Investigation. Is
that correct?"

"Yes."

"Professor Cramer, are you currently employed?"

"Yes. I am the Sidney Paton Professor of Accounting at the
Wharton School of the University of Pennsylvania."

"Is it an honor to hold a professorship?"

"Yes, professorships in accounting are reasonably rare." Lenny
often wondered why the 'honor' wasn't accompanied by a com-
mensurate increase in salary. The real money, of course, was in
being designated an 'endowed chair.' Lenny was still searching for
a chair designation at an agreeable university.

"Professor Cramer, are you a Certified Public Accountant?"

"Yes, I have been licensed in the state of Pennsylvania since 1984,"
Lenny responded.

"Are you a member of the American Institute of CPAs?"

"Yes, also since 1984."

"Do you serve on the Board of Directors of any major corporations?"

"Yes, I serve on the Board of Directors of two *Fortune 500* companies and for three mid-tier companies."

"Dr. Cramer, are you an outside consultant?"

"Yes, I have my own forensic accounting firm here in Philadelphia. I started it about seven years ago."

"Please estimate how many professional articles you have published."

"About 70." Lenny shifted slightly in the wooden witness chair. He was careful to speak to the jurors rather than the attorney.

"Thank you." The attorney shuffled several pages and then continued, "Now, have you ever appeared as an expert witness in the courtroom?"

"Yes. I have been an expert witness in forensic accounting matters on about eleven different occasions—two oil companies, two banks, one insurance company, a manufacturer, an accounting firm, the Internal Revenue Service, the SEC, and two-family divorce cases."

"What is the SEC?"

"Sorry." Lenny's face reddened. "The SEC refers to the Securities and Exchange Commission. The SEC was created by the Securities Exchange Act of 1934. The government agency has the legal authority to prescribe accounting guidelines for firms whose shares of stocks and bonds are sold to the investing public on the stock exchanges. The law requires that such companies make reports to the SEC, giving detailed information about their operations. The SEC regulates the amount and type of information to be included in annual and quarterly reports and the methods to be used to develop the information. For the most part, the SEC has followed many of the standards established by the FASB concerning the methods used to develop the required accounting information."

"What is the FASB?" the lawyer asked.

"FASB stands for the Financial Accounting Standards Board which began to issue financial accounting standards in 1973. Before that, the official standard setting body was the—"

"Dr. Cramer," the attorney interrupted, "please confine your answer to the question asked."

"Right. The FASB. Well, the SEC has charged this seven-member independent nongovernmental body with the responsibility of developing and issuing standards of financial accounting affecting the private sector of the United States. Committee members include public and nonpublic accountants as well as non-accountants. In short, the FASB is our current source of U.S. Generally Accepted Accounting Principles, for which accountants use the acronym GAAP."

The attorney turned to the judge and said, "Your honor, we present to this court Dr. Cramer as an expert witness in the area of forensic accounting."

The robed judge turned to the opposing attorney and said, "Mr. Henderson, do you have any objections to this request?"

The opposing attorney stood up and spoke loudly, "No, your honor."

The judge turned to the court reporter. "Let the record reflect that the plaintiff's counsel did not challenge the *bona fides* of Dr. Cramer as an expert witness in forensic accounting. Counselor," the judge said to the attorney conducting the direct examination, "you may proceed."

Lenny then answered a number of technical questions for which he had previously prepared. As the defendant's attorney returned to his seat, the opposing attorney rose to begin his cross-examination. His questions focused on how income taxes should be reported on the financial records of the oil company involved in the lawsuit.

"Professor Cramer, I would like to start by asking you about a FASB pronouncement. I understand that even though the long name for these pronouncements is 'Statement of Financial Accounting Standards' that the shorthand notation your profession uses to refer to them is FASBs. So, my question to you is under FASB 69 are the terms *net income* or *net profits* ever mentioned?"

"Not in FASB 69. Although," Lenny said, "it is generally understood that results of operations are approximately equivalent to net income and net profits, and that some companies, in fact, use the term net income and net profits in their FASB 69 disclosures."

"Are those companies the exception, rather than the rule?" Mr. Henderson asked.

"I really can't say. While I have looked at the financial reports for several companies, I haven't done a comprehensive study of terminology use." Lenny paused and then turned to the judge. "FASB 69 is a pre-codification standard and is no longer considered authoritative. May I clarify?"

"Counselor Henderson?" the judge said as he motioned to the plaintiff's lawyer.

The attorney whispered to the co-counsel on his right and then turned back to judge. "No objections."

"Dr. Cramer, enlighten us."

Lenny cleared his throat. "I'm sorry if I confused the court. I didn't mean to imply that the underlying fundamentals of FASB 69 are no longer applicable or that the accounting guidelines have been superseded. What I was trying to say is that all standards issued before July 1, 2009 have been subsumed into what is now referred to as the Accounting Standards Codification or ASC. The last and final FASB—*Statement of Financial Accounting Standards No. 168*—established the ASC as the source of authoritative GAAP for all nongovernmental entities. This includes all for-profit companies and not-for-profit organizations. Of course, for public companies that are SEC registrants, SEC rules and interpretive releases are also considered GAAP and still apply."

"Dr. Cramer, you said FASB 69 has been subsumed. Subsumed how?" the judge asked.

"The evolution of U.S. Generally Accepted Accounting Principles has been an organic undertaking spanning eighty some years of research bulletins, opinions, statements of positions, interpretations, and standards from various standard setting bodies. The result is the massive 25,000-plus pages of minimally-organized jumble we call GAAP. If we had to do it over again, GAAP would look much leaner, be topically organized, and more understandable."

Lenny paused to get his breath. "But with a multi-trillion-dollar economy that uses GAAP for financial reporting, starting over isn't an option. Instead, in the early part of the 2000s, the FASB enlisted over 200 professionals from multiple organizations to abridge the evolved body of authoritative literature into a single, consistent, searchable format. It took five years. The Codification kept the underlying content of the official pronouncements, but not the original pronouncements themselves. Redundancy was eliminated. Nonessentials removed. Only the essence remains. The previous standards-based approach has been subsumed into a comprehensive collection of roughly 90 topics."

Lenny knew he was putting the jurors to sleep, but he continued since the judge had asked the question. "Topics are divided into subtopics, subtopics into sections, and sections into subsections. FASB 69 is now ASC 932-235-55, or *Extractive Activities-Oil and Gas—Notes to Financial Statements—Implementation Guidance and Illustrations.* The 900 series of topics address specific industry standards, in this case, oil and gas."

"Thank you, Dr. Cramer," the judge smiled. "Mr. Henderson, you may proceed with your cross-examination."

"Very well, your Honor." The plaintiff's attorney picked up his notes. "Professor Cramer, you testified earlier that income taxes are one of several costs in the computation of net income and net profits and are deducted along with other taxes on, or measured by, profits or income. Are you saying that classification of expense items is irrelevant for accounting purposes?"

Lenny thought for a moment and then spoke, "Well, to paraphrase an early accounting theorist, A. L. Littleton, from the 1940s: All costs have equal standing as far as being recovered in the determination of income. I agree with Littleton. I don't believe that any one particular cost is somehow superior to another from an accounting standpoint."

"Professor Cramer, I didn't imply any kind of qualitative superiority. I am asking whether the classification of costs itself, the various items of cost under GAAP, is irrelevant."

Lenny shifted in the hard seat and replied, "Well, it depends on the circumstances. I have seen expenses lumped together. I've seen them aggregated at extremely high levels of detail. Personally, I believe there are certain minimum standards on some items with respect to how they should be disclosed, but as far as what level of detail is required, everything depends on the specific situation. I mean, you have to give me a situation with a specific example."

"Perhaps," the attorney posited as he walked towards Lenny, "you should tell us what an income statement does."

"The income statement is the financial report that measures the profitability of the operation of an enterprise for a distinct period. It provides investors, creditors, and other stakeholders with information that helps them predict the amount, timing, and uncertainty of future cash flows."

In a half-question, half-statement, the attorney then said, "And the income statement consists of revenues less expenses, does it not, Professor Cramer?"

"Yes."

The attorney cleared his throat and then asked, "Well, does FASB 96 require a separate reporting of income taxes on a separate line?"

"FASB 109 superseded FASB 96. FASB 109 has been codified into several topics in the ASC, generally ASC Topic 740 Income Taxes. For Extractive Activities—Oil and Gas, income taxes are codified as subtopic ASC 932-740."

"I am sorry. I meant ASC Topic 740," replied the attorney.

Lenny turned to the half-listening judge and stated, "ASC 740 is concerned primarily with timing differences—the difference between income tax expense as reported on the financial statements versus what's on the corporate tax return, and I would have to refresh my memory by looking at the specific provisions to see exactly what it says."

"Professor Cramer," the plaintiff's attorney continued, "could you explain what timing differences are?"

Lenny sighed. "The late Ed Deakin, a notable University of Texas professor of accounting, described this well. A timing difference, he said, arises when there is a different method used for recognizing a revenue or expense for financial reporting purposes from the method used for reporting taxes. An example would be depreciation. The total amount to be depreciated is the same for both financial reporting and tax reporting. The allocation of depreciation expense each year, however, will differ if the same depreciation method is not employed. The difference between the two methods is a timing difference that causes the amount of reported income tax expense each year to differ from the amount of income tax actually paid."

"Well," the attorney said, his voice rising, "it is true that ASC 740 does address the question of the timing differences in the reporting of income tax, but to know what taxes you have to account for, you have to know whether they are treated as an income tax under ASC 740, isn't that so?"

Lenny hesitated and then stated, "I think you're asking me to draw a conclusion about ASC 740, which at this point I'm not prepared to draw. As I mentioned earlier, I would like to look at ASC 740 and see what it says, and then perhaps I can help you with the interpretation."

The attorney acted offended. "Well, I believe you cited ASC 740 in your report, did you not?"

"Yes, but I don't believe I cited a provision which says you have to report income taxes on a separate line in the income statement."

At this point Lenny began to get irritated with the attorney. Lenny knew in general that ASC 740 dealt with accounting for income taxes, and he knew the general provisions, but he was not a walking encyclopedia who could quote every single word of every financial accounting standard.

"Professor Cramer, I've had marked for identification a portion of the FASB Accounting Standards Codification Topic 740 on Income Taxes entitled *Income Taxes-Overall-Disclosure-General-Income Statement Related Disclosures.* I ask whether you'd be able to respond to my question after examining that exhibit." The attorney got permission from the judge and walked to Lenny and handed him the codification excerpt for Topic 740.

After reading ASC 740-10-50-9, which was highlighted, Lenny looked up and began speaking slowly, distinctly, and firmly. He knew that everything that was said by a witness was taken down by the court reporter. "If I may, I'll restate the question for the record, since it's been a bit of time since we went through it. The question was about does ASC 740 require reporting of income taxes on a separate line of the income statement. In Topic 740, Subtopic 10, Section 50, Paragraph 9 it states—if I may, I'll quote it and let it stand for itself:

> "The significant components of income tax expense attributable to continuing operations for each year presented shall be disclosed in the financial statements or notes thereto."

Lenny looked up from the exhibit. "The answer to your question is No. GAAP does not require disclosure of income tax expense on a separate line of the income statement." Lenny chuckled to himself. The one thing about a courtroom, he thought, is that sometimes it can be very esoteric and even occasionally boring.

The attorney smiled. "Well, within the variations of timing differences, are income tax expenses under the income statement reported separately?"

"I have seen them reported as a line item, Income Tax Expense, which includes part of the income tax expense, but not all of it. Until 2015, I've seen extraordinary items reported gross with the income tax subtracted from them. I've seen extraordinary items reported net of the income tax effect. Based on my experience, under U.S. GAAP income tax expense can be disclosed in a variety of ways, not just as a separate line item on the income statement."

The attorney took a drink of water and then stated, "Professor Cramer, I understand your answer to be that income taxes *may* be reported under operations, under extraordinary items, *or* in corrections of errors on the income statement. My question to you is as follows: Are income taxes under GAAP reported on a separate line in determining income from operations?"

"I can say this," Lenny answered. "Generally, there is a line item that is labeled income tax expense that's related to the results of operations for—let's say—the financial statements. Also, after 2015, extraordinary item reporting has disappeared."

The attorney interjected, "Including the income statement, when you refer to financial statements?"

Lenny replied, "Yes, including the income statement."

"Does ASC 740 require separate reporting of income tax expense in determining income from operations?" Mr. Henderson looked directly at Lenny.

"Let me review ASC 740 again." Lenny read for a moment and then explained, "ASC 740 does say that the components of income tax expense should be disclosed. The standard says that there should be an allocation of the items, and it gives some options on how they are disclosed."

Lenny paused and then continued, "I believe it was the late University of Chicago Professor Sidney Davidson who wrote about the depreciation problem. He correctly cited it as a major contributor to timing differences between what companies report and the income tax that they actually pay, when in fact these same companies have this large contingent liability of deferred taxes that is going to catch up with them some day when the timing differences reverse."

Lenny caught his breath and then continued. "That was the focus behind FASB 109, now ASC 740, and today you are asking me to attempt to convert that to a statement of whether ASC 740 requires some specialized disclosure of income tax expense when the standard itself allows options in the way in which taxes are disclosed.

"I'll share my own feeling on this, and I'm just thinking out loud here, is that *yes*, ASC 740 requires a disclosure of income tax expense as defined within the standard."

Lenny stopped, poured a glass of water, and took three small sips as he thought. "However, it allows a variety of disclosures. It certainly requires some reconciliation between what has been reported on the income tax statement and the income as it is reported on the financial statements. To the extent that there is no material difference between the income tax expense as reported on the financial statements and the income taxes reported to the IRS, ASC 740 simply would not apply. There is no material difference, and hence, there is no problem here."

"Professor Cramer, please try to speak in laymen's language. When you refer to options available under ASC 740, aren't you really talking about the way the components of the income tax expense are either disclosed on the face of the income statement or explained further in footnotes?"

Lenny sensed that the attorney was trying to discredit his testimony, so he quickly responded. "If I understand your question, what you're saying is that there has to be a disclosure of those tax expenses. When they are material, they are disclosed in the statements in *some* form, and there is a subsequent disclosure either in the statements *or* in the notes thereto which explains what's going on with the income taxes that are covered by ASC Topic 740."

Lenny paused and then continued, "But, again, if the income tax expense under ASC 740 is the same for financial reporting purposes as it is on the tax return, then a simple disclosure of the amount is sufficient, and that disclosure can be on the face of the income statement or it can be someplace else in the notes to the financial statements."

"Professor, are you familiar with the reporting of income tax expense by oil companies—integrated oil companies—on their income statement?"

"Yes, I am," Lenny responded.

"Are you familiar with windfall profits tax?"

"Of course. Windfall profits taxes have been imposed from time to time by the U.S. Congress on companies that experience a sudden increase in profit margins—say, when there is an unexpected jump in crude oil prices like we had in the summer of 2008. The price per barrel almost doubled, spiking to $140, with retail gas prices climbing above $4 a gallon at the pump. That year there were several bills before Congress to reinstate the windfall profits tax which had expired back in 1988."

"Do you know of any oil company that reports the windfall profits tax as an income tax expense on its income statement?" the lawyer fired back.

"When it is listed, typically windfall profits tax is listed as a separate line item from the other income tax expenses," Lenny answered calmly. "Remember, the windfall profits tax was an *excise* tax—not *an income* tax. Today there is no windfall profits tax."

"The answer is you're not aware of any oil company that reports windfall profits tax as an income tax expense on its income statement or financial statements?"

"It's been awhile since companies have been required to pay a windfall profit tax, but if my memory serves me, the answer is Yes. That's correct," Lenny answered firmly.

A few more minor questions followed before Lenny's testimony was complete. From his previous experience as an expert witness, he had learned it was always best to rephrase the interrogator's question to make the point to which he was testifying. Today he felt things had gone smoothly at the hearing.

After exchanging pleasantries with some people he had met earlier in the courtroom, Lenny quickly grabbed a cab to go back to his university office. He needed to review his lecture on dividends for preferred stock. In the back of the cab, he pulled out his iPad and began reading the *CPA Letter Daily*, an electronically delivered briefing of top stories impacting the accounting profession published by the American Institute of CPAs. He spotted a conference he had hoped to attend and added a note in his calendar for November: "AICPA National Forensic & Valuation Services Conference, Orlando, FL." He loved Florida in the fall. Not so muggy. He also browsed through aicpa.org, the AICPA store for practice aids and continuing professional education courses. An on-demand webinar on cash management entitled "Optimizing Company Cash: A Guide for Financial Professionals" caught his attention, so he purchased a 6-month access to the webcast. He blocked out two hours in his schedule for the coming week to view the presentation. The title of the web training event reminded him of Dana Scott's cash problem and the unclear status of his personal relationship with Dana.

———————

"Lenny, you're back early," the building manager assigned to Steinberg-Dietrich Hall said.

Lenny turned around and smiled. He recognized Woody's voice right away. "My testimony ended quickly, and I figured that I would come back to campus and prepare my lecture for tomorrow."

"What's the lecture on?" inquired Woody.

"Dividends for preferred stock."

"I'll give you a hand with it," Woody smiled.

Lenny was familiar with the pattern of Woody's behavior. Woody often would hang out in Lenny's office to avoid working. Most people knew that if they needed someone from facilities, they should come to Lenny's office because Woody would probably be there. On more than one occasion, Lenny had come to his office and found Woody asleep in Lenny's easy chair.

"Tell me how this sounds, Woody. Preferred stock is like bonds payable, because both securities pay investors a percentage on their respective par values."

"Nah. Too technical," grumbled Woody as he eased back in the easy chair. "What's par value, anyway? Is it a golf score or what?" Lenny smiled.

He enjoyed going through class preparation with Woody, who had a decidedly layman's perspective of the business world, but more street smarts than Lenny hoped to ever have. Lenny was confident that if Woody could understand what he was talking about, any student could too. Well, most students.

"Par value does nothing more than establish the maximum responsibility of a stockholder in the event of insolvency. Par value is used to record the preferred stock when it is issued. From the par value of preferred stock dividends are calculated," Lenny said.

"How's that?" Woody asked as he stuck a piece of sugar-free gum in his mouth.

"Give me a second, Woody," Lenny said laughingly. "I didn't realize that your desire for knowledge was so strong."

"Yeah, I'm that way about accounting for preferred dividends," retorted Woody with a sheepish grin.

"I'm always happy to quench a student's thirst for knowledge," replied Lenny, becoming more serious. "Let's see. To calculate preferred dividends, all you must do is multiply the par value by the dividend percentage associated with the preferred stock. For example, if a company has 8 percent preferred stock with $100 par value, all they do is multiply 8 percent by $100, giving them $8 in annual dividends per preferred share. If a company has 1,000 shares of preferred stock outstanding, then the total annual preferred dividends the company would pay would be $8,000."

"What if your stock is not outstanding—like the stock my brother-in-law bought three years ago that is now totally worthless?" grumbled Woody as he put his feet up on Lenny's desk. "That stock was certainly not outstanding."

"That's what your brother-in-law gets for listening to his so-called friends with hot tips," said Lenny, referring to Woody's brother-in-law who often boasted that he had friends in the mob. "*Outstanding*, my friend, has a different meaning when it comes to stock. There are three terms you should know. *Shares authorized* are the maximum number of shares the corporation could possibly sell as specified in the company's corporate charter. *Shares issued* are the number of shares of stock actually sold to the public by the corporation. And *shares outstanding* refers to the shares of a corporation's stock that are outside of the control of the corporation."

"What's the difference between the number of shares issued and the number outstanding?"

"You're paying attention today, Woody," remarked Lenny with a grin.

"Always do," garbled Woody, as he placed an unlit cigar in his mouth.

"Once stock is originally sold, it is issued and outstanding. If the stock is repurchased in the market by the company and held as treasury stock, the stock is still issued, but no longer outstanding or available for purchase in the marketplace by individuals like your brother-in-law or other investors." Lenny paused and stared at Woody. "Are you ever going to smoke that cigar? You've been putting that same cigar in your mouth for three months without lighting it up."

"It's healthier this way." Woody fingered the cigar, looked at it, and then stared back at Lenny. "Besides, this is a smoke-free campus. They took away my rights. Where is the ACLU when you need them? There doesn't seem to be much to preferred stock dividends, does there? That calculation you went through was a piece of cake."

"Nuances, Woody. There are always nuances. I haven't even mentioned what to do if the preferred stock is cumulative." Lenny took a deep breath and continued. "My previous example assumed that the preferred stock was non-cumulative. If the preferred stock is cumulative, the stockholder is guaranteed a dividend each year. If we go with the previous example and require dividends to be cumulative, the preferred dividend of $8 per year is guaranteed to be paid at some point. If the corporation fails to pay out dividends for one year, then the dividends are one year in arrears. That would mean that preferred stockholders would receive $16 per share the next year. If there was no cumulative feature, the preferred shareholder would only receive $8 per share regardless of whether dividends were in arrears. And don't forget, that common stockholders can receive no dividends until the obligation to preferred stockholders is completely satisfied."

"I'll keep that in mind," Woody replied in the middle of a yawn. "Is that it?"

"Yes, that's it. Pretty easy, huh?" asked Lenny, eyebrows raising. "I think I got it."

"Good. Then, you should be able to answer a couple of multiple-choice questions I've been working on for the midterm exam."

Woody groaned. "Not one of your multiple guess-questions, Doc. If you just had four possible answers, I'd have at least 25% chance of getting it right. But no, you always make them so hard by having 'none of the above' as a possible answer."

"Exactly! Reduces the likelihood of guessing to which you jokingly referred. We'll start with the easy one first."

Which of the following terms refers to the largest number of common shares of a corporation?

a. Shares authorized
b. Shares issued
c. Shares outstanding
d. Repurchased shares held in the treasury for reissue
e. None of the above.

"Most of the time the longest answer is the right one," Woody said. "So, if I guessed answer 'd' — "

"You'd guess wrong," Lenny said. "In fact, treasury shares would usually be the smallest number of common shares for a corporation and the answer is what?"

"Lenny, you didn't let me finish," Woody interrupted. "I was going to say answer 'a' based on the mini-lesson you gave. As a great teacher once told me, *authorized shares* are the maximum number the corporation could legally sell. You can't get any larger than maximum." Woody smiled in satisfaction.

"And if you answered 'a' you would be right. You're one for one, Woody. Care to stop now?"

"Nah, I like to play the odds. Hit me with question 2, Doc."

Lenny handed Woody a spare calculator he had picked up for free at one of the vendor booths at the last Mid-Atlantic Regional meeting of the American Accounting Association. "You might need this for the next one. It involves some numbers."

> At December 31, 2018, and December 31, 2019, Wasatch In-
> dustries, Inc., has 4,000 shares of 10%, $25 par value, cumula-
> tive preferred stock and 240,000 shares of $1 par value com-
> mon stock outstanding. The Wasatch Board of Directors
> declared and paid a total of $8,000 in dividends to sharehold-
> ers in 2018. In 2019, the board declares and pays a total of
> $36,000 in dividends. What are the dividends received by the
> preferred stockholders in 2019?
>
> a. $24,000
> b. $10,000
> c. $8,000
> d. $4,000
> e. None of the above.

"My longest answer strategy usually doesn't work with answers containing numbers because numbers are so short, so I'm going to eliminate answer 'e,'" Woody said. "And I can eliminate $24,000 because the first answer is usually the sucker answer for students not willing to check all the possibilities. That leaves 'b,' 'c,' or 'd' so I have a one in three chances of getting this one right. I like 'b,' and I don't even need a calculator for that one: 4,000 shares times $25 per share times 10% equals $10,000. I'm going with 'b,'" Woody said as he put his unlit stogie back in his mouth.

Lenny smirked. "Close but no cigar," he chuckled.

"Don't tell me it's 'e,' Doc," Woody complained.

"Let's look at your answer first," Lenny suggested. "It's true that the annual dividend for 4,000 shares of 10% preferred would be $10,000. On the face of it, 'b' would seem to be the right answer."

"I thought so," Woody said.

"Answer 'b' is partially right but doesn't take into consideration the fact that the preferred stock is cumulative and that there were dividends in arrears from 2018. Like I said, you were close, Woody."

"So, we have $10K preferred dividends per year but only $8K paid in 2018. That leaves $2K unpaid," Woody said.

"Yes, Wasatch had $2,000 dividends in arrears as of December 31, 2018 that it owed to preferred shareholders going forward. With the Board of Directors declaring $36K dividends in 2019, that more than covered the $10K 10% annual dividend to preferred shareholders plus the $2K back dividends. That makes a total of $12,000 to preferred in 2019, leaving $24,000 for common shareholders."

"So, 'a' was a trick answer? I was right."

"Yes, answer 'a' was what we call a plausible distractor."

"And I suppose $8,000 and $4,000 are also plausible destructors because you mention $8,000 dividends for 2018 and 4,000 shares?" Woody speculated. "That leaves answer 'e,' the longest answer."

"Bingo!" Lenny said. "You shouldn't have been so quick to dismiss the longest answer though your guessing strategy is very flawed. *Destructors* ... very clever."

"*None of the above*," Woody muttered as he leaned forward in his chair. "Sounds like the name of a long shot winner at the track. I may not have gotten question two right, Doc, but I'll have you know I was a big winner at Harrah's Chester Racetrack the other day. It paid 8 to 1."

"What was the horse's name?"

"Dana's Revenge."

Dana. It had been several days since he had seen her last. Lenny wondered how she was doing. Woody continued to ramble on about his day at the races and his love for the ponies. Lenny, half listening, continued to think about Dana as he cleaned up his exam notes for the midterm and put his papers in the proper order for his lecture tomorrow.

Five

Accounting is the system for gathering data about an entity's economic activity, processing and organizing the data to produce useful information about the entity and communicating the information to people who use it to make decisions. Communication is often an important but challenging part of the process.

—John Friedlan

Frank Harrison was scheduled to testify as an expert witness for Jane Braswell in the Superior Court of Philadelphia. She was the wife of a wealthy heart surgeon in Philadelphia. Frank did a great deal of divorce work for attorneys, but few of the cases ever reached the courtroom. This messy marital split-up was the exception. Frank felt qualified to testify about the valuation of a service-type business, plus the Braswell's extensive collection of jade carvings and rubies.

However, nothing today could be as dramatic as what happened yesterday afternoon, when Frank was in the courtroom waiting to be called to testify. A morning newspaper article best described the bitter dispute with this headline: "Tales of Money, Sex, Intrigue Spice Up Braswell's Divorce Drama."

Apparently, Jane Braswell had signed a prenuptial agreement with Benjamin Braswell, which limited Jane to twenty percent of the money made by the 48-year-old heart surgeon. A major question of this trial concerned the validity of the prenuptial agreement.

Yesterday, Frank had watched as a Mrs. Daniels testified about her sexual encounters with Ben Braswell. She said that the rendezvous had taken place during the lunch hour at her home while her husband was at work in the same hospital that employed Ben Braswell.

Frank had watched Jane Braswell toy with a gold bracelet when Mrs. Daniels started to complain that she was having difficulty breathing because it was so tense in the courtroom.

Suddenly Mrs. Daniels fainted and fell out of the witness chair, smashing her face on the counter enclosing the witness box. The judge cleared the courtroom, and called for an emergency recess until the following day. When the paramedics arrived, they efficiently lifted the woman onto an EMT stretcher. While they were carrying the woman through the crowded Superior Court hallway, she began to moan loudly.

———————

"All rise," the bailiff said to the reassembled court. "The Honorable Judge Gantmann Mundy presiding."

"You may be seated," Judge Mundy said. "Members of the jury, in light of yesterday's excitement, I want to thank you for your patience. We will resume this case by hearing testimony from the next scheduled witness."

Frank was asked to take the stand. A few minutes later Jane Braswell's attorney approached Frank, who was now sitting in the witness chair. The jury was to the left of Frank and the judge was to Frank's immediate right. "Mr. Harrison, have you testified in divorce cases in the past?"

"Yes, about twenty-five such cases."

"Would you please state your credentials?"

Frank leaned forward in his seat and began. "I am president of Kuaker City Consulting, one of the largest consulting firms in Philadelphia. We specialize in valuations, pensions, insurance, and employee benefits.

"I am a Certified Financial Planner—CFP for short—and a Chartered Financial Consultant. I am also a member of the Financial Planning Association. Several members of my firm are actuaries."

"Mr. Harrison, what is required to become a CFP?"

"A CFP designation is provided to individuals who have a bachelor's degree, specialized education in over 100 integrated financial planning topics, successfully completed a 10-hour exam on risk management, investments, taxes, retirement, employee benefits and estate planning, and three years of qualifying work experience."

"Mr. Harrison, what is an actuary?"

Frank smiled broadly and looked at the jury. "Some people maintain that it is a graveyard for dead actors. But seriously—." Several jury members smiled and one older gentleman in the courtroom actually laughed aloud.

"Mr. Harrison," the judge said. "Please stick to the question."

"Yes, Your Honor. An actuary is a professional statistician that calculates insurance and annuity premiums, reserves, and dividends."

"Mr. Harrison," the attorney continued, "do you have any business experience with jade and rubies?"

"Yes, I have taken and passed both the diamond and colored stone courses of the GIA—Gemological Institute of America. I am currently a one-third owner of the Jade & More Shop here in Philly. I purchase rubies frequently in Bangkok, Thailand, and in Myanmar."

"You have a business degree from Temple University, is that correct?"

"Yes, sir."

"Mr. Harrison, you were engaged by Dr. and Mrs. Braswell to determine the value of their assets, were you not?"

"Yes, I was."

"What value did you arrive at?"

"I estimate their total net worth, including Dr. Braswell's medical practice, to be approximately $9,332,000. If it pleases the court, I would like to explain how I arrived at this figure."

The judge nodded. "Please, proceed, Mr. Harrison."

Frank turned to the judge. "I have prepared some charts for the court. May I move the charts where I can show them to the jury?"

"Please do," the judge said, pointing to an easel with poster-sized charts.

Frank moved the easel closer to the witness chair to a position that enabled the jury members to see his financial illustrations. Frank then handed the judge a copy of the charts.

The opposing counsel jumped to his feet. "Objection, Your Honor. May we see what the witness has given you?"

Frank handed another copy to the judge. The court clerk retrieved the copy from the judge and delivered it to the attorney who was still standing. The attorney thumbed through the document before returning to his seat.

With the theatrical outburst over, Frank removed the blank cardboard covering his deck of posters to reveal the first chart showing the total estimated value of the Braswells' assets:

Cash	$25,400
Accounts Receivable	8,400
Marketable Securities	129,000
House	574,000
Autos	96,000
Business	7,600,000
Jade/Ruby Collection	941,600
Miscellaneous	15,600
Liabilities	(58,000)
Net Worth	$9,332,000

Frank allowed the jury members to absorb the total net worth figure that was prominently displayed in large blue numbers near the bottom of the slick, professional-looking visual aid.

He then explained, "Dr. Braswell was not co-operative. My firm had extreme difficulty getting reliable information from Dr. Braswell, especially with respect to his medical practice. Let me start with cash first," Frank gestured toward the chart.

"There may be more than $25,400 of cash available, but this is the figure at about the time Dr. Braswell removed many of the records from the Braswell home.

"The current amount of the receivables—$8,400—is the discounted amount of cash we estimate will be collected using appropriate interest rates at the date Dr. Braswell left Jane Braswell.

"The marketable securities were valued at estimated current market price based on the latest stock and bond market listings.

"The house is valued at $574,000, which is what the Braswells could realize from its sale—the estimated sales proceeds, net of brokerage fees and closing costs. We used a certified appraiser to value the property.

"The two automobiles are based upon their blue book value, taking into consideration their condition and mileage." Frank pointed to the $96,000 figure.

"Dr. Braswell's closely-held business is probably worth at least $7.6 million. Mrs. Braswell had first-hand knowledge of the weekly cash flow into his business. Therefore, I used the cash flow method to value the business. This method determines cash flow to Dr. Braswell from his business more than the compensation that he pays to his employees. I calculated six years of cash flows and year six is considered the future value of a perpetual annuity for all later years. Since Dr. Braswell is young, I projected cash flow for 20 years, using a discount rate of 7 percent." Frank turned to the second chart that showed the cash flow calculations in elaborate detail. The nodding jury members did not seem interested in the numerous calculations.

"Now for the jade and ruby collection," Frank said. "Our appraisal effort was hindered somewhat by the fact that Dr. Braswell removed the jade collection from his home the night he moved out. He also took all of the rubies from the family safe deposit—"

"Objection, your Honor. That is hearsay. My client asserts, instead, that Mrs. Braswell removed and hid the jade and ruby collection."

"Objection sustained. Please strike the last statements from the record." The judge waved his right arm at the court reporter. "Mr. Harrison, please limit your remarks to the appraisal and avoid any extraneous remarks."

"Yes, sir. I apologize to the court." Frank tried to look humble. "Anyway, Mrs. Braswell does have photos of many of the jade items, and I personally sold many of the items held in the collection to Dr. and Mrs. Braswell—usually Mrs. Braswell." Frank paused and looked toward the jury box. During testimony he always tried to look at each of the jurors several times to appear friendly and honest. He was careful to speak to the jurors and not the attorney.

"The same for the rubies," Frank said. "In addition, most of the stones had been professionally appraised for insurance purposes." Frank turned to a summary chart of many of the most valuable pieces. "Using the photos, invoices, and my personal knowledge of the jade and ruby markets, I estimate their current market value to be $941,600.

"There is approximately $15,600 of miscellaneous assets," Frank continued. "And I estimated payables and liabilities at the discounted amounts of cash actually expected to be paid. After deducting the $58,000 of liabilities, the total current net worth of the Braswell family is at least $9.3 million—quite possibly much more."

Dr. Braswell's attorney then began to question Frank in a thick Irish brogue. "Mr. Harrison, why did you not use the market comparable approach to value Dr. Braswell's medical business?"

"Well, I considered the market comparable approach, but decided not to use it because Judge Nims, in a U.S. Tax Court decision, rejected the use of the market comparable approach. However, even using this approach, you'll get almost the same value.

"Using the market comparable approach or market multiples approach, you must identify comparable companies which can be used to value companies with high growth potential but have limited prior history. Dr. Braswell's business is established with a record of accomplishment. I believe the discounted cash flow approach is the best approach to value this business."

"Mr. Harrison, why did you not reduce your value of the company by a lack of marketability discount—say 30 or 40 percent?"

"I don't believe it is appropriate to reduce the cash flow valuation by any type of discount. We are looking at the cash flow to be earned by a service company. The company's cash flow is based upon Dr. Braswell's efforts. I don't expect him to stop working. If he does, the medical practice is worth little. A discount for lack of marketability (DLOM) factor would be more applicable when valuing a non-service type business that is closely-held—say something like a small manufacturer.

"Keep in mind that under the cash-flow approach, I did not place a value on Dr. Braswell's goodwill—goodwill is an intangible asset. If you insist on a DLOM, we would need to factor goodwill into the business value raising the figure considerably above the $7.6 million estimate I've provided the court."

Frank smiled in satisfaction at the attorney. He knew his testimony had been convincing because he could see it in the jurors' faces.

But he also knew that although there was good money to be made in doing business valuations, being an expert witness wasn't without its own risk. Business valuations, particularly, exposed him to the threat of litigation. Worse, some professional liability coverage explicitly excluded valuation work. Risk-reward trade-offs, he thought. But if he ever wanted to hit a home run, he had to be willing to swing for the fences. Frank liked the idea of hitting the ball out of the park.

———————

On the way back from his court appearance Frank read an Associated Press story about an accident at a jade mine in Hpakant, Myanmar. At least 15 people were killed and dozens injured in a landslide from a giant mound of discarded earth at a jade mine in northern Myanmar. A search was ongoing for more miners, but the searching was hindered by heavy rain. The article indicated that such accidents are not rare because scavenging for jade remnants is dangerous and not regulated. At least 100 people were killed by a single landslide in November 2015. Frank wondered if there were lawyers around that would use forensic accountants to determine the damages. He knew that a jury trial was available in Myanmar.

Another story in the New York Times was about a reporter who was jailed because he challenged the prosecutor's account of how he and a colleague were arrested. He was arrested while investigating violence against the persecuted Rohingya ethnic minority.

Six

___

Most accountants are dull bean counters without many new ideas. Business needs creativity, innovation, and the willingness to be bold.

—Richard Rampell

Lenny stepped off the bus at Seventeenth and Chestnut and took a deep breath as he proceeded down Chestnut Street. What a beautiful day for early September in Philadelphia. It was a comfortable 72 degrees Fahrenheit with a mild breeze and bright sun; the oppressive humidity that can make Philadelphia so unbearable during the summer was absent.

Lenny was still uncertain of his plan, so he wanted to walk a few blocks to calm his nerves. He saw the Philadelphia Stock Exchange in the distance and thought about stopping in and talking to Bill Nicholson, a friend of his who was also a bond dealer. He decided not to stop.

It was still hard for Lenny to believe that Bill was a bond dealer; one time, Lenny even had to explain to him that bond discounts and premiums represent adjustments to bond interest expense for the company issuing the bond. Lenny carefully explained to Bill that a bond sold at a premium if the market rate of interest was less than the rate of interest paid by the bond, and that if the market rate of interest was greater than the bond interest rate, the bond sold at a discount. As his mind shifted away from Bill Nicholson, Lenny wondered if he would be able to smile as easily later in the day once he went through with his plan.

Lenny was so wrapped up in his thoughts that he was oblivious to things going on around him. At Fifteenth and Market, he completely ignored the giant 45-foot steel clothespin statue created by Claes Oldenburg. The Split Button, another of his works, is displayed at the University of Pennsylvania. At Twelfth and Chestnut, Lenny almost ran into a mounted patrolman's horse.

As Lenny approached Jewelers' Row, he could feel a cold sweat on his hands. He had been thinking about Dana constantly, ever since their last encounter. He was worried that somehow, he was misreading the acquaintance, that the relationship with Dana was more casual than serious. His big fear was being utterly embarrassed and humiliated if it turned out Dana didn't share his feelings. So, he had devised a plan, an alibi for showing up at her jewelry shop unannounced. He knew Dana was probably smart enough to see through his pretense, but in his awkward way he had to try.

Calling upon some inner strength, Lenny began to execute his plan. He opened the door to Jade & More and walked in.

"Yes, sir. What can I help you with today?"

Lenny turned and was disappointed to see a neatly dressed, twenty-something blond-haired man with a pleasant smile greeting him. It had never dawned on him that Dana might not be in the shop. *How stupid is this?* Lenny thought.

"Uh, I, uh, well, I'm looking for, uh, a locket," Lenny stammered softly.

"Lockets are a very popular item," beamed the sales clerk confidently. "If you'll walk this way to our display, I'm sure you'll be able to find something that will fit your taste."

Lenny looked around. There was no other person in the store. No sign of Dana.

"Now tell me, sir, who is the locket for?" inquired the salesperson. "Is it for your wife, significant other, your mother—"

"It's, uh, for my daughter for her birthday," Lenny said.

"That's a wonderful gift for a daughter. I know she will treasure it."

"I hope so," uttered an unenthusiastic Lenny.

"How old is your daughter?" the salesperson inquired.

"She'll be fourteen on September eighth," came a voice from behind Lenny.

Lenny turned around quickly and saw a smiling Dana. "That's right, isn't it? Your Rebecca is going to be fourteen, isn't she?" Dana said in a way which suggested that she already knew the answer.

"Why, uh, yes. That's right. But—"

Dana held up her hand. "Give me one second, Professor Cramer," she said. "Phillip, I think I can take it from here. I'll help Professor Cramer. Why don't you head to the back office and help Janet with the aging of our receivables," Dana suggested.

"Whatever you say, Ms. Scott. Nice meeting you, sir." The sales clerk walked behind a purple curtain into a back room.

"How did you know Rebecca was going to be fourteen on September eighth?" Lenny asked. He was surprised Dana knew such intimate details about his daughter.

"She told me in Myanmar. Girl talk. That kind of thing."

"Yes, but you remembered. I'm surprised."

"Lenny, I have a good memory. In fact, I have a surprisingly *good* memory. Maybe too good."

Lenny's plan wasn't going exactly how he had envisioned. He smiled politely before quickly changing the subject. "I'm impressed that you know about aging receivables," he said. "Last time we talked you were still pretty worried about cash flow."

"It was Frank's idea. Aging is fairly easy to implement. All I had to do was categorize all my accounts receivable by the number of days they are outstanding. The longer they are outstanding, the less likely I will be able to collect the cash. Each age category has a percentage associated with it that Frank worked out. The percentage represents the portion of accounts receivable outstanding for that period that I more than likely will never collect. I then take the total amount I estimate as uncollectible and compare it with the amount already in my allowance for bad debts account. And voilà! That's French for the difference represents my bad debt expense for the reporting period."

Lenny smiled. "I wish all my students were as smart as you. Of course, the whole purpose of estimating bad debt expense is to allow the cost of uncollectible credit sales to be matched in the same reporting period with the revenues they generate. Did Frank also tell you that the allowance method is not available for tax purposes? For the IRS, you can only use the specific charge-off method."

There was a long pause. Dana was staring at Lenny. In the meantime, Lenny, with his head down, appeared to be studying a glass display case of chains and lockets. Only the hum of the fluorescent lights overhead could be heard. Dana decided to break the silence.

"Well?"

Half startled, Lenny replied, "Well, what?"

"Well, have you decided upon a locket for Rebecca yet?"

"Oh, that. Well, uh, what do you suggest?"

"These over here are quite nice for a fourteen-year-old girl," Dana said, pointing to a group of lockets.

"Yes, they are nice," repeated Lenny quietly.

Once again there was a long pause, although not quite as long as before. Dana again was the one to break the silence. "Lenny, this is rather out of the way for you, isn't it? If you wanted to buy Rebecca a locket, there are shops much closer to where you work or live than here. Why did you choose my shop?"

Lenny paused and swallowed hard. He was ready with the alibi he had practiced as part of his plan. "I happened to be in the neighborhood, and I knew that you were honest, and that I wouldn't get cheated."

"How do you know if I'm honest?" Dana said. "For all you know I might be a jewel thief. Have you checked with the Better Business Bureau? Done a background check on Google? After all, as I remember from our conversation in Myanmar you don't like to take chances."

"You are honest, aren't you? Somehow, I can't imagine you being a crook," Lenny said.

"Why not? Because I have such an innocent face? I thought a good accountant had to be skeptical—a good detective."

"I'm sure that's it," Lenny said. "Dana, you don't need to be sarcastic. I know I haven't known you for long, but I've just always thought of you as honest."

Dana didn't respond. Lenny's shifted his eyes away from Dana, back towards the lockets.

"This one looks like a nice one here." Lenny pointed to a slender silver chain with a heart-shaped locket.

"I think someone Rebecca's age would like that."

"Well, I'm not sure. Maybe it's too young? What about an oval-shaped locket? Or—"

"I didn't think you could make a decision," Dana said. "There's a pattern—"

"I'll take it," Lenny interrupted. It was clear where Dana was going with the subtext.

"I don't want to force you to buy it. I wouldn't want to rush you—*again*."

Lenny tried to sound assertive. "You're not rushing me. I think Rebecca would like it."

"Fine. I'll wrap it up for you."

There was a long period of silence as Dana placed tissue paper around the locket and placed it in a box. She then wrapped the box in silver foil paper with a red ribbon around it.

"Will there be anything else?" Dana asked mechanically, as if she were following a generic retail sales clerk script.

There was no immediate response from Lenny. Finally, he cleared his throat, took a deep breath, and said, "Dana, I haven't been able to get you out of my mind since we last met."

Dana looked stunned. Before she could say anything, Lenny had put his head down, pretending to look at the display case. The conversation stalled. None of this was going the way Lenny had hoped. He wasn't ready to make eye contact again which was really kind of strange. When he was in the classroom, he could lecture to hundreds of students at a time, with calm and aplomb. He could look into the eyes of students, sense whether he was making a connection, and adapt his pace and his presentation to the crowd like a master. One-on-one was where he felt bumbling and inept.

Dana gently tapped Lenny on the shoulder. "Friends, Lenny. I don't have any problem with us being friends."

Lenny looked up. He searched Dana's eyes for clues on the nature of this friendship she referred to, whether it was it was "just friends" or something beyond that. By Dana's tone he was almost certain it wasn't friends-plus.

"By the way, Rebecca is going to love that locket," Dana said, switching the subject easily.

"I hope so," Lenny sighed. Back to the banter, he thought.

"So, Lenny, what have you been doing? Have teaching and consulting been keeping you busy?"

"For the most part. The semester is just starting, and my consulting work has grown. How are things with you?"

"Fine, I guess." Dana paused and glanced outside the window. "Are you in a terrible rush?"

"No," Lenny said quickly.

"Why don't you come back to my office for a second," Dana suggested. "Phillip!"

After Dana called Phillip in from the back room to wait on customers, Dana and Lenny went through the back room to Dana's office. On the way back, they passed Janet, the bookkeeper, who remembered Lenny from the trip to Myanmar.

After exchanging pleasantries with Janet, Dana and Lenny went into Dana's office, and Dana closed the door behind them.

"Nice office," Lenny said, trying to make conversation.

The office had two solid cherry-wood desks. The larger of the two was Dana's. A smaller one was at the far back of the room. Lenny noticed a coffee cup on the back desk with the saying "Love an Accountant. It's Less Taxing." There were no windows in the room, which had a distinct aroma of cigarette smoke. The room was illuminated by overhead, full-spectrum fluorescent lights. The dark-colored wooden floors made the room appear to be more dimly lit than it really was but still gave the office a classy feel.

"It's all right. Nothing special," Dana replied smugly. "You can probably tell from the coffee mug, that desk over there is Frank's. We share the office since there is not much room. I apologize for the smell of cigarettes. Frank is trying to quit smoking, but occasionally, he sneaks a puff or two."

Dana motioned for Lenny to sit in one of the side chairs. She sat down behind her desk. Leaning forward, Dana said in almost a whisper, "Lenny, I know you're busy, but do you think you could spare some time and look at our books? I'm concerned. We're not making the type of profit I anticipated. Janet and Frank handle the books since I don't know much about accounting. Frank has given me some good personal investment advice, but when it comes to the business I don't like being at his or Janet's mercy. I feel like I'm in the dark. I need someone that I can trust to go through the books."

Lenny's face lit up. "I have a lot going on at the moment, but I think I can come in for a day every other week, if that would work for you." Lenny pulled his phone from the inside pocket of his sport coat and tapped in a note on his calendar.

"I would really appreciate it if you could," replied Dana. She sounded relieved. "I've been trying to check some things on my own. I know that our sales are up, but for some reason cash is down from last year."

"Have there been any large increases in expenditures? New equipment, for example?"

"No more than last year. We did buy more inventory, but that isn't unusual if our sales are increasing. Right?"

"Absolutely. Sales, cash, and accounts receivable should move in the same direction." Lenny looked up at the white plaster ceiling as he thought through some options. "Maybe we ought to make an estimate of your inventories using the gross profit method. I—" Lenny stopped, turned to his right, and saw Frank Harrison entering the small room.

"Well, look who strayed from the hallowed halls of academia," Frank said, interrupting Lenny midsentence. "I thought eggheads like you just sat in a library, surrounded by stacks of books, thinking great thoughts all day long. What brings you here from your precious ivory tower?"

"He was buying a gift for his daughter," Dana interjected. "And, if you must know, we were just reminiscing a little about the trip to Myanmar."

Frank was smiling, one of those insincere smiles that often accompany a biting tone. Some might even call it a facial sneer. "I see," he said. "I have some advice for you. Watch yourself, professor. You stray too far from your ivory tower, and you're liable to get your fingernails dirty or, heaven forbid, maybe even develop a callus! Then what would all your rich, spoiled students think? They'd be horrified at the sight and might even think you know something useful. That could be career ending."

"Good advice. I'll be careful to remain an academic egghead," Lenny said. The jocularity that was usually present was now absent from his voice. Lenny stood up and looked at Dana. "I really should be leaving now."

"Ok, Lenny, and I'll be sure to give Rebecca a call tonight and wish her a happy birthday."

"Dana, you don't need to do that."

"Expect my call." Dana looked directly into Lenny's eyes, hoping that he could catch on that she wanted to continue their talk about the books.

"Will do," replied Lenny with a wink that only Dana could see. Lenny turned to Frank and extended his hand. "Nice to see you again, Frank. Always a pleasure."

Frank shook Lenny's hand. "Good seeing you again, professor. I surely hope you aren't taking public transportation back to Penn. That would require you to mix with the common folk."

Lenny smiled, waved to Dana, and departed. Frank shut the door. Dana looked at Frank and said, her voice quite raised, "Was it necessary to be so derisive with him? Why so scornful? What did he ever do to you?"

"I don't like him. The professor thinks he knows everything, but in reality, he's lost once he leaves campus. We call guys like that *street stupid*," Frank said.

"Frank, that's not fair! You hardly know him," Dana countered.

"Maybe. Maybe not. But I still don't like him." Frank cracked his knuckles, relaxed a bit, and then said: "What was he doing here, anyway?"

"I told you, Frank, he was buying a gift for his daughter."

"Really? Seemed like more than that. Anyway, Dana, here's my point. I don't like that guy hanging around here." Frank balled up his fists, then relaxed his hands, rubbing them together, then changed the subject. "By the way, I looked into those two companies you asked me about the other day. You were right about them being good investment possibilities. The location-aware social apps industry is going to grow quickly. Smart phone and tablet sales are off the charts."

"Which of the two do you like the best?" Dana asked as her concentration shifted to her investment portfolio.

Frank paused for a moment and then said, "I think you would be better off with SoshNET. It has a better cash-flow statement."

"I looked at that statement, Frank, but how do you gain information from it? I know that a balance sheet reports a firm's position at a single point in time by looking at its resources and debts. An income statement reports performance of a company over a period of time by looking at its revenues and expenses. But I have real trouble following the cash-flow statement."

"Even I have trouble understanding the cash-flow statement," Frank replied, pointing to himself. "SoshNET has a positive cash flow from operations. That means that SoshNET is currently taking in more cash than it is paying out from its normal business activities. With the anticipated growth in that industry, SoshNET should be in a stronger financial position than Cosmogo."

"So, the key to the cash-flow statement is to look at the cash flows from operations?" asked Dana as she shifted position in her chair.

"Not entirely. A cash bottom line is rather meaningless. The change in cash from one period to the next is no mystery. All you must do is compare the totals from the two periods and take the difference. What's important is what caused the change in cash. Was it due to operating activities, financing activities, or investing activities?"

Dana gave an understanding nod. "I see. If a company had a negative cash flow from operations, then the company likely has to borrow money to continue operating."

"That's right," said Frank. "Likewise, positive cash flows from investing activities can be a bad sign, because it could indicate that the company is liquidating its assets."

The two continued to discuss Dana's portfolio and their disagreement over Lenny's presence was temporarily forgotten.

Lenny went back to his faculty office and worked energetically for three hours on a pressing client matter. Next, he sorted through his mail, and three items caught his attention. The invoice for his company's malpractice insurance showed that the cost of the insurance had risen dramatically again. He always paid his malpractice insurance in one annual payment at the beginning of the year; he then adjusted the prepaid asset account monthly to record the insurance expense in his company's income statement. Lenny believed that within a short period of time there would be no small practitioners left in the accounting profession. The malpractice insurance premiums would be too high, and most of the accounting work would end up being done by the "Big Four" CPA firms: Ernst & Young; Deloitte; PricewaterhouseCoopers; and KPMG.

Premiums were escalating, coverage was shrinking, and many insurance carriers had stopped all coverage for malpractice insurance. Lenny's insurance premiums had increased by a factor of five within the last three years, while the available commercial coverage had been cut in half. Lenny still remembered what former Chief Justice Warren Burger had said in a speech to the American College of Trial Lawyers: "We may well be on our way to a society overrun by hordes of lawyers, hungry as locusts, and brigades of judges in numbers never before contemplated." Burger had been right. There was a stampede of malpractice cases going to the courtroom.

Just under the malpractice insurance invoice was a plain white envelope with no return address. Inside was a clipping from the classified advertisement section of *The Philadelphia Inquirer.* Someone had circled one help-wanted ad:

> FORENSIC ACCOUNTANT. This position requires 7 to 10 years of experience in internal auditing, preferably in the banking industry, and/or an investigative accounting-type background and experience with the IRS or FBI. The successful candidate must have a thorough understanding of and experience with operational procedures, particularly in contractor audits and compliance with agreements. The individual must be able to demonstrate and document familiarity with and identification of suspicious situations, with primary emphasis on fraud detection.

Lenny placed the ad in his circular file along with the other unsolicited mail he received. Though at one time he may have considered taking a full-time position, he enjoyed too much the variety offered by his teaching, consulting, authoring, and board of director memberships. His forensic practice also kept him quite busy and allowed him to stay current by getting his "hands dirty" helping real clients.

Next Lenny filled out his Continuing Professional Education (CPE) reporting form. A CPA license is issued by an individual state; Lenny was licensed in Pennsylvania. A CPA in public practice in Pennsylvania must take 80 CPE hours every two years to maintain a CPA license. Lenny still needed about six more hours this year.

With the three items requiring immediate attention out of the way, Lenny began to focus on more important matters. One of his accounting clients, Bigg Smiles, a local orthodontia group, had recently applied for a bank loan to purchase the professional building where the three doctors practiced. He was pleased that his client had finally followed his suggestion to acquire the medical office building to shelter taxable income through depreciation write-offs. As a trusted business advisor, Lenny felt it was his responsibility to help his clients hang on to as much of their earnings as possible; otherwise, the doctors would see their hard-earned profits disappear on a one-way trip to Washington, D.C. He always liked what famed U.S. Supreme Court Justice Learned Hand had said about tax planning in *Gregory v. Helvering* (1935):

> Anyone may arrange his affairs so that his taxes shall be as low as possible; he is not bound to choose that pattern which best pays the treasury. There is not even a patriotic duty to increase one's taxes. Over and over again the Courts have said that there is nothing sinister in so arranging affairs as to keep taxes as low as possible. Everyone does it, rich and poor alike and all do right, for nobody owes any public duty to pay more than the law demands.

Before approving the loan, the bank had asked the three doctors running the orthodontia group for a financial statement compilation. The American Institute of CPAs (AICPA) defines a compilation as a professional "service, the objective of which is to assist management in presenting financial information in the form of financial statements without undertaking to obtain or provide any assurance that there are no material modifications that should be made to the financial statements in order for the statements to be in conformity with the applicable financial reporting framework." Because a compilation does not require assurance services such as those provided in a review or full-blown audit, compilations are much less expensive for clients. Fortunately, many banks are satisfied with a compilation as supporting documentation for a business loan.

Lenny remembered when he first started working with Bigg Smiles, LLC. He was hired to help the three organizing orthodontists select the organizational form that would be the most beneficial for them; they were particularly concerned about reducing taxes and protecting their personal assets from business creditors. Given their concerns, Lenny knew the limited liability company (LLC) business structure would work well for these doctors; an LLC would avoid the double taxation of a corporation while offering the owners limited liability for business debts.

Like many of Lenny's clients, Bigg Smiles, LLC, kept its accounting records on a tax basis. Similar to cash-basis accounting, tax-basis accounting recognizes revenues when received rather than billed and expenses are recorded when paid rather than incurred. Depreciation expense is computed under MACRS—the modified accelerated cost recovery system. To bring Bigg Smiles in conformance with Generally Accepted Accounting Principles, Lenny would have to book several adjusting journal entries (AJEs). GAAP requires accrual basis accounting. Lenny made the following AJEs for the year:

Date	Account and Explanation	Dr.	Cr.
Dec 31	Accounts Receivable	$725,000	
	Revenue from Orthodontia Services		725,000
	To record revenue for the year on an accrual basis. $725,000 billed to patients but not yet collected.		

| Dec 31 | Orthodontia Supplies Expense | $63,000 | |
| | Accounts Payable | | 63,000 |

To record supplies expense on an accrual basis. $63,000 supplies received from vendors but not yet paid.

| Dec 31 | Accumulated Depreciation—Equipment | $37,500 | |
| | Depreciation Expense—Equipment | | 37,500 |

To record depreciation on a straight-line basis using the industry standard depreciation method, useful lives, and salvage values. $37,500 adjustment required to reduce MACRS depreciation to straight-line.

Once he finished with Bigg Smiles, Lenny spent the next three hours on some detailed accounting work for a couple of his other clients. He then made his way home. Later that evening Dana did, in fact, call and wish Rebecca a happy birthday. She was kind enough not to mention to Rebecca the locket Lenny had bought his daughter earlier that day. Lenny and Dana then chatted for about 45 minutes on several subjects. At the end of the conversation, Lenny set up an appointment to look at Dana's books. He debated whether he should take on a new client, given his existing practice load, but accounting was like any professional service business where it was hard to regulate the volume of work. It was always "feast or famine." He'd rather have too much work than too little.

That evening Lenny drafted an engagement letter for future consulting services he would provide to Dana's Jade & More shop. The letter referred to each party's responsibilities, the general nature of Lenny's investigative services, his hourly rate, and information regarding payment expectation. Lenny always received a signed engagement letter from a client before beginning any professional work. Many accountants have lost malpractice disputes because they did not have an engagement letter.

———

"Hello, Cramer here."

"Lenny, this is Frank Harrison. How are you doing today?"

"Fine. How about yourself?" It was an automatic response. Lenny was surprised to receive this phone call, since it was obvious from meeting Frank in Dana's office that Frank didn't like him.

"Not so good, Lenny. That's why I'm calling. I wanted to apologize for my behavior yesterday. You see, when I saw you with Dana, I thought that you were trying to move in on her and break up our relationship. Yesterday after you left, she assured me that nothing was going on between the two of you. But she wasn't pleased with my outburst, and she insisted that I call you today and explain my behavior. I hope you don't hold a grudge."

Lenny was stunned. He had no idea that Frank and Dana were seeing each other. When Dana had called him last night and expressed her distrust of Frank, she hadn't mentioned that she and Frank were anything more than business partners. This changed everything. *How could he have been so stupid.* "No problem. Apology accepted," Lenny said, trying to hide the disappointment in his voice.

"Lenny, let me make it up to you. Why don't you come out with Dana and me tonight for dinner? Bring your daughter along, too. I know Dana would like to see her."

"That's nice of you, Frank, but I am afraid I can't make it tonight. Perhaps another time." Lenny was being diplomatic. There was no way he would place himself in such an awkward social situation as to go out with a dating couple when he was single.

"That's too bad. I hope there are no hard feelings," Frank said. He could be incredibly friendly on the phone.

"No hard feelings, Frank. So long."

"Good-bye."

———

Frank Harrison put down the phone, leaned back in his executive chair, and thought about lighting a cigarette. A big smile covered his face.

There was a knock on his door and his secretary entered. "Here are those files you wanted, Mr. Harrison."

"Thank you, Wendy."

Wendy stared at him for a second. "You certainly seem pleased with yourself, Mr. Harrison."

Frank stood up from his chair, "Wendy, I am pleased. Very much so. I just convinced someone with more initials after his name than there are letters in the alphabet into believing a complete fairy tale— a romantic fairy tale at that. This guy fell for it hook, line, and sinker." Frank started to chuckle. "I wonder what I would have done if he had actually accepted my dinner invitation. Man, it's a good thing I had him figured out right from the beginning!"

Lenny arrived at the jade shop on Tuesday, September 23. It was a gray, dreary fall day in Philadelphia. Lenny closed his red and blue umbrella, which he had purchased at the University of Pennsylvania bookstore, and unbuttoned his tan London Fog raincoat.

Lenny smiled at Phillip, the young Jade & More sales clerk who was behind the jewelry counters and proceeded to the back room. Lenny felt that his relationship with Dana was becoming more confusing each time he encountered her. Nothing made sense. He knew he liked her, and she was comfortable enough with him to ask him to help her gain some insight into what was causing her cash-flow difficulties. She had told him that she did not trust the explanations Frank had given her, but then she was dating Frank. *How could she go out with someone she doesn't trust?* Maybe he'd misjudged her. Maybe Dana really wasn't the kind of person he thought she was. Maybe the fantasy was all in his head.

"Hello, Professor Cramer."

Lenny turned around and saw Janet sitting behind her desk with a pleasant smile on her face. "Hi, Janet. How's life in the world of bookkeeping?"

"Fascinating, as always," replied Janet as both she and Lenny began to laugh. The telephone rang at Janet's desk, providing an interruption that allowed Lenny to exit conveniently and make his way to Dana's office. He knew she wouldn't be there until later. She had told him not to wait for her but to go ahead and get started on the work he had planned.

Based on his experience—assuming embezzlement wasn't the problem—Lenny had found that cash-flow problems often start with out-of-whack payables or receivables. The payables arise from the purchase of merchandise on credit from suppliers, and receivables arise from granting credit to customers. Both receivables and payables are closely tied to inventory transactions. If payables and receivables weren't the cause of the problem, another possibility would be recent acquisitions of property, plant, and equipment (PP&E). PP&E can use up a great deal of cash.

Lenny decided to tackle the payables first. Aside from minor payables for utilities, equipment rentals, and the store lease—each of which was rather constant in amount—the payables largely consisted of five major suppliers. Lenny wrote them down.

- East Asian Importers, Inc.
- Carson Denig Gem Importers, Inc.
- International Jewel Importers, Inc.
- Nu-Sang-Wan Gems, Ltd.
- Southeast Precious Artifacts, Inc.

Of the five suppliers, Carson Denig Gem Importers and International Jewel Importers were the two suppliers with whom the jade shop conducted by far the most business. On the surface, Lenny saw nothing unusual with any of the five suppliers, with maybe one exception. All but one of the suppliers granted credit with terms of 2/10, n/30. These numbers meant that Jade & More's account balance was due to the supplier in 30 days from the date of invoice; however, if payment was made within 10 days, Jade & More could take a 2 percent discount. A practice of always taking discounts is good cash management and can often result in significant savings for a company. Lenny's examination of the cash disbursement journal revealed that, with rare exceptions, Jade & More always took advantage of payment discounts.

The one exception was Carson Denig Gem Importers. Unlike the other suppliers, Carson Denig did not grant Jade & More discounts. Invoiced amounts were due in 15 days rather than the 30 days that was the normal practice of the other suppliers. Lenny made a mental note to check with Dana as to why they would do so much business with a supplier with such restrictive credit terms.

Contrary to the stereotype, Lenny knew that accountants did much more than simply keep the books. A good accountant or accounting firm makes recommendations to improve a client's accounting systems and the related internal controls. The accountant will typically provide information to the client concerning tax advice and financial planning as well. In short, a good accountant typically becomes the company's single most trusted business advisor. Helping the client improve its future cash flows was par for the course. It was with this in mind that Lenny had noticed the credit terms granted by Carson Denig Gem Importers even though the accounting for the Denig Gem purchase transactions seemed to be completely proper. Normally, under a perpetual inventory system in which the gross method is used to record both inventory and accounts payable, when a discount is taken, the Purchase Discounts Taken account is credited for the discount, the Cash account is credited for the amount paid, and Accounts Payable is debited for the full amount of the invoice. For the Denig Gem invoices, no discount had been taken, so the Cash and Accounts Payable accounts were recorded for the same amount. Janet was doing everything correctly.

Lenny glanced at his watch. He couldn't believe it was 4:30 already. Going through the payables had taken up most of the day. He had hoped to see Dana before he left, but she had told him that she had a dental appointment that afternoon and might not be in the shop until later. As Lenny began to pack his briefcase, he was surprised to see Dana walk hurriedly into the room.

"I tried to get here as quickly as I could," an out-of-breath Dana said as she shook the rain from her umbrella. "But the traffic is always bad this time of day. Don't you just hate going to the dentist. They love inflicting pain and making you feel grateful for it. Anyway, I was so relieved to get out of the dental chair that I forgot my umbrella and walked half a block in the rain before I realized it." Dana inhaled sharply. "Lenny, I don't mean to be so wrapped up in myself. How did it go today?"

Lenny smiled. He was amazed at how Dana was able to spew forth so many words in such a short period of time. "With the books? Not too bad."

"Good, let's celebrate my getting out of the dentist's office in one piece by going out to dinner, and you can tell me all about it.

I'm starved. I skipped lunch because I was so worried I was going to have to have a root canal." Dana put her purse on the desk and began going through her mail.

Lenny paused before replying. "Well, I'm not sure about dinner."

"Oh, come on. Live a little, Lenny. I won't bite."

"What about Frank? Shouldn't you see if Frank can make it."

"Frank!" Dana made a face of disdain. "Why would I want him to come along?"

Lenny put his head down and shifted his feet. "I don't know."

"Good, then, it's settled. We're going to dinner. I hope you like French food, Lenny. There's a great place only five minutes from here."

Lenny grabbed his briefcase and raincoat, and along with Dana headed for dinner. The rain had stopped, so Dana and Lenny were able to get to Le Ciel in a short time. After a brief wait, they were seated. Suddenly, Lenny exclaimed, "Dana, I've got to go back to the shop."

Dana looked startled. "Why, what's wrong?"

"My umbrella. I left my umbrella at the shop." Lenny looked at his watch. "I'd better go get it."

Dana sighed and rolled her eyes. "Really, Lenny. I don't know what I'm going to do with you. Your umbrella isn't going anywhere. You can grab it later."

Lenny settled back into his seat. "You're right. Let's get this celebration started. What would you like to drink?"

After both had ordered drinks, Dana leaned back in her chair and inquired, "Well, Lenny, did you find anything important today?"

Lenny began fiddling with his napkin. "It's going to take a little time, Dana. I'm just getting—"

"Oh, I know that. I hope I don't seem too impatient."

Lenny saw the worried expression on Dana's face. "You have a right to be concerned. Cash flow worries are the bane of a small business. I may be just getting started, but I already have some ideas for you." Lenny noticed that Dana look somewhat reassured. "Tell me," he said, "why do you do business with Carson Denig Gem Importers?"

"Denig Gems? Why, what's wrong with them?"

"It's their credit terms." Lenny put down his napkin momentarily and continued. "All of your other suppliers have credit terms such as 2/10, net 30. Carson Denig only gives net 15 terms."

"I don't understand. What does 2/10, net 30 mean?"

Lenny smiled. "I'm sorry. Sometimes I'm so used to being around accountants and accounting students that I forget the jargon I use is unknown to people outside the profession."

Just as Lenny was about to explain, the waiter brought over their drinks and took their dinner orders. Refreshments now in hand, Lenny filled Dana in on what 2/10, n/30 meant. While payment terms are written 2/10, n/30, they were pronounced as "two-ten" and "net-thirty" when spoken.

"I see," Dana nodded. "The rationale for granting a prompt payment discount of two percent is that the suppliers feel that by getting the money twenty days earlier, they can invest it and can make up for the two percent discount taken."

"Exactly. There is also less chance that an outstanding receivable will become a bad debt and it shortens the company's operating cycle." Lenny resumed fiddling with his napkin. "You really are bright. It's amazing how you catch on to things so quickly."

"No, it's not," Dana said jokingly. "I'm just a natural genius." Dana started laughing at herself, unable to maintain a straight face. Lenny joined her. He couldn't keep a straight face either. Dana finally returned to being serious. "Sarcasm aside, I see what you mean, though. The net 15 credit terms are lousy. I don't really know why we do business with him. I'm going to have to ask Frank about it."

"You really should because you do more business with Carson Denig than you do with any other supplier."

Dana looked surprised. "I've seen the name on a few things, but I never realized we did that much business with them. I really am going to have to check with Frank about this."

"Hopefully, I'll be able to come up with some more clues for you after a few more visits. But forensic accounting sleuthing takes time. We ignore the materiality concept and examine both small and large transactions." Lenny began to turn the spoon on the table continuously and put his napkin down.

Dana smiled broadly. "Lenny, I really appreciate you doing this for me and carving time out of your hectic schedule to fit me in." Dana leaned over and kissed Lenny's cheek. He blushed. There was a period of awkward silence before the two of them were interrupted by the waiter.

"Excuse me, mademoiselle and monsieur. These drinks are from the gentleman seated over there."

Dana and Lenny both looked in the direction indicated by the waiter, where they saw a grinning Frank stand up and begin to walk over to their table.

Frank extended his right hand to Lenny and said as they shook hands, "I sure didn't expect to see you two here. I'm really surprised." Frank looked directly into Lenny's eyes. Lenny swallowed hard. It was clear that Lenny was struggling to think of what to say. Dana came to his rescue.

"Just a social gathering for a few drinks and dinner. No big deal, really. Why don't you join us?"

"Yes, Frank," Lenny said as he finally was able to spit out some words. "Please join us."

"No, thanks. I was on my way out when I saw the two of you. I have some work to do." Frank paused and continued. "So, you two just decided to get together here, huh?"

Dana quickly responded, "That's right. Lenny called me and said he was going to be downtown, and I suggested we meet here for dinner and drinks. Isn't that right, Lenny?"

Lenny looked at Dana and nodded in agreement.

"What brought you here, Frank?" Dana asked.

"Oh, I had a late business luncheon—very late—with a client." Frank stood up and adjusted his tie. "If you'll excuse me, I must be going. Lenny, good seeing you again," Frank said,

After it was clear that Frank had left the restaurant, Lenny turned to Dana and asked, "Why did you tell him that story about my being downtown and meeting you here?"

"I don't want Frank to know you're looking at our books. Besides, it wasn't a complete fabrication. You were downtown, and it was my idea to come here."

"I would just hate for him to get the wrong idea," Lenny said.

"What do you mean by that?" Dana raised her eyebrows.

"Well, I just wouldn't want him to feel that I was trying to ruin things between you and him." Lenny continued to fidget with his napkin, tearing it into little pieces as he spoke.

"Understood," she said. "That's why I told him that you and I were meeting socially rather than professionally. I don't want him to know that you are examining our financial records, Lenny, because you're right: If Frank knew that you were looking at our books without his consent, our partnership would be over."

Lenny was getting more confused as the conversation continued. When he had mentioned to Dana about not ruining things between her and Frank, he was not talking about Dana and Frank's partnership in the jade shop. *Maybe she feels that her personal life is none of my business.* Lenny didn't know what to think at this point.

The waiter soon brought them their dinner. The conversation shifted to talking about Rebecca and life at Wharton. After dinner, they went to their own homes, taking separate cabs.

Frank left Le Ciel and immediately headed for the Jade & More shop. He hadn't thought Lenny would have the courage to go out with Dana after their phone conversation the evening before. He was sure that Dana was having Lenny poke around the books. If that was true, then Frank needed to make sure things were in order. Plus, he had to develop a plan to slow Lenny down if he found out too much too soon.

When Frank got to the jade shop, the street was rather quiet. People were still milling about, but nothing like the large crowds that normally shopped Jeweler's Row between 9 and 5. The store was closed. Frank took out his keys, opened the door and walked in. He locked the door behind him.

Frank walked into the office area and looked to see if anything had been touched. It appeared that the payables ledger and cash disbursements journal might have been examined, but he couldn't be sure. Everything else seemed to be just the way he had left it. He flipped through a few more files and books but saw nothing else out of place. Frank was beginning to think that maybe he was jumping to conclusions.

To be on the safe side, Frank pulled out his cell phone and took several pictures of the work area where the accounting records were stored. He then wrote down the exact order from top to bottom of all the books in the filing cabinet. The photos would allow him to know in the future if any of the books were examined or if anything had been moved.

Frank assumed that no one, not even Lenny, would be careful enough to return records such as the cash receipts journal for last year back to exact same position from where it had been retrieved. Frank then took out an invisible marker and began numbering some files and documents in sequential order. Once the ink dried it would not be visible to the naked eye except under a special light. Convinced that he had taken adequate safeguards to allow him to know if anyone was looking at the books, Frank closed his briefcase and prepared to leave.

He looked at his watch. He was surprised to discover that he had spent an hour and a half arranging things. He was about to turn off the light when he saw something that caught his eye—a red and blue umbrella. Frank walked over to it and picked it up. He read the price tag which was still on it. "The University of Pennsylvania Bookstore," he said aloud in the empty office. *So, Lenny was here.*

That changed things. Now that he knew for sure Lenny was snooping around, Frank wanted to make sure that he could control what Lenny saw. Then, if Lenny did find anything, he was sure to hear from Dana about it. It was getting late. Frank determined that he couldn't do anything more about the situation for now.

Frank walked out the door, locking it behind him. He decided to head over to his consulting office to work on a couple of things as well as to figure out what to do about Lenny. The streets were virtually deserted around Sansom Street at this hour, so for safety reasons he walked toward Chestnut, which would have more people on it this time of night. Frank was relieved to reach the more populated and brightly lit Chestnut Street.

"A coupla' dollars for a cup of coffee, sir?"

Frank turned to his right and saw a panhandler walking alongside him. The urban beggar had a dirty gray beard and hair to match. He was dressed in threadbare clothes and smelled of urine.

"Get a job, you bum. It's because of street people like you that the stock markets are so volatile—down one day, up the next. Why the government supports people like you I'll never know." Frank had little tolerance for the homeless and other "leeches on society," as he called them. He, himself, had come from a poor background, so he knew what it meant to be down on your luck. But he had worked hard to make himself a success. He could not understand why others could not or would not do the same.

"It wasn't me, sir. I ain't got nothing to do with the stock market. I just need a cup of Joe," the panhandler insisted.

"Get away from me, you leech, or I'll call a cop," Frank ordered. The vagrant backed off a step or two. Frank couldn't fathom what a derelict like that could know about the stock and bond markets. He, on the other hand, had earlier in the day, calculated the amount of a bond discount to amortize for one of his clients. It was a simple calculation really, requiring nothing more than the effective interest rate method.

The first step involved multiplying the book value (or carrying value) of the bond by the market rate of interest to compute actual interest expense. Next, he needed to calculate the coupon interest paid on the bond. He found this amount by multiplying the face value of the bond by the stated interest rate printed on the bond. The last step was to take the difference between the actual interest expense and the cash interest paid to arrive at the amount of the bond discount to be amortized. In his client's case, the market rate of interest was much higher than the interest rate on the bond, re-sulting in a large bond discount amount recorded at the purchase.

"I can tell you about takeovers," the panhandler mumbled, in-terrupting Frank's train of thought.

"Takeovers? What could you possible tell me about something like that?" Frank said sarcastically.

"I hear things," the panhandler insisted, extending his empty hand, palm up, toward Frank. "And I really could use a cup of coffee. Just a few dollars."

"I'm calling a cop," Frank started to walk away pulling out his phone.

"What if I was to tell you that MFZ Industries is gonna take over Marsupial Services?"

Frank stopped and stared at the panhandler. "Where did you hear that?"

"At lunch today—on Rittenhouse Square. I was going through the trash cans there and ..." The man smiled broadly. "You get good things to eat there around lunch. People throw out really good food—"

"Get back to the takeover," Frank snapped.

"Well, this man said that he was going to announce his plans to take over Marsupial tomorrow afternoon at 5 p.m."

"What was the guy's name?" Frank asked, the sarcasm now completely gone from his voice.

"I don't know his name, but the other man called him Vince."

"Describe him."

The panhandler stopped for a second and asked, "What about my coupla dollars?"

"Don't worry about that," Frank said. "Tell me about the guy. What did he look like?"

"He was short with a gray Van Dyke beard. He was bald up top with hair on the side, wore a bowtie, and ... and he smoked a pipe."

"Vincent Mayville!" Frank uttered in disbelief. "Everyone's speculating that his announcement tomorrow would be about his retirement. That was going to be the big news. There hadn't been an inkling that he was going to try and take over Marsupial." Frank eyed the panhandler warily and asked, "Have you mentioned this to anyone else?"

"No, not a soul."

"And you're not making up this story, are you?"

"No, I swear."

Frank took out his wallet. "Here's twenty dollars for the info, and here's another twenty not to mention it to anyone else."

"Thank you, sir, thank you. I won't mention it to a soul. You have my word." The panhandler tucked the bills into his frayed coat pocket.

"One more thing," Frank said as he pulled out a card and began writing his cell number on the back of it. "Here's my card. If you ever hear of anything like this again, you give me a call or come by my office and show my secretary this card."

The homeless man accepted the card, cradling it in both hands like a small treasure. As he read the face of the card, he mouthed the words engraved on the linen card stock. "Mr. Frank Harrison, CFP. Thank you, sir. Of course, I'll keep my ears open."

"Great," Frank said, walking away at an increased pace. His priorities had suddenly shifted for the time being. Deterring Lenny Cramer's investigation would have to wait so he could take advantage of this valuable information he had just been given. *This information could not be considered "inside information," could it?* Frank wondered.

Seven

To the contrary, GAAP is not divine in origin; it is, instead, something of a chimera derived from economics, law, mathematics, the behavioral sciences, ethics, and communications. Over the past forty years [plus] the accounting profession has endeavored to codify this body of knowledge.
—Abraham J. Briloff

Dana looked up from her desk when she saw Frank walk into the office. "Frank, I haven't seen you for a week since you ran into Lenny and me at Le Ciel."

"I've been busy."

"Yes, I saw the little item about you in *The Philadelphia Inquirer.* The piece said you did very well on the takeover of Marsupial."

Frank adjusted his tie, then sat down at his desk and began to sift through some mail as he spoke. "I took a bit of a gamble. I would have included you in it, but there was so much uncertainty involved with the deal that I did not want to run the risk of it falling through and friends of mine losing money."

"Oh, I understand," replied Dana.

"Anything unusual going on here with the jade shop?" inquired Frank, changing the subject.

"Nothing, really. Although, I did have a question about something I noticed the other day."

"What's that?" Frank asked as he finished separating his mail.

Dana tried to be very casual in her tone as she spoke. "I was going through some papers, and I noticed that we do a great deal

115

of business with Carson Denig Gem Importers. Why do we do so much business with them when they grant us such lousy credit terms?"

Frank immediately put his mail down and glared at Dana. "Carson Denig Gem Importers is the foremost importer of Burmese gems in the country. We could rely more on our other suppliers, but then we would be substantially lowering the quality of much of our jade goods. We also would lose a significant portion of our clientele who come to our shop expecting the highest quality in jade."

"I was just curious." Frank's icy glare made Dana uncomfortable, and she added, "I felt there had to be a logical explanation. Thanks."

Frank soon left the office. Shortly thereafter, Dana called Lenny and told him about her conversation with Frank. She mentioned to him how uncomfortable Frank appeared to be about her questioning Carson Denig as a supplier. Lenny responded that he would be at the jade shop in two days and would examine the receivables and start on the inventory to see if he could find any red flags.

Dana punched the End button on her phone and then called a local merchant on Jeweler's Row, Irv Moskowitz. Now 64 years of age, Irv was regarded by some as the Dean of Jeweler's Row. He had continued a business started by his father, and the Moskowitz name had been on Jeweler's Row for over 78 years. Jewelers Row was established in 1851 and is America's oldest diamond district.

"Hello, Mr. Moskowitz. I'm Dana Scott of Jade & More."

"Call me Irv. Everyone else does. How are you today, Dana?"

"I'm fine, thanks. How about yourself?"

"Eh, you do not want to know, my dear."

"What's wrong?" Dana asked with alarm.

There was a slight pause. "Don't get old," he said. "A beautiful young girl like you should be married. You should not run a jade shop, miss out on life, and become old like me. Get married. Settle down. Have a family."

"But you're already taken, and all the other men pale in comparison to you," giggled Dana.

"You flirt with an old man like me? You must have something important to ask me. What is it, darling?"

Dana laughed. Whenever she spoke with Irv he always told her to get married, and she would always express her devotion to him. It was their little ongoing inside joke. "Irv, I do have something to ask you. It's about Carson Denig Gem Importers. What do you know about them?"

"They have excellent merchandise, if that's what you mean."

"Is it among the best?"

"It is good, but there are some suppliers with better quality. I will tell you, my dear, that we still do business with them, and we have no complaints."

"What type of credit terms do you get from them?"

"One moment, my dear, let me look that up for you." There was a rustling of papers that could be heard over the phone. Then Dana heard Irv yell, "Sylvia, get me our Carson Denig file." After a few more seconds Irv got back on the phone.

"Dana, our terms with them are the same as most others—2/ 10, net 30."

"2/10, net 30?" Dana repeated in surprise.

"Yes. What's wrong, my dear?"

"Nothing. I was just curious to know what you knew about them, that's all," Dana said in consternation.

"The only suspicious thing I hear about them, and don't repeat this to anyone," Irv said as his voice lowered to a near whisper. "I hear that Denig Gems sometimes offloads stolen jewelry and smuggled gems. But they do this only with private customers and not with people like you and me. I always check for the title of all the items I receive from them to make sure they're legitimate. I have never had a problem with Denig so far on the merchandise I've purchased. Like I said, my dear, that is what I hear. It could be gossip."

"Well, I appreciate your giving me the inside scoop. Thanks a lot, and take care of yourself, Irv."

"Dana, now you can do something for me."

"What's that?" Dana asked, anxious to return the favor.

"Make an old man happy and get married."

"You just won't give up, will you?" said Dana laughingly.

"Take care, my darling. Good-bye."

Dana looked at the clock on her desk. It was almost five, too late to call Carson Denig. She opted not to do anything further until Lenny came in on Thursday.

———————

Frank decided he couldn't wait any longer. He was surprised that Dana had asked him about Carson Denig. He had to do something to slow Lenny down. Late that night, Frank went back to the jade shop. He checked through the accounting records he had catalogued a week ago. Everything was exactly as he had left it. That gave Frank an idea. He spent the next 30 minutes fabricating purchase orders, receiving slips, and vendor invoices. Taking care to notice exactly where in the files he was placing the items, Frank inserted the fraudulent documents in with the originals. For the time being that should keep him in the clear or, at least, buy him some time until he devised a better plan for stalling Lenny.

———————

Dana looked at her watch. It was 10:03 a.m., only a minute later than it was the last time she had looked. "Where could he be?" she said aloud, alone in her office. Lenny was supposed to come by the office around 9:30 this Thursday morning, but he'd not yet arrived.

Dana stood up and started to pace the office. She wanted to call him to see what was keeping him, but she felt she could not do that since Lenny was helping her in his spare time as a favor to her. She hoped that he hadn't taken the bus but had driven instead. Now she was beginning to think otherwise, that Lenny might have taken the bus to avoid paying the fee to park in downtown Philadelphia. Accountants are so cheap, she thought. For all she knew, Lenny had probably spent the last 20 to 30 minutes waiting for a bus since most of the Philly buses were not expresses. Add to that the stops at every corner. Every accountant she had ever met was the same—cheap and a lousy dresser. Accountants looked decent if they were in a suit, but they had to be kept away from sports coats. They did things with plaids and pastels that bordered on illegal. But times were changing. Most professional accountants were now schooled in formal etiquette and business fashion during CPA firm training and orientation sessions. But Lenny, on the other hand, was a professor. And, absent-minded or not, he belonged to the ranks of academics who had an uncanny knack for fashion faux pas.

Dana's thoughts were interrupted by a knock on the door.

"Come in," she said.

"Hi, Dana," said Lenny breathlessly as he walked into the office. "I'm sorry I'm late, but I barely missed the bus at 34th and Chestnut, and I had to wait another 20 minutes for the next one to arrive. The bus was packed with senior citizens since they can ride free at this hour. I swear the bus stopped at every corner to either pick up people or let them off. If that wasn't bad enough, it took even longer since many of the senior citizens took a long time to get on and off the bus."

"That's okay," Dana replied as she tried to contain her smirk. She couldn't help herself given Lenny's attire. He was wearing a rumpled yellow and black plaid sport coat which looked as if it had been packed in a duffel bag for a year. Under the coat he wore a blue shirt with green stripes accessorized with a solid brown tie. Lime green trousers and white shoes finished off the wardrobe. Unable to control herself, she turned away from Lenny and started to giggle.

"What's so funny?" Lenny inquired innocently.

"Nothing, really. Just something I was thinking of when you came in," replied Dana sweetly.

Dana then told Lenny about the conversation she'd had with Irv Moskowitz and how she planned to phone Carson Denig Gem Importers that day concerning Jade & More's credit policy. She also told Lenny about the contradictory view Frank held concerning the quality of the goods provided by Carson Denig compared to what Irv had expressed. She finished with the rumor that Denig was dealing in stolen and smuggled jewelry.

Lenny smiled. "I think I know someone who might be able to verify the stolen-goods rumors. But before I contact him, I'd like your opinion. Who do you think is right about the quality of Carson Denig's merchandise—Frank or Irv?"

"Irv said that Carson Denig has *very good things*, but that they weren't the best around as Frank says. I don't think it's a matter of who is right or wrong, but more of a professional difference of opinion."

"That makes sense. I could see where it's not a question of 'either-or' but a case where two experts might disagree," Lenny said. "Even so, I still think you ought to call Carson Denig about their credit terms."

"Lenny, I hate doing that behind Frank's back," Dana said. "It's possible he could find out."

"It's up to you," Lenny sighed. "But if you want to know—"

"Okay, okay. I'll call," Dana said with resignation. She called out to Janet to look up the phone number for Carson Denig Gem Importers, Inc. Dana called Denig, but she got their voicemail asking callers to leave their name, phone number, and a brief statement concerning the nature of the call. And, of course, a customer service representative would call back as soon as possible. Instead of hanging up like she normally would, Dana left a message. Five minutes later the phone rang with a customer service representative from Denig Gems on the other end.

"You have a question concerning your account with us, Ms. Scott?" the woman on the other end of the line asked.

"Yes. I want to know why my shop only gets credit terms of net 15 while other shops that do business with you have terms of 2/10, net 30."

"I'm afraid I can't answer that for you," the customer service representative replied. "You are going to have to speak to Mr. Denig about it, but he's not available at the moment. Can I have him call you back when he returns?"

"Yes. Please do."

After Dana hung up, she recounted her conversation to Lenny. He was already sitting at Frank's desk and had begun looking through the receivables. Lenny nodded in acknowledgment a couple of times and encouraged Dana to keep him informed. Dana then slipped out to the front of the store to help with some customers.

———

Based on the preliminary work he had done at Dana's shop a week ago, Lenny decided to start his investigation with notes receivable thinking that it might be relatively simple given there would not be too many notes to examine. Lenny knew that notes receivable can occur when a company loans money to another company or to an individual and, usually, interest is charged, or a note receivable may be acquired from a customer who cannot pay an existing account receivable. The only unusual notes receivable were a series of notes received from Denig Gems. The notes were for a wide range of amounts extending over a long period of time. Lenny traced the notes to the Sales Journal and the General Journal. About 70 percent of the notes were associated with the sale of merchandise to Denig. Apparently Jade & More not only purchased inventory from Denig Gems but also occasionally sold merchandise to Denig Gems. Oddly, though, Lenny did not find any corresponding entries in the General Journal recording the cost of goods sold and reducing the inventory. Jade & More recorded inventory using the perpetual method, so each sale transaction should have two parts: recording the sale and recording the inventory reduction. Lenny made a note to investigate this further.

Lenny then examined each individual entry in the General Journal related to the remaining notes receivable from Denig. It took some time, but in the end, Lenny was able to account for the remaining 30 percent of the notes. They weren't for merchandise but for services performed for Denig Gems.

Suddenly, Dana ran into the office. "Lenny, you've got to get out of here. Frank's on his way."

Lenny looked surprised. "I thought you said he rarely stops by before four o'clock."

"Have you been daydreaming?" Dana inquired with a smile on her face. "It's 3:55. I just got off the phone with Frank. He said that he would be here within fifteen minutes. You have to hurry."

Lenny had totally lost track of the time while searching for the various notes received from Denig Gems. He began to pack up and hurriedly put the books and files away, disappointed that he did not have the opportunity to look in the files for the documentation in the form of a receipt indicating what services the jade shop performed and who performed the services.

"Did you find anything?" Dana inquired as she glanced again at her watch.

"Perhaps. Tell me, Dana, did either you or Frank ever do any work or consulting for Carson Denig?"

"I surely didn't," Dana replied with bewilderment. "I've never even met him."

"Why don't you call me tonight at my office," Lenny suggested. "I'll be working there until eight o'clock. We can talk about it more then. In the meantime, I'd better leave. I don't want Frank to see me here."

Lenny said good-bye to Dana and headed onto busy Sansom Street, whose sidewalks were congested with people. Unbeknownst to him, Frank was across the street on the corner from where he had phoned Dana earlier. He had a perfect view of Lenny departing.

Frank and Dana chatted amicably for the hour or so that they were together in the office that afternoon. Frank never said a word about seeing Lenny, and Dana never brought up Carson Denig's name. When Dana left, Frank immediately checked and saw that someone had been looking at both the books and the files. This activity confirmed his suspicions. Dana might be curious and ask lots of questions, but Lenny was the one digging into the records. Frank knew that he had to slow Lenny down, and he hoped that his series of plans would work.

Frank gathered his belongings, left the jade shop, and walked to his car. He ripped off his nicotine patch, lit a cigarette, got into his car, and drove to Dorney's Tavern. It was only a five-minute drive, but he wanted to make sure that he was there by 7:30 p.m. He found a parking spot in a public garage, took the self-service parking stub from the dispenser at the lift gate, and eased into an empty stall. As he walked toward the bar, Frank checked the time on the stub. It was stamped 7:19 p.m.

Dorney's was a place that Frank frequented on occasions. He knew all the bartenders and most of the servers, so it was not at all unusual that he was recognized and greeted when he walked into the tavern.

"Frank, how are you doing?"

Frank looked at the large man behind the bar who greeted him. Al was about six-feet-four-inches tall and weighed about 260 pounds.

He had played football at Philly's Frankford High School, but a knee injury his senior year effectively ended his football career. Now, at the age of 42, Al was the head bartender at Dorney's.

"I'm doing pretty good, Al. How about yourself?"

"Not bad." Al grabbed a mug. "You want the usual, Frank?"

"That sounds good." Frank sat down at the end of the bar. It was an active night, but not especially crowded. Frank looked up at the bank of flat panels TVs. The college football game was just beginning.

"You going to watch the game?" Al inquired, already knowing the answer.

"You know what a Temple fan I am," Frank responded. "Owls are going to take the American Athletic Conference this year."

"They may have a tough time knocking off Akron tonight, Frank."

"Al, there won't be any zip left with Akron after Temple is through with them." They both chuckled over Frank's pun on Akron's nickname, the Zips. "Can you imagine having a nickname like the Zips? You know, Al, it's short for the Zippers."

"Get out of here."

"I'm serious. They were originally called the Zippers and their name was shortened to the Zips."

"I wouldn't touch that line with a ten-foot pole," Al replied as both he and Frank bellowed with laughter.

Frank then saw a tall blonde walk in and sit alone at a table. He looked at the burly bartender and raised his eyebrows. "Al, I think I just found a good table to watch the game from."

"Yeah!" replied Al with a wink.

Frank looked at his watch, and then said to Al, "Hey, Al, can you tell me what time it is? My watch must have stopped."

"It's 7:38."

"Thanks. Make sure you send someone over to the table to serve drinks."

"No problem. Happy hunting, Frank."

Frank smiled at Al and walked over to a table where a blonde was sitting, struck up a conversation, and sat down to watch the game.

"Cramer, here" Lenny said, picking up the phone on the second ring.

"Hello, Professor Cramer, this is Carson Denig. Dana Scott said I might be able to reach you at this number. She suggested I speak to you to explain about the consulting work Jade & More does for me."

"Sure, I'd like that. I did have a few questions for you."

"Dana mentioned that you might," Denig said. "Professor Cramer, perhaps we can talk in person. I'm staying at the Sheraton, just around the corner from your office. I can meet you in the lounge and show you some of my papers which detail the work they did. I know it's short notice, but I'm free this evening."

Lenny looked at his watch. It was 7:25 p.m. "I can be there in about five minutes, but I can only spend about a half hour with you."

"That should give us enough time," Denig said. "Dana Scott described you to me so I should be able to find you in the lounge. Professor Cramer, I look forward to meeting you."

"That will be fine, Mr. Denig. I'll be there in about five minutes."

Lenny hung up the phone and gathered his work together, deciding what he was going to take home with him and what he was going to leave in the office. He looked outside the window. It was already dark outside.

Lenny knew Dana had left a message with Denig's office and was expecting a call back, but he was surprised Dana had not called him first to let him know Carson would be calling. He also was curious about what records Carson Denig was going to show him. This impromptu meeting could be helpful, Lenny thought. He might learn something from Carson Denig that would solve Dana's problem at the jade shop.

Lenny locked his office door, turning the doorknob several times out of habit to make sure that the door was locked. He walked down the two flights of stairs and stepped out the door into the chilly fall night. As he approached his car Lenny was struck from behind with a blunt object. He dropped his briefcase and tried to break his fall, but it was too late. The force of the blow, combined with his head hitting the cement, knocked him out.

"Look! He's starting to move around. Dad, are you okay? Can you hear me, Dad?"

Lenny recognized Rebecca's voice and smiled. His head was throbbing, and he found it difficult to concentrate.

"Mr. Cramer, this is Dr. Miltiken. Can you hear me?"

"Yes," Lenny garbled as he tried to sit up.

"Don't move, Mr. Cramer. Just keep still."

"Ok," Lenny said. He rubbed the back of his neck and then lightly touched the swelling knot on his forehead. "What happened?"

"We were hoping you could tell us that," the doctor replied, as he checked Lenny's eyes with a small flashlight.

"I remember going to my car, and then I remember falling."

"Anything else?" inquired the doctor.

"Nothing else until I just now heard Rebecca's voice," answered Lenny, squeezing Rebecca's hand.

"Well, Mr. Cramer, we believe you were mugged. In the struggle, you took a direct hit to the back of your head, and, then fell face down. The gash in your forehead required six stitches," the doctor continued in a calm voice. "Between the blunt force trauma and the fall, it appears to me that you may have suffered a slight concussion. Now I don't think it's serious, but I would like to keep you overnight for observation."

"I understand," Lenny said. He closed his eyes for a moment and then asked, "What hospital is this?"

"University Hospital," the doctor replied. "The police brought you here when they found you lying face down on the street. They are in the waiting area and want to question you about this, but I'll have them return tomorrow. Now I want you to rest."

"Rest sounds good," Lenny said weakly. He hoped sleeping would relieve the pounding in his head. Lenny looked over at his daughter. "Rebecca, I want you to take a cab—"

"That's not necessary, Dad. Dana will take me."

"Dana?"

"She picked me up and drove me here. She's outside in the waiting room."

"How did she know I was here?" Lenny asked.

"She tried to reach you at your office," replied Rebecca. "Then she called our house to see if you were there. And then she called again later to check. She told me to call her if I heard anything. When I called to let her know you were at the ER, she offered to drive me over here. Dad, I was pretty scared when you didn't come home." Rebecca eyes were glistening from trying to hold back tears. "Dana said I could stay with her tonight. Is that okay, Dad?"

"Sure, honey. Don't worry about me. I'll be fine." Lenny squeezed Rebecca's hand once more. "Thank Dana for me, and I'll see you tomorrow, Rebecca."

"Night, Dad. Get better."

"Mr. Cramer, that's it for visiting hours," the doctor said. "I want you to take these two pills and get a good night's sleep. Doctor's orders."

Lenny willingly complied and spent the night sleeping in the hospital. The next morning when the doctor examined him, Lenny was feeling much better. The doctor told him that he could leave the hospital and that he should go home and rest for about three days before returning to work. Lenny called his accounting department head at Wharton and made arrangements for a graduate student to teach his classes.

Prior to his discharge, Detective Calhoun of the Philadelphia Police Department paid Lenny a visit. Lenny was so tired and concerned about the throbbing in his head that he had not thought about the mugging until now.

"Professor Cramer, did you see the person who attacked you?" Calhoun asked.

"No."

"Do you have any idea who it could have been?"

"No," Lenny responded.

"Was anything stolen?"

"To the best of my knowledge, no," replied Lenny. "My wallet was intact and from what my daughter said you recovered my briefcase."

"Let me make sure I understand the facts," Calhoun said, looking at his notepad. "You left your office around 7:30 p.m. and were on your way home when you were hit from behind just before getting in your car."

Lenny nodded. "That's right, except that I was on my way to meet someone and then I was going home."

"Did you notice anyone around the office building last night? Calhoun inquired.

"No, I was all alone."

"I wish I could help you, Professor Cramer, but to be honest with you, I don't see how we have enough leads to possibly apprehend the individual since nothing was stolen from you and you never saw the person." Calhoun closed his notepad and placed it in his inside coat pocket. He was a large black man about forty years of age. He looked imposing at about six-foot-two in height and two hundred pounds in weight. "If you think of anything else, give me a call at this number." He handed Lenny a P.P.D. business card.

"I'm sorry I couldn't be of more help, Detective," sighed Lenny. "It just happened so fast."

"No problem at all. Just be grateful it was only a couple of stitches. Take care."

Lenny was discharged from the hospital later that morning. Dana picked him up outside the hospital and drove him to his car, which was still parked outside his office building.

"You know what's a real shame about this whole thing?" Lenny posed. He and Dana had talked about the mugging at some length on the way over.

"No, what?" Dana responded.

"I was all set to meet with Carson Denig concerning the consulting work that he did for Jade & More and the notes that you have. I was going to meet him when I got hit."

"What notes?" Dana inquired.

"I forgot," Lenny said with a smile. "I was going to tell you last night about the large number of notes receivable you have from Carson Denig for sales and services rendered. That's why I asked you about it yesterday."

"How did you get in touch with Carson Denig? I called there yesterday, and he never returned my call. I was going to call him again today," Dana said as she parked behind Lenny's car.

"Wait a minute!" Lenny said incredulously. "Carson Denig never called you back?"

"No."

"He told me that he spoke to you."

Dana shut off the engine and turned towards Lenny. "He never spoke to me." There was a brief period of silence before Dana continued. "Did he say that we had talked when he called you last night?"

"Yes. In fact, he told me that you asked him to call me."

Dana paused. A look of anguish crossed her face. "Oh, Lenny, are you thinking—"

"What's that?" Lenny said, cutting her off before she could finish the sentence.

"That the attack last night was no accident. That Carson Denig was the one who hit you." Dana looked pale and moisture began to form around her eyes. She took a handkerchief and dabbed at her eyes.

"That's entirely possible," Lenny responded with some anger in his voice.

"I'm afraid, Lenny," Dana almost cried. "Who knows what he might do next?"

Lenny tried to console her. "If he wanted to do more harm to me, he could have done it easily. And if it is him, I think he only wanted to scare me off, not hurt me seriously."

"I feel so guilty," Dana insisted. "I was the one who got you into this mess, and now look what's happened!"

"Don't worry, Dana. I'm going to call Detective Calhoun when I get home and tell him about this. The Philly Police Department will take care of Carson Denig." Lenny unfastened his seat belt and opened the car door.

"Promise me you'll be careful," Dana implored as she gripped Lenny's hand tightly.

"Yes, Dana, I promise." Lenny looked into her worried eyes. "I know I haven't said this before, but I appreciate you looking after Rebecca last night and bringing her to the hospital."

"What else could I have done? She was scared," Dana whispered.

Lenny leaned over and kissed her on the cheek and quickly got out of the car. He walked over to his car and started it up.

Dana rolled down the window of her car, waved, and shouted, "Make sure you get plenty of rest."

Lenny waved back and headed home.

There was not much traffic at that time of the morning and Lenny arrived at the house within ten minutes. It felt good to be back. He had missed the simple comforts of home during his brief stay at the hospital. Lenny walked over to his desk in the study and looked at his familiar AICPA desk set. He toyed with the high-quality pen awhile before sitting down at his desk. Lenny removed his phone from his pocket and dialed Calhoun. He was pleased to hear the detective's voice on the other end.

"Detective Calhoun, this is Lenny Cramer. I have some information that might be useful."

"Professor Cramer, I'm listening."

Lenny told him about the Carson Denig phone call and the subsequent discrepancy between what Carson had said and what Dana had told him. Calhoun thanked Lenny for the tip and told him that he would keep him informed. Feeling slightly fatigued from the events of the last twenty-four hours, Lenny got up from the desk chair and plopped himself into his overstuffed recliner near the bookshelf. He started reading the latest issue of *The Journal of Accountancy.*

One story on "Family Business Transition Planning" suggested that one could maximize a company's value by making sure financial accounting systems are in good order, family expenses are not run through the business, there are no unusual accounting practices, and full audits of financial statements are completed annually. He started another article about the value of Apple's iPad as an accounting tool, when he gently drifted off to sleep.

"Frank, I didn't expect to see you here so early today!" Dana said. She was surprised to see Frank as she walked into her office.

"I have a business meeting later in the day, but I also wanted to talk to you," Frank said sternly.

"What about?" Dana was curious but cautious.

Frank took a deep breath and looked at Dana sincerely. "Last evening around 6:15, I received a long-distance phone call from Tucson, Arizona. Carson Denig was returning a phone message that he got from his secretary saying that you had phoned him earlier in the day about the credit terms that Denig Gems offers us."

Dana was stunned. Not only had Frank caught her checking on Carson Denig behind his back, but worse, *Denig was in Arizona.* That meant he couldn't possibly have been the one to attack Lenny.

"I told him that you called by mistake," Frank continued. "You see, Dana, I know that he gives better credit terms to other shops, but he always gives us his best merchandise. In exchange for giving us first crack at his inventory, I agreed to the more restrictive credit terms. While it's true that as a partner in a general partnership, I didn't legally need you to agree to the arrangement because any contract signed by one partner is binding on the other, I still should have told you about it. At the time I agreed to the arrangement, I intended to tell you, but things have been crazy around here and I forgot. I'm sorry. Anyway, I agreed to the credit terms without consulting you because I thought you trusted my judgment. If I hadn't agreed to the credit terms on the spot, Carson said he would have taken the proposition to someone else."

Dana felt embarrassed. "I'm sorry, Frank. I should have never suspected anything. Will you forgive me?" Before Frank could answer, Dana asked, "Did you say that Carson Denig called from Tucson?"

"Yes. He called from the Holiday Inn there. Why?" Frank inquired.

"Nothing, really. I'm thinking of a trip to Arizona for the holidays," Dana lied.

"Dana, I get the sense that you don't trust me. You didn't even give me a chance to accept your apology before you launched into questions about Denig's whereabouts," Frank said. "If you are not going to trust me, then we should end our partnership. This business is a hobby for me, Dana. It's certainly not my meal ticket. I don't want to be in a partnership where my partner is checking up on me. We can end it right now, dispose of the assets, settle the liabilities, and share the gain or loss the same way that we shared the profits in the past. It's up to you."

Dana felt extremely awkward. She did not trust Frank, but she was currently not in a financial position to buy him out. Like it or not, she knew that she could not afford to have Frank end the partnership now. "Frank, I do trust you," Dana said as sincerely as she could. "And I apologize for questioning your judgment."

"Well, that's what I was hoping you would say," Frank responded. "We make a good team, you and me."

Frank finished gathering up the work on his desk and packed it in his briefcase. He was on his way to his consulting office for a meeting with a client. As he stepped from the entrance of the jade shop onto Sansom Street, he smiled broadly and said aloud, "Frank, you're a genius. An honest-to-goodness genius."

"Hello," Lenny said between yawns as he picked up the ringing phone.

"How are you feeling, Lenny?"

Lenny recognized Dana's voice and smiled. "Pretty good."

"I was just talking to Frank. I'll tell you about the whole conversation later, but the most important thing is that he got a phone call yesterday evening from Carson Denig."

"Did Frank get mugged, too?" Lenny said sarcastically.

"No," replied Dana.

"Too bad," retorted Lenny.

"This is serious Lenny," Dana sniggered. "Carson Denig called Frank from Tucson, Arizona, from the Holiday Inn there. Denig could not have been the one that attacked you!"

"Hmm. You're right, he couldn't have done it himself, but he still could have had someone else attack me."

"There's that," Dana admitted. "It's possible."

Lenny thanked Dana for calling and told her that he would call Detective Calhoun about the latest development. While he was looking for Calhoun's phone number, the telephone rang. Calhoun was on the other end.

"I was just going to call you," Lenny said. "I found out that Carson Denig was in Tucson, Arizona, last night."

"I know," Calhoun replied. "We've cleared him completely. We pulled the lugs. According to the local usage details from the phone company the call to your office was placed locally through an untraceable cell phone. The only long-distance call Denig made into Philadelphia yesterday was to Jade & More."

"Jade & More. That's how I found out he was in Arizona. From the folks at Jade & More," Lenny interjected.

"While Carson Denig may no longer be a person of interest, I do believe I have a much better suspect, Mr. Cramer," Calhoun added.

"Fantastic! Who is it?"

"Dana Scott," Calhoun answered.

Eight

The only act which a CPA can perform, and which is denied to all others, is the rendering of an opinion on the fairness of financial statements. The audit function has, more than any other activity performed by CPAs, bound the profession together during its first century.
—Stephen A. Zeff

"Dana Scott!" Lenny repeated incredulously. "That's ridiculous! She—"

"Before you jump down my throat, hear me out," Calhoun said in a calm voice.

Lenny wanted to hang up the phone on the spot or ask Calhoun where he got his police training. The thought of Dana being the one behind his mugging was incomprehensible to him, but he decided he would listen to Calhoun anyway. "I'll hear you out, Detective Calhoun, but I'm telling you right now that there is no way Dana could possibly be the mugger. She's too petite. Whoever hit me, clipped me hard enough to knock me out with a single blow."

"I'm not saying she's personally guilty," cautioned Calhoun. "I'm only saying that she is our prime suspect. There is a whole lot of difference between being a suspect and being guilty. The evidence makes her a person of extreme interest."

"What evidence?" Lenny asked.

"I grant you, it's circumstantial," Calhoun emphasized, "but let me finish before you say anything. First point. The only ones to know that you were working in your office last night were your daughter Rebecca and Dana Scott. Right?"

"Right."

"Second point. Carson Denig had no way of knowing who you were or your connection to Jade & More unless Dana Scott told him. Right?"

"Right."

"Third, no one else could have known that you had focused your attention on Denig Gems as part of your consulting work. And you and Dana Scott were the only ones who could have known that a phone call from Carson Denig would interest you."

Lenny felt uncomfortable. "Maybe her partner found out."

"You mean Frank Harrison? We're in the process of checking him out. At the moment he appears to be in the clear. We know he was in a bar last night at the time you were mugged," Calhoun said.

"You didn't let him know that I was working for Dana, did you?" Lenny asked. He was worried that alerting Frank would compromise his investigation into Dana's cash flow problems and complicate his relationship with her.

"No," replied Calhoun. "We can be very discreet when we have to be. But let's suppose that Frank Harrison did find out that you were looking into Carson Denig. How would he have known that without Dana Scott telling him? Or, more interesting, how would Frank Harrison have known you were in your office last night at 7:25 p.m. when you received the phone call unless Dana Scott told him you would be there? In short, either Dana Scott is involved, or she is lying to you about who she told what regarding Denig Gems. Of that I am fairly confident."

Lenny did not know what to say. There was a long pause and all that could be heard on the phone was occasional static. Perhaps Calhoun was right that Dana was either lying or involved. There had to be some explanation. Then it came to him. "How about Dana's bookkeeper, Janet? She has seen me go in and out of the jade shop. So, has Phillip, the sales clerk. They could have mentioned it to Frank—"

"But neither of them could have tied you to Carson Denig," Calhoun interrupted, "and neither knew that you were in your office last night. P.P.D. is still going to check them out, but listen, Professor Cramer," Calhoun's voice became calmer, "I want to repeat that Dana Scott is only a person of interest. She may or may not be guilty. Her biggest crime might be that she mentioned something that was overheard by someone else. But, at this point in our investigation, just looking at what we have pieced together, she appears to be involved in some way."

Lenny shook his head. He had listened to Calhoun's arguments but wasn't convinced.

"Professor Cramer, normally, it is not departmental practice to provide a victim with information concerning a suspect. But, in this case, since you have frequent contact with the suspect, we would rather be safe than sorry. I would recommend that you be extremely cautious when in Dana Scott's presence. It might be wise to avoid her until this thing gets settled. There is one thing in Dana Scott's favor, though, Professor Cramer."

"What's that?" asked Lenny anxiously.

"I haven't thought of a possible motive for why Dana Scott might want to do you physical harm," Calhoun revealed. "Of course, that's if she is acting rationally. If she is under some type of emotional stress, then there is no telling what might motivate her."

Lenny sighed. "Detective Calhoun, may I ask you to keep me informed of anything else that arises?"

"Sure. I'll be in touch," Calhoun said. "Be careful, Professor Cramer."

Lenny ended the call and sat down in his chair. He did not know what to think. He cared deeply for Dana and did not want to believe that she could be involved in his mugging. Last night, he had even trusted her to take care of his young daughter. There was just no reason he could think of why she wanted to do him harm. Then, again, he couldn't argue with Calhoun's logic, either. Lenny could feel his natural skeptical accountant's instincts starting to take over, warning him to be cautious.

Between the unsettling conversation with Calhoun and the constant throbbing in his head from his concussion, Lenny was now exhausted. Soon he dozed off in his chair, more perplexed than ever as to what to think about Dana.

———————

Monday morning, Lenny returned to his university office. He was feeling better and believed that the weekend rest had recharged him. Dana had called to check up on him, but he received no further reports from Detective Calhoun. The Carson Denig episode had stayed on Lenny's mind over the whole weekend, and now he was anxious to begin puzzling through the connection with the mugging.

When he got to his office, one of the first things he did was to get in touch with Woody. Most anxious to oblige, Woody joined him in his faculty enclave. Woody leaned back in the extra chair next to Lenny's desk.

"Woody, I want to call upon your vast expertise to assist me with an important matter," Lenny said, trying to withhold a grin.

"I'm at your service, sir," Woody replied, twirling his ever-present, always unlit cigar.

"Have you ever heard of Carson Denig or know anybody who might know of him?" Lenny inquired. "I hear that he may deal in stolen jewelry."

"You've come to the right place, Dr. Cramer," Woody replied, leaning forward to make a point. "He's one bad dude, Doc. I don't run with the same brothers I did when I was younger, but from what I hear around the 'hood,' I wouldn't be surprised if he deals hot merchandise, among other things."

"Do you know how I could get in touch with him?"

"I know where his warehouse is—back in the old neighborhood in Southwest Philly." Woody paused and looked Lenny in the eye. "Doc, take my advice. Stay away from Denig. Get yourself better from that conk on the head you took."

"You heard about that?"

"Everyone around here has been talking about it," Woody reported. "Must have been intense from that knot on your head. What were there, ten stitches?"

"Only six, Woody," Lenny said. He then recounted to Woody how, after receiving the phone call from Denig, he was hit on the head coming out of the building, and how Calhoun suspected Dana of being behind the attack.

"Um huh. I think that dame's involved," Woody said.

Lenny refused to accept that Dana had played a role in his mugging. "I don't think so. I think Carson Denig is worried about me finding something in his or Dana's records. I don't know how he found out about my activities or whereabouts, but I don't think Dana is intentionally involved."

Woody turned both ways to make sure no one down the hallway was within earshot and said to Lenny in a near whisper, "Doc, I can get us into that warehouse if you want to do some snoopin'. I know the guard there, and if we agree not to boost anything, he'll let us in."

Lenny thought for a while. "I'm up for a little midnight forensic auditing. When do you think we could get in?" he asked anxiously.

"Probably tomorrow night, just before midnight, when the night shift comes on. One thing, though," Woody warned.

"What's that?"

"You can't tell that fine lady friend of yours anything about this. If you're wrong and she is involved, I don't want Carson Denig having a reception committee for us," Woody said with caution.

"Understood, Woody. Tomorrow night at Carson Denig's warehouse. A hunting we will go."

Dana put down a jade dealer's advertisement she had received in the mail and began to pace in her office. Things were getting wild. Usually, her life went according to a plan—no surprises. At least, no unmanageable surprises. She liked it that way. She liked being on top of things. Free spirited—*yes*. Wild—*no*. But lately she believed that the events of the past weeks were speeding recklessly out of control.

She had grown fond of Lenny and was naturally worried about him after the mugging outside of his office. Still, she was not quite sure where they were in their relationship or even what kind of relationship they really had. She did notice lately, ever since the attack, that Lenny seemed very distant each time they spoke. She couldn't help feeling that she was responsible for Lenny's injuries. After all, she was the one that had convinced Lenny to look at her books and records with the intention of finding a solution to her cash-flow shortage. She never dreamed then that she would be placing Lenny in physical danger.

She glanced over at Frank's desk and shook her head in disdain. Clearly, she didn't trust a single thing Frank had told her about the arrangement the jade shop had with Carson Denig. In fact, she privately believed that Frank was getting some type of kickback under the table from Carson in exchange for steering business to Denig Gems. She had heard of similar situations in other industries and thought it might be happening to her. She remembered from her accounting classes that one of the best ways to steal was to establish some type of illegal arrangement with a vendor. But she also knew that she didn't have the expertise to prove it. "If only Lenny hadn't been hurt," she moaned.

Dana looked at the large wall calendar she had received from one of the vendors during the holidays last year. There was a different type of jade carving on it for each month. She knew that it would be some time before Lenny would be able to come by and continue his investigation. She also knew that it would be far more difficult for Lenny to spend extensive time here during the day. If Frank wasn't suspicious before, he was definitely suspicious now. Dana felt that drastic action would be needed if she was going to regain control of the situation.

She walked over to Frank's desk and began rifling through the drawers. She didn't know what she was looking for, but she just felt that she had to do something, anything. All she saw, however, were bundles of papers, neatly rubber banded, that dealt with the day-to-day business that did not appear to be very important.

Dana closed the last desk drawer. She looked around the backroom and decided to start taking a physical inventory. Lenny had asked her to do this when she got a chance. Dana figured that the work would help to ease her restlessness. She grabbed her bar code scanner and walked out into the shop.

Frank had decided that Jade & More would use the specific identification method for inventory instead of the more common FIFO, LIFO, or weighted-average cost flow assumptions. Dana knew that the acronym FIFO stood for first in, first-out. As she approached the closest jewelry display case, she mouthed the term silently, pronouncing it "fi" with a long "I" sound like in wi-fi and "fo" with a long "o" like in foe. "Fifo," she muttered. Under the FIFO flow assumption, the first items purchased were assumed to be the first items sold. Lenny had told her FIFO was a good choice if one were selling fresh produce. This method ensured that the older produce was sold before it spoiled. The result was that the first items in were the first sold, and the last items purchased were the ones which remained in inventory at the end of the period.

Similarly, the acronym LIFO stood for last-in, first-out. The last items purchased were assumed to be the first ones sold. Lenny had said the use of LIFO would be appropriate if one were in the business of selling coal. Spoilage wasn't an issue. As the new coal is off-loaded from railroad cars or coal trucks, it would, likely, be placed on top of the old coal pile. That way, any coal that would be sold would come from the top of the coal mound, so that the most recent shipment of coal would be the first to be sold. The LIFO cost flow assumption is the exact opposite of that for FIFO.

Dana remembered that Lenny had explained that the third cost flow approach—weighted average—took the total cost of goods available for sale, something he said was the sum of beginning inventory plus purchases and divided that total by the number of units available for sale. This approach would give a weighted average cost per unit. By multiplying the number of units in ending inventory by this weighted average cost per unit, you could calculate the cost of ending inventory. Weighted-average, Lenny said, was a solid choice for fungible inventories like chemicals and commodities, where the products are physically indistinguishable.

Among the three cost flow assumptions, Lenny also had reminded Dana that in a period of rising prices, using the FIFO method results in the lowest cost of goods sold and the highest reported income. No wonder FIFO was the most popular of the three methods for financial reporting. Contrariwise, in a period of rising prices, using the LIFO method results in the highest cost of goods sold and the lowest reported income. For this reason, some companies elect LIFO because this method results in lower taxable income and, therefore, lower taxes paid to the government. Dana liked the idea of lower taxes, but Lenny had said there was a catch to using LIFO. Under the IRS conformity rule, companies that elected LIFO for tax reporting also had to use LIFO when issuing financial statements. Companies couldn't have it both ways—LIFO to reduce taxable income and FIFO to increase reported earnings to shareholders. Rather, a company that chooses LIFO for tax purposes must also use LIFO for financial reporting purposes; according to the IRS, you cannot have your cake and eat it, too.

Dana started to laugh. She recalled that Lenny had made a crack about a fourth cost flow assumption—FINO. He hoped that Jade & More wasn't using that approach, and if so it could easily explain the cash flow shortage. "Lenny, what's FINO?" she had asked. "First In, Never Out, darling," Lenny had said. "It's a very poor business practice. Try to avoid—"

Of course, she remembered most of her accounting from college. Accounting was like riding a bicycle. You never forget. Lenny had told her that LIFO probably would disappear if the U.S. switched over to international financial reporting standards. He called it "IFRS" or "eye-furs." Good name.

She wished she had not played dumb with Lenny. She liked the guy, strange clothes, and all. But she had used the "dumb blonde" approach so many times to get what she wanted from a man, it was second nature to her, and the ploy most often worked with men. Lenny had been putty in her hands. The same with Frank. Make them think you are helpless, and they'll do almost anything for you. She learned that ploy while serving as president of the Women's Student Government at Pfeiffer University.

The scanner beeped as Dana ran it over the bar code for a tasteful jade and diamond ring set in white gold. Frank was right. Dana knew that they had no choice but to use the specific identification method of inventory rather than the more common FIFO, LIFO, or weighted average methods. The big three were only appropriate when dealing with inventories that consisted of many of the same type of goods. Their jade shop did not have many items which were identical. For the most part, each item was unique—meaning that no cost flow assumption was necessary at all. Specific identification allowed Jade & More to keep track of every single item of inventory and how much each one cost, piece by piece.

Computers helped ease the task of using the specific identification method. Rather than having to search through the accounting records for the original cost of each inventory item, Dana could instead scan in the bar code of the item into the computer, and within seconds the exact cost of the item, when it was purchased, from whom it was purchased, and a brief description of the item appeared on the screen.

Dana continued her walk around the store scanning the tag of each item in the shop. It took much longer than she expected, since she had to remove every single piece of jewelry from the various display cases to scan them. Simply counting all the items visually was not an option as it would be when taking inventory under any of the other three methods.

By five o'clock, Dana had finished scanning two-thirds of the inventory. She hoped that the information would be useful in finding out more about the shop's cash-flow problems, and she also hoped that she would be able to see Lenny soon.

She took out her phone and called Lenny's office, but got no answer. The same was true for Lenny's cell. She then tried to reach him at home. She could hear someone pick up on the other end of the line.

"Hello, Cramer residence."

Dana recognized Rebecca's voice immediately. "Hello, Rebecca. How are you? This is Dana Scott."

"I'm fine, Dana. I bet you're looking for my dad."

Dana could hear a mounting tone of affection in Rebecca's voice. She knew that Rebecca liked her, and she, in turn, had grown fond of Rebecca. "You're right, Rebecca. Is he home?"

"You just missed him. He's gone out for the night with someone from school—I mean the university."

"Oh," Dana said, clearly disappointed. She knew things between them weren't quite what they had been before the mugging, but she never suspected it was because of another woman. She had thought, instead, that Lenny might, at some level, be holding her responsible for getting him mixed up with Carson Denig. Dana was stunned by Rebecca's revelation.

"He said he was going to be late," Rebecca continued. "Do you want me to have him call you when he gets back?"

"No, that's fine," Dana replied in a dispirited voice. "I'll talk to him later, Rebecca. Take care."

Dana put down the phone and walked over to the coat rack to put on her coat. She grabbed her briefcase and left the shop, feeling depressed and sorry for herself as she went out into the crowd of people going home from work.

Lenny took Woody to dinner at a small diner close to where Woody lived in Southwest Philadelphia. It was not a part of the city with which Lenny was very familiar. Most of the homes were either row homes or twins. A good number were well kept although there was not much in the way of green, elaborate lawns. The owners of those houses that had grass rather than cement in front had not invested in trees or plants. The area consisted mostly of people with low-paying service jobs and blue-collar workers, many of whom were employed at nearby plants in the area, the Philadelphia International Airport, or the many oil refineries across the Schuylkill River in South Philadelphia. Lenny was particularly dismayed over two features of the area. One was the horrible condition of the streets. Potholes were plentiful—there were at least five in every block, and they weren't insubstantial.

The other unusual characteristic of Southwest Philly was the large number of trolleys in use. It seemed to Lenny that when he wasn't driving around or over potholes, he was driving on or over trolley tracks. There were trolleys on Woodland Avenue, which used to be an old run-down shopping area. The trolleys along this route went underground near the University of Pennsylvania and provided service to Center City and the suburbs. There were similar trolleys on Island Avenue and Elmwood Avenue, which were also in Southwest Philadelphia. All three of these trolley lines were within two blocks of one another. Many visitors climb aboard a burgundy and green Victorian-style trolley to take a one and one-half hour narrated, round-trip tour.

Later, Woody explained to Lenny that part of the reason for all the trolleys was the large number of manufacturing plants that used to be in the area many years ago. Another reason was the local trolley barn designed to house many of the trolleys of SEPTA—the public transportation authority in Southeastern Pennsylvania.

To kill time after dinner, Lenny and Woody went to the South Philly Bar & Grill, a neighborhood sports bar which was a favorite hangout of Woody's. Lenny did not drink much, but he enjoyed watching Woody in his element with many of his local buddies.

"They were bums!" Woody proclaimed about the 1964 Philadelphia Phillies baseball team. "Leading by six games with twelve games left to play and they blew it. They're bums. I've never gone to another game since."

"Me neither," a burly redheaded man in his late fifties added. "And the Phillies' manager, Gene Mauch, was the biggest bum of them all!" Woody and others nodded their heads in approval.

"Woody," Lenny said in a low voice. "That was over fifty years ago and since then the Phillies have won the World Series twice—once in 1980 and not too long ago in 2008. Why are people still talking about the '64 season?"

"Because it still hurts, and I'll never forgive them. Besides, how could the Phillies lose to the wildcard Cardinals in 2011? They had a 102–60 season but couldn't get by the first round. Right, guys?"

Sounds of affirmation and nods came from the others at the bar. Similar conversations went back and forth for another hour, migrating from pro-baseball to pro-football, then college football, pro-basketball, college round ball, high school basketball and finally, pro-ice hockey than by the time.

When the subject turned to ice hockey, Woody motioned to Lenny to leave. Although it was well past 11:00 p.m., Lenny had an impression that Woody was motivated to leave more by his lack of interest in pro-ice hockey than by the time.

Lenny was glad to leave the smoke-filled tavern and the din of blaring TV screens. He was starting to get nervous about this entire late-night escapade. Although the joke around the staff room when he was a first-year associate for one of the Big 4 was that only the best "newbies" were assigned to do the midnight audits, Lenny knew the story was more urban myth than reality. Nowhere in Auditing Standards was an after-dark, illegal search for documentation standard practice for field work, and now here he was, getting ready to break into Denig Gems. Lenny knew that the Sarbanes-Oxley legislation (now known as SOX) became effective in 2002 following the disclosure of several massive corporate frauds. One of the SOX provisions established the Public Company Accounting Oversight Board (PCAOB) to oversee the audits of public companies to protect investors and the general public. The PCAOB also has authority to establish auditing standards.

Lenny had never broken into a place before, although he rationalized this adventure was not really quite the same thing, inasmuch as the guard was going to let them in as a favor to Woody. Still he did not have a criminal record yet, and definitely wasn't looking to get arrested and lose his CPA license. Lenny wondered if this crazy plan was worth it. Maybe Detective Calhoun was right. Maybe Dana was involved in some way. Why should he stick his neck out for her and risk his entire career with a felony charge for trespassing? Lenny could not come up with an easy answer. It didn't matter anyway; it was too late to back out now.

Woody and Lenny climbed into the car. Lenny drove; Woody navigated, giving Lenny GPS-style turn-by-turn directions to the warehouse from memory. It was a short drive from the bar. The area was dark, absent street lights. At first glance, Lenny didn't realize that the large brick building they had just passed was the warehouse. Lenny kept driving and parked his car a block away. He and Woody walked back from there to the front of the building they had just passed.

The warehouse looked more like a large garage than a typical warehouse. Woody explained to Lenny that a small taxicab company had once used the building to house its cab fleet. Lenny estimated that the garage/warehouse could hold about ten cars.

"Don't move!" a voice from the dark warned.

Woody and Lenny stopped in their tracks. A flashlight beam scrolled across their faces.

Lenny and Woody covered their eyes. "Hey, Tommy, is that you?" Woody asked. "Can you kill the light, you're blinding us."

"Woody?" The guard flashed his light directly on Woody's face, laughing. "Hey, I thought you two were a couple of crack heads."

The guard led them into the warehouse through a side door. The light was better. Lenny was shocked when he caught a glimpse of the guard. He was ancient—maybe in his late seventies. The man could not have been much taller than five-foot four, nor could he have weighed much more than one hundred pounds. He was not the type of guard Lenny had envisioned. He was expecting more of a nightclub bouncer or the football-player type.

"Doc, I want you to meet Tommy McLaughlin. He was one of the top lightweight boxers in his day," Woody boasted.

"How ya' doin'," growled Tommy, extending his right hand.

Lenny tried to withhold his smile at the sound of Tommy's gravelly voice. "Lenny Cramer, pleased to meet you," Lenny said, reaching out to shake Tommy's right hand.

Rather than shake hands, Tommy pulled back his right hand and brought it back up over his right shoulder with his thumb sticking out and said, "Go hang it on a wall." Tommy started to cackle uncontrollably. "I told you I'd get him on it, Woody! Gets 'em every time."

Lenny stared at the scene, unable to conceal a grin. He had heard the expression "Hang it on a wall" in some really old black and white movies, but he had never actually heard anyone use that expression before. Tommy was clearly getting a big kick out of the situation, and Woody was enjoying it, too. Lenny really didn't care as long as he got a chance to look around the place.

"What's that up there?" Lenny asked, pointing to a glass-enclosed room on the second floor visible from the first floor.

"That's an office. You want to have a look?" Tommy asked.

"Yes, please," replied Lenny.

After reminding them not to take anything and to leave things as they found them, Tommy led Woody and Lenny up the steps to the office. Woody decided to keep Tommy company, leaving Lenny to explore on his own.

Lenny went straight to the filing cabinets. There were several. After locating the four-drawer cabinet that contained all the customer files, he checked under the letter "S" to see what was kept under Dana Scott's name. Nothing. Lenny next checked the J's. That worked. Jade & More's file was one of the largest in that drawer. Lenny pulled the file and opened it up on the desk next to the bank of metal four-drawer filing cabinets. Inside he found several invoices for shipments of jade to the Jade & More shop. But aside from invoices, the only other document in the file was a letter signed by Dana, in which she had agreed to credit terms of n/15 for all purchases from Denig Gems. That was odd since Dana had led him to believe she didn't know anything about why Jade & More didn't receive a purchase discount of 2/10 like Denig's other customers. But he couldn't think about that right now. The midnight forensic audit was underway. He had to keep looking.

Lenny decided to see if Denig had a separate file on Frank Harrison. That proved to be interesting in a convoluted way. While there was a large file for Frank, none of the papers in the folder dealt with jade or the retail shop. Instead there was a good deal of correspondence concerning a corporation called Denright, Inc. of which Carson Denig, Frank Harrison, and U.S. Speaker of the House, Jim Bright, were the owners. All the stock of Denright, Inc was owned by those three individuals, but Lenny could not find anything that indicated the nature of that company's business. Lenny wondered if Dana was aware that Frank also shared a business relationship with Denig and Bright through this limited liability corporation. This information meant that Jade & More and Denig Gems were related parties through their shared ownership of Denright, Inc. This undisclosed related party relationship was a fraud red flag.

Next up were the accounts payable files. Lenny wanted to see who Carson Denig did business with. Interestingly, there weren't many files besides those that dealt with office supplies. That was going to make it easier for him; fewer files to review. As he was rummaging through the payable file cabinet, Lenny was quick to spot that there was one for Jade & More. In the folder were copies of the notes that Carson Denig had outstanding with Jade & More. Lenny was about to put them back when he spotted Dana's signature at the bottom of one of the notes payable. He then looked at the other notes in the file, carefully inspecting the signature blocks.

On each of the notes the only signatures were those of Carson Denig and Dana Scott. That was perplexing. Dana had previously told him that she did not know of any services performed by Jade & More for Carson Denig, and that she had never met him. Yet here was her signature on the notes Denig had used in payment of whatever services Jade & More had provided.

This situation wasn't looking good for Dana. First her signature on the credit terms agreement and now her signature on the notes, both of which she claimed she knew nothing about. Dana was not telling him the truth ... or at least not all of it. Maybe Detective Calhoun's contention that Dana Scott was a prime suspect had some merit after all.

Lenny closed the Jade & More file, leaving the Js. As he thumbed through the rest of the alphabet, he noticed there was another thick folder in the payables drawer—this one in the Ts. The Tijuana Imitation Gem Importers' file revealed that Denig Gems did a great deal of business with the Mexican firm, but there was little detail on the invoices aside from the number of items Denig purchased and their cost. Lenny searched to see if Denig kept a hardcopy ledger for its accounts payable records, but he could not find the A/P ledger, General Ledger, or any of the accounting books. It figures. Most small businesses had gone to a computerized system for their accounting records. The only problem was that without access to the Denig's side of the purchase transaction he would be unable to determine for what this merchandise was used.

Lenny closed the last of the file cabinets. There wasn't anything else in the office that appeared to be important enough to warrant further looking. He checked his watch. It was well past one in the morning. Where had the time gone? He walked out of the office and saw Woody and Tommy sitting on some wooden crates, talking about, of all things, the 1964 Philadelphia Phillies.

Tommy looked up. "Ya find what ya was looking fer?" he growled.

"Never know with these kinds of things," Lenny said, walking down the steps. "Mr. McLaughlin, would it be a problem if I look in some of these crates? I'm thinking that—"

Before Lenny could finish, Tommy shouted: "No problemo, per-fesser, as long as you pack everything back up."

Lenny started walking around the warehouse, looking at the address of origin on many of the crates, as Woody and Tommy watched him.

"You need a hand, Doc?" Woody asked. "What supplier are you looking for in particular?"

"Tijuana Imitation Gem Importers."

"That begin with a T?" Tommy inquired.

Lenny turned around quickly and was surprised to see that Tommy was not joking.

"Here's a couple over here," Woody called, saving Lenny from having to answer Tommy's question. Lightweight boxing had definitely taken its toll on the retired contender, slowing down not only his physical but mental reflexes. Lenny felt a little sorry for Tommy.

Woody found a crowbar nearby and carefully opened the crate. It contained various knick-knacks and baubles which looked like they were made of jade. "Look at this thing!" Woody said, holding up a green figurine of a squirrel eating a nut.

The other crates contained similar merchandise. Nothing in any of them helped Lenny get any closer to understanding why Jade & More did so much business with Denig or if Frank was behind the cash flow shortage. If anything, the midnight audit escapade had made Lenny more suspicious of Dana. He kept seeing her signatures on all those notes.

Woody carefully nailed the tops back onto the crates, so no one could tell that they had been opened. Once that was done, Lenny thanked Tommy and slipped him two fifty-dollar bills for his help. Woody and Lenny walked outside into the starry night. One midnight auditor was still frustrated about a long past major league baseball season; the other was frustrated at how little he had learned.

Frank looked out of the window of his office, trying to determine his next course of action. It was a beautiful October day in Philadelphia. There was not a cloud in the sky. The statue of William Penn atop City Hall was clearly visible to him. Until the construction of some office towers a few years back, the statue could be seen from almost any part of Broad Street on a clear day.

The thoroughfare called Broad Street is aptly named. It is an incredibly wide arterial street with many sections having four lanes running in both directions. Most major Philadelphia parades are held on Broad Street. Frank would often take friends up to his office on New Year's Day to take advantage of its great view of both City Hall and the Mummers Parade as it marched up Broad Street.

But the Mummers Parade and New Year's Day were far from Frank's mind at this moment. Last night at the jade shop, he had discovered that, once again, someone had been going through both his desk and Jade & More's books. He was now certain that Lenny was the one responsible. Frank was disappointed that the slight concussion that Lenny had suffered had not been enough to slow Lenny down or deter his zeal for examining the books at the jade shop. Frank felt that the time had come for him to play his next card.

"Betty," Frank said over the intercom to his secretary. "Get Bob Hawkins for me on the phone. I believe we have his number on file."

Dana looked at her watch: two in the afternoon. She had finally completed the physical inventory count of all the items in the jade shop, a meticulous and lengthy process she had started yesterday morning. She was glad it was finished. She picked up the phone to call Lenny to let him know the physical inventory was done. The fact that Lenny was out last night with another woman had disheartened her, but she wasn't one to mope for long. She had made up her mind this morning that she would not let Lenny's womanizing ways interfere with their business relationship.

"Hello, Lenny. This is Dana Scott," she said matter-of-factly. "For your information—I just finished taking the physical inventory as you asked. I still have to get a computer printout of all the merchandise, but I wanted you to know that the physical count is done."

Lenny was a bit surprised. Dana rarely started a conversation in this manner. She normally engaged in some small talk before getting to the point. Worse, he also noticed the tone of her voice was rather impersonal. "Uh … ah … OK, Dana," Lenny said through a yawn. "I'm sorry. You'll have to excuse me. I had a late evening last night."

"Yes, I heard. I tried to reach you yesterday evening and Rebecca told me you were out late with someone."

"It was late, but you'll be pleased to know that I was working on your problem the entire evening. Sorry to say, though, I didn't find any answers."

"I may be a blonde but I'm not stupid, Lenny. Don't patronize me," Dana said coldly. "I know very well you weren't doing anything last night that is even remotely related to the jade shop. There's no reason to lie to make me feel better. I get it. This is business. What you're doing for me is only a favor. Something you do in your spare time. I can't expect you to be putting in all types of hours for me. You're entitled to your own life. No need to make excuses about where you spend your time."

Lenny thought about what Detective Calhoun had said to him. Calhoun suspected Dana as being his assailant, but could not come up with a motive unless, of course, Dana was clinically irrational. She definitely sounded irrational to Lenny now. "What are you talking about, Dana?" he said cautiously.

"Lenny, if you want to go out with another woman, what can I say? We're adults," Dana replied.

"Whoa! What other woman? What are you talking about, Dana?" asked Lenny quizzically.

"Professor Cramer, there's no reason to be cagey about it," Dana said. Her voice lacked any sign of patience. "I trust Rebecca. When I called, she said you were out, that you were not alone, and that you would be very late."

"Dana, I swear, I didn't go out with another woman." Oddly enough, Lenny started to laugh. "There must be some kind of mis-understanding," he said. "I went out with—" Lenny suddenly re-membered his promise to Woody not to tell Dana anything about going to Carson Denig's warehouse. "I went out with ... LOLA in the Penn Law Library" Lenny said. "LOLA is the system name for the online catalog. Stands for something like 'legal on-line archive'— but nobody seems to know for sure, not even the circulation desk staff. So, yes, I was with LOLA almost all night in the Biddle Law Library searching through old auditing cases to see if there were some approaches to your cash-flow problem that I might be over-looking. The stacks are deep in the bowels of the Biddle and the best time to get to that stuff is late at night," Lenny lied. "Rebecca thinks I spend too much time with LOLA. But, as a practicing forensic accountant, I can't live without her," Lenny chuckled.

"You don't have to be accountable to me," Dana said. She had softened her tone somewhat, and she felt embarrassed about accusing Lenny of having a relationship with a computerized card catalog. "I'm sorry, Lenny. I must sound a little crazy the way I invaded your privacy. I really did not have any right to do that."

"No need for an apology, Dana. It's a simple misunderstanding." Lenny paused for a moment and changed the subject. "So, you've got the inventory done. I bet that took a while."

"It wasn't too bad. I spread it over two days." Dana was relieved that Lenny had changed the subject. "Lenny, when do you think you'll be able to stop by to see what I came up with?"

"I've got a free day on Thursday of next week. In the meantime, spot check the computer inventory printout against a sample of the physical inventory just to make sure that there are no scanning discrepancies on the SKU numbers and quantities. The stock-keeping unit numbers should match exactly." Lenny paused for a moment as he considered whether he should repeat a question he had asked Dana a couple of days before the mugging. He decided he had to do it. "Dana, I think I may have raised this before, but just to be certain, did you ever meet Carson Denig or sign any agreement with him for services that either you or Frank performed for Denig Gems?"

"Not that I know of," Dana said. "I may have signed a contract that Frank gave me for the shop to do business with Carson Denig, but I have never met the man in person nor have I done any work for him or his company. Why?"

"And you never signed any notes either?" Lenny continued. "Notes receivable, or I.O.U.s from Denig."

"No." Dana was growing impatient. "Are you going to tell me what's going on?"

"I wish I knew, Dana. It's all so murky." Lenny was still cautious about what he should say in front of Dana given Detective Calhoun's warning and especially considering what he had found at Denig's warehouse. "I'll see you next Thursday," Lenny said. "Hopefully we'll be able to get some things straightened out then."

Lenny ended the call. He leaned back in his overstuffed office chair, more confused than ever. He didn't know what to think. In his heart he wanted to believe Dana. She could be caring, fun, and was good with Rebecca. But she had lied to him. He decided that it really didn't matter at this point what he thought. What did matter was getting some answers. Who had attacked him? What was the relationship between Denig and Dana? Where was Frank in all this? Which one of these three was the guilty party or was his mugging just one of those "wrong-place, wrong-time" random acts of violence?

Lenny's curiosity was getting the best of him. He was determined to find out the who, what, and why. While he may not be a private detective, he knew that as a forensic specialist he had considerable investigative skills. And he had wits and experience. From that point forward, Lenny no longer looked at himself as working exclusively in Dana's best interests. The client-professional relationship was important, but it didn't trump finding the truth. Lenny's interest in the case had evolved. He now viewed himself instead as an independent investigator trying to unravel a cover-up of some sort.

In a fraud investigation, materiality is not a factor. Although the materiality concept frees an auditor or accountant from worrying about minor problems, a forensic accountant looks for even small red flags to follow to catch a suspected fraudster. As he told his students, uncovering fraud is a marathon, not a sprint.

Nine

There is growing evidence in the marketplace that historical cost-basis information is of ever-declining usefulness to the modern business world. The issue for the financial accounting profession is to move the accounting model toward greater relevance or face the fate of the dinosaur and the passenger pigeon.

—Robert K. Elliott

"Yo, talk to me" Robert Hawkins said gruffly. He was working out of his home office in his pajamas, eyes glued to his three computer monitors cluttered with electronic spreadsheets. The telephone call was clearly a distraction from what he was doing.

"Yo yourself, Bob. This is Frank Harrison. How are *yo* today?" Frank kidded.

"Oh, hi Frank. Sorry about the *crusty* hello. I'm crunching some worksheets that don't want to behave. I'm a little edgy." Bob held the phone away from his face and sneezed twice. "So, what's up with you, Frank, and your Kuaker City Consulting outfit? You ready to toss me some more crumbs?"

"Yes," Frank answered. "More work ... but it's not exactly for the consulting practice that I need your free-lance skills. Got a slight problem with my exposure in the jade shop. I need some help reducing my risk. Bob, didn't you attend some of Professor Lenny Cramer's classes at Penn several years ago?"

"Sure. Two accounting courses. He was tough. A couple members of my study group didn't pass his classes and dropped out of the program. Why do you ask?"

"I'm getting to that," Frank said. "Did you have to write any accounting cases for Cramer?"

"At least three," Bob replied. "Everyone had to create three cases from scratch for his MBA accounting course."

"Do you still have copies of them?"

"Probably, have the originals. He always gave them back. Margin comments in red. The whole *shtick*. Why?"

"Bob, see if you can find them for me. If you can, then my problems go away, and you make a great deal of money in the process. Do you still have the same printer that you used in college?"

"Yes, but Frank you're starting to freak me out with strange questions like that. What are you up to now? In this economy, I can always use the money, but I run a legit shop."

"Right, Bob," Frank smiled. "Listen, I'll tell you all about it tonight at your apartment. Say 7:30. Find the three cases and get your old printer hooked up and ready to go. One more thing: go by the campus book store and purchase a copy of the latest edition of Lenny Cramer's accounting case book—the one they use in the MBA course now. Can you do that?"

"You got it. Anything else?"

"No, that's enough for now."

"7:30 p.m. My place. I'll be waiting," Bob said. He heard a click and the line went dead.

———————

In response to a call late Monday afternoon from the business school's dean's administrative assistant, Lenny had set up a meeting with Dean Davidson for 10:00 a.m. on Tuesday. She had said it was urgent that Lenny talk to the dean that morning. Lenny had a theory that academic administrators only wanted to see faculty when there was trouble. Chairs, deans, and provosts hardly ever brought good news.

Lenny walked into Dean Donald Davidson's office at 10:03. Don looked up from the letter on his desk, but he did not smile when Lenny said hello.

"Sit," the dean motioned to Lenny with a wave of his hand. Lenny took a seat in one of the two office chairs positioned in front of the six-foot expanse that was the dean's executive work surface. "Lenny, you have a problem," he said, as Lenny eased himself into the chair. "Did you ever have a Robert S. Hawkins in your classes?"

"Oh, I don't know. There's always a possibility. I've had many students in my classes over the years. I can look it up. I've kept all my grade records since I've been here. Why?"

"Well, an agitated Robert Hawkins, Wharton MBA alumni, class of '16, came in yesterday with some disturbing information. He claims that you copied some accounting cases which he turned in to you three years ago and that you used them in the latest edition of your case book." The dean opened a manila folder and shoved its contents toward Lenny.

The dean continued, "You'll notice he also included copies of three cases from your new accounting case book for comparison. What I find particularly disturbing is that the three cases in question are almost identical to the work which Hawkins turned in to you when he was your student. You only changed the names of the companies. For goodness sake, Lenny, you have a Ph.D., and you're a licensed CPA. How could you be so stupid? You didn't even change the names of the cast of characters in his submitted work."

Lenny bit his tongue trying to avoid shouting at the dean. "Wait a minute, Don. I do admit that near the end of my MBA courses I ask each student to develop three original accounting cases. By that time, students know how to do analysis; where they're weak is synthesis. Creating whole cloth out of disparate threads. It's how I move the needle along Bloom's Taxonomy of Learning to get my graduate classes to do higher-order thinking. But I have never copied *in toto* a case submitted by a student. Yes, some of the student cases provide a springboard for what I write for each new edition of my textbook, but I would never steal a student case outright. I may look stupid, but I'm not dumb. My cases are my own. I wrote them. I'm the author."

"Ok, Lenny," the dean said. "And now you're going to tell me you don't keep the graded cases for your records, but you hand them back to the students—red-pen comments and all."

Lenny nodded. "Timely feedback is an important part of learning. You force us to hand out those student evaluation questionnaires every semester. Students can be very damning if they don't get their papers back on a timely basis *with* comments."

"You don't have to be sarcastic with me, Lenny. You're the one in the hot seat, here. So, explain to me this. How is it that Robert Hawkins has the original paper he submitted with your grade and corrections on it—corrections in your handwriting—*for a case that you say you wrote?*" The dean snatched back the folder with the photocopied material.

"Look here, Lenny." The dean opened the folder and rifled through the pages. "Hawkins' first case involves a company which records the collection of accrued interest separately from the bond proceeds. My background is in Organizational Behavior, so don't expect me to understand how he computed the discount or premium between interest payment dates, but it doesn't take a forensics expert like yourself to see that you copied this student's work word-for-word. Look," he pointed to the first page of the marked-up assignment, "there's your grade. And here is where you made suggested changes in his wording." The dean then reached in his bottom drawer and pulled out Lenny's new case book.

Don turned to the first paper clip in the book. "On page 102 of your text is this same case. You have even made the changes that you had written on Hawkins' paper." The dean slammed the book shut. "How could you do this, Dr. Paul Leonard Cramer? Passing off a student's case as your own. No attribution. No credit for the student's work. That's plagiarism and a gross violation of campus policy on academic honesty. Wharton faculty know better. I always suspected you were a questionable hire."

Lenny was shocked. He remembered writing the "Deficiency in Accounting for Bonds" case. But the handwriting in the margins of the student's paper surely looked like his own. There was his distinctive and unmistakable slanted l's.

Lenny looked back at the dean and said softly, "Don, I do know better. In every one of my syllabi I have a paragraph that explains the importance of giving credit where credit is due. In class when we talk about long-term assets such as intangibles, I link plagiarism to copyright infringement and theft of intellectual property. Believe me, I know what plagiarism is. I didn't plagiarize. There must be some simple explanation. Dean Davidson, I can assure you that I have never copied a student's paper intentionally. Ever!"

"I certainly hope you are right," the dean said. "I worry about the word 'intentionally.' You do understand that perception is reality? Mr. Hawkins alluded to a lawsuit if you don't give him a cash settlement for his portion of the book royalties and a sizeable sum for damages. And he wants a byline for the case in the next printing. Call him and clear this matter up immediately. We cannot afford this type of publicity. I've marked his telephone number on the front of this manila folder. In the interim, I am suspending you indefinitely until you can settle this. Get one of your colleagues to cover your classes."

"But Don," Lenny protested. "You can't—"

The dean held up both hands and cut him off. "I have no choice, Lenny. This is serious business for the Wharton brand. We can't afford to have it tarnished. Settle out of court ... and fast. And Lenny, I didn't just read the bond case. I compared every single word in your three textbook cases against the student's three graded cases. They are word-for-word. We have a zero-tolerance policy for student plagiarism. Consequences are worse for faculty. Am I clear?"

"Clear," Lenny tried to say but gulped noticeably instead. It sounded more like "cluhp."

"Now, if you'll excuse me, Lenny, I have to go to a meeting. Please keep me informed as to the status of this messy problem. I'll give you two weeks before I take this matter up with the university provost's office." The dean stood and walked over to his coat rack to retrieve his suit jacket.

Lenny knew he was dismissed. He took the folder the dean had given him back to his office and began his own comparison of the student's papers with the cases in his recently published book. They were identical, except for the company names. The second case in question involved a medium-sized company that was the victim of a classic liquidity squeeze. The company's sales were increasing rapidly, but the bank was unwilling to provide additional short-term loans to purchase more inventory.

The third case focused on the embezzlement of money from a bank by the chief financial officer. The CFO had simply made monthly journal entries to cover up personal expenses paid by the bank using ACH transfers that settled through the Federal Reserve's Automated Clearing House. No one reviewed the entries because the internal audit staff reported directly to him. The internal controls were weak.

Lenny knew he was the author. He remembered writing all three cases one summer, but he had not retained his pencil drafts. He had long since discarded them. The grades on the copies of Mr. Hawkins' three cases were B+, A–, and B, respectively. The markings and margin comments on the cases appeared to be in his handwriting. Lenny pulled out his 2015 grade book, and sure enough, the grades were the same: B+ on the bond case, A– on liquidity squeeze, and another B for the CFO embezzlement. Hawkins' final grade for ACCT 620 Financial Accounting was a B. This mark was an average grade for graduate students. In today's climate a professor had difficulty giving Cs to graduate students even if they deserved a D. Grade inflation had taken its toll on evaluating students for future employers. What was the saying? *'You pay your fees, you get your Bs.'*

Lenny could not remember Robert Hawkins, nor could he re-member any of the cases he might have submitted. He wanted to kick himself for returning the graded originals instead of handing back a copy of the submitted cases with his comments.

Lenny dialed Hawkins' phone number. He heard a recording, but he did not leave a message. He then searched for Hawkins' phone number in the white pages of the phone book and jotted down his address on the manila folder. He'd drop by Hawkins' place later to clear up this plagiarism mess in person.

Lenny glanced back at the student's paper. Hawkins' three cases were identical, all right, but they were written too well. Lenny knew he was a good writer, but the book publisher's editor made his prose dance. Editors made many changes. Where were the editor's changes? Hawkins' cases danced the same dance. Elegant, refined, polished. Graduate student writing never approached this level. Then there were Lenny's handwritten remarks in the margins. They kept jumping out at him. The red pen was the same, but something was off. *Something was rotten in the state of Denmark,* Lenny thought.

Lenny's mind began to wander, his thoughts turning morose. He had a dreadful thought. Could he lose his CPA license? He brought up the AICPA Code of Professional Conduct on his computer. The Code consisted of four parts—concepts, rules of conduct, interpretations, and ethical rules. He quickly read the five enforceable ethical standards:

1. Independence, Integrity, and Objectivity
2. General Standards—Accounting Principles
3. Responsibilities to Clients
4. Responsibilities to Colleagues
5. Other Responsibilities and Practices

Failure to follow these ethical rules could result in admonishment, suspension, or expulsion from the American Institute of CPAs.

The Professional Ethics Division Executive Committee issued ethical rulings. Rule 501 caught Lenny's eye. "A member shall not commit an act discreditable to the profession." A felony, signing a false tax return, issuing a misleading audit opinion, and failure to return client records were considered discreditable acts. Plagiarism wasn't specifically mentioned in the code. And Lenny knew it wasn't a felony because copyright law violations were civil offenses rather than criminal. But then he remembered a presentation at the Accounting Ethics Boot Camp last year where accounting ethicist, Steven Mintz, had discussed the applicability of the AICPA Code of Conduct to AICPA members who were accounting academics rather than practitioners. He had pointed out that Interpretation 102-5 addressed accounting faculty directly:

> Educational services such as teaching at a university or engaging in research and scholarship are professional services subject to AICPA Rule 102. This rule provides

that the member shall maintain objectivity and integrity, shall be free of conflicts of interest, and shall
not knowingly misrepresent facts or subordinate his or
her judgment to others.

Committing plagiarism definitely showed a lack of "integrity"
and it "misrepresented facts" concerning the true author of the cases
that Don Davidson had given him. If the dean was right, he would
be expelled from the AICPA. Expulsion didn't mean he'd lose his
CPA license *per se*, but the situation was almost as bad. It would
be like a doctor getting kicked out of the American Medical
Association or a lawyer out of the American Bar Association. *How
would he be able to attract new clients or hang on to the ones he had
if he wasn't a member of the largest voluntary professional association
of accountants?*

By now Lenny had a migraine. "Time to go home," he said to
himself as he rubbed his temples. Tomorrow he was scheduled to
testify in Washington before Congress as a member of an expert panel.

––––––––––––

Lenny leaned forward in his chair, repositioning the microphone
on the witness table so that it was directly in front of him. He was
the third in a panel of six experts who had been asked to speak
today in room 2123 of Rayburn House Office Building.

"Good morning, Chairman Dingell," he began. "Thank you,
for allowing me to testify today concerning your proposal to
expand the Securities and Exchange Commission's disclosure regulations. Let me start by saying that I do not believe there is a
need for such an expansion of the SEC's disclosure program at
this time."

Lenny was testifying before the Subcommittee on Oversight of
Investigations of the House Energy and Commerce Committee,
chaired by Congressman Greg Walden (R-Oregon). These hearings
had been scheduled to review the SEC's role in the supervision and
promulgation of accounting standards and to examine the existing
structure for establishing disclosure requirements for publicly held
companies.

"Professor Cramer," Representative Walden interjected, "you are aware that Professor David Albrecht has indicated before this committee that there is a crisis of confidence in the accounting profession?"

"Yes, sir," Lenny replied, "And before the advent of the accounting blogosphere and its so-called luminaries, there was Professor Abraham Briloff who testified before Congressional committees on numerous occasions about the failings of the Accounting Establishment. I am aware that certain people have made and continue to make shrill statements about the accounting profession, but I believe that further disclosure regulations are unnecessary. In fact, I believe that the current large regulatory apparatus is both cumbersome and costly, especially post-Enron.

"The formation of Financial Accounting Standards Board or FASB in 1973 was designed to establish standards of financial accounting and reporting. The tripartite structure of the FASB in concert with the Financial Accounting Foundation (FAF) and the Financial Accounting Standards Advisory Council (FASAC) lessened the need for governmental regulations. The establishment of the Public Company Accounting Oversight Board (PCAOB) in 2002 under the Sarbanes-Oxley Act was a step backwards, which only added to the regulatory burden.

"My position is simple. I believe that the SEC's budget is determined by politicians who are primarily concerned with appearance. This position was the stance of Professor Ross L. Watts in 1980, when he stated that the SEC spends a small fraction of its budget on estimating costs and benefits, but that a much larger fraction is spent on lawyers who produce and enforce regulations. Thirty-plus years have passed, and what we have learned is that the more things change the more they stay the same. Over-regulation continues to hamper economic growth and encourage capital flight. In today's global capital markets, one can just as easily launch an initial public offering (IPO) on the London or Hong Kong Stock Exchanges rather than go public in the U.S. No wonder our country's best entrepreneurs are fleeing the oppressive U.S. regulatory landscape for greener pastures."

Lenny paused for a moment, then looked at Congressman Walden and proceeded. "Allow me to elucidate. Two major reasons are often given for the need for the regulation of corporate financial disclosures, and both arguments are based upon the so-called *market failure* notion.

"The first argument involves the 'public-good' nature of information. As this argument goes, information for users is under-produced because insufficient disclosure leads to suboptimal resource allocation. Since financial information is a public good, one may argue that without regulation, an insufficient amount of financial information will be produced."

Lenny raised his voice. "I believe this argument is unfounded. Proponents underestimate both the corporate incentives to provide and the power of market forces to demand financial information. There is ample empirical evidence that companies publish financial statements long before they are required to do so. A corporation benefits from disclosure because it is more efficient for the corporation to provide information about their current operations and future plans than for the stakeholders to obtain the information themselves. In fact, there is much more likelihood of too much information being prepared—not too little.

"Congressman Walden, I encourage the Albrechts and the Briloffs of the world and their followings of academic extremists to present empirical evidence that too little information is currently being produced or that increased regulation yields higher quality data."

The congressman held up his hand. "Just a moment, Dr. Cramer," he said. "We had a witness yesterday, Mr. Frank Harrison, who testified that corporate insiders know much more about their companies than do outsiders. That is, they have information that isn't required to be divulged through current regulation. And with that privileged information, many of these unscrupulous insiders manipulate stock prices. Have you forgotten the high-profile cases of late in which major insiders were sent to jail? Remember television celebrity Martha Stewart in her orange jump suit? Or, how about the 2011 conviction of billionaire Wall Street Insider Raj Rajaratnam over his $25 million of ill-gotten gains at Galleon?"

Lenny raised his hand and his voice. "Yes, yes, I'm aware that insider trading is a high priority area for the SEC's Enforcement Division. And, Congressman, I'm also aware that there is considerable controversy surrounding whether members of the House, the Senate, or their staff who trade stocks on nonpublic information heard in the halls of Congress are *also* subject to these same SEC insider-trading rules." Lenny paused for a second to watch several members of the Oversight Subcommittee shift uncomfortably in their seats. "This subject provides a nice segue into the second argument for regulation.

"Commonly accepted wisdom is that managers have incentives to waste, misuse, or divert corporate assets to maximize their own self-interest. Most investors understand this problem and know professional managers often act in ways that reduce shareholder wealth. To effectively counteract this tendency, shareholders must be convinced that the current financial disclosures are accurate and complete. Information signaling to shareholders may be done by installing a system of accounting controls and hiring certified public accountants to ascertain that this system is working. The CPA can state whether the financial information generated from the internal control system is reliable. The use of stock underwriters and the adoption of high-dividend payout policies are two other signaling mechanisms.

"In conclusion, Congressman Walden, my testimony before this subcommittee is that there is no need for additional disclosure requirements for U.S. publicly held companies. The two primary arguments in favor of increased disclosure do not hold up to serious scrutiny. The bottom line is that free market forces induce adequate levels of disclosure and provide sufficient protection for investors. Thank you for this opportunity."

Congressman Walden smiled and turned toward the C-SPAN camera. "Professor Cramer, the committee would like to thank you for your testimony and for taking time out of your busy schedule to appear before us," the congressman said. "Before we move to the next panelist, I would like to get your views on a point Mr. Frank Harrison raised in his testimony, yesterday. He told the committee that, during a period of rising prices, the traditional historical cost concept currently required under U.S. GAAP can cause an overstatement of real income and an understatement of asset values. He argued that the current accounting model is deficient when dealing with uncertainty. Can you comment on this gap between historical costs and current market values?" Congressman Dingell then smiled as he looked at Lenny. *Touché*, Lenny thought. His jab at the congressman over Washington politicians trading on insider information to line their wallets had not gone unnoticed. He sensed the congressman was attempting to get back at him by setting Lenny up to look like a fool over his well-known position on the primacy of historical cost.

"Sir," Lenny began slowly, deliberately. "Financial accounting has chosen to ignore changing market values and uses cost as the predominant measure of value for assets and liabilities. And with good reason! Historical cost data is relatively objective and can be verified easily. Our built-in conservative bias as accountants can be seen in the adherence to the lower of cost or market rule and the deferral of unrealized gains until a realization event—such as a sale or exchange. Historical cost has served us well except in times of rapidly rising prices as we experienced during the 'Great Inflation' of the mid-70s and early-80s. In a classic case of overreach, the Financial Accounting Standards Board responded to the surging 11.5% inflation of 1979 by issuing FASB 33.

"Statement of Financial Accounting Standard No. 33 required the disclosure of current value information on one of two bases—price-level adjusted or current cost. Not surprisingly, surveys of the business and investment communities suggested that users did not find the information helpful. Of course, preparers of such current value information complained that it was a total nuisance to assemble. In 1986, the FASB backpedaled from the onerous disclosure requirements, replacing SFAS 33 with SFAS 89. In this standard, also titled 'Financial Reporting and Changing Prices,' the FASB made price level reporting voluntary.

"For the record, let me add that the current FASB position is more or less unchanged. SFAS 89 was codified into the Accounting Standards Codification in July 1, 2009. ASC Topic 255-10-50 *Changing Prices-Overall-Disclosure-General* encourages, but no longer requires, disclosure of supplementary information on the effects of changing prices. Entities are not discouraged from experimenting with other forms of disclosure. As a practical matter, with inflation under control since the mid-1980s, few companies provide price-level adjusted accounting supplements to their annual reports anymore. But with our incredible $22 trillion-dollar U.S. debt problem, hyper-inflation may be just around the corner.

"A better approach to historical cost and current values would be found in IFRS. International Accounting Standard (IAS) 29 mandates CPPA in the event of hyper-inflation. Constant Purchasing Power Accounting enables financial capital maintenance when the stable monetary unit assumption fails. Of course, because IFRS is a global standard used in over 160 countries worldwide, the likelihood of having to report financial information in a country troubled by hyper-inflation is higher. Politics is politics, and the ability to print money to pay for goods and services a country can't afford is a temptation for the undisciplined." Lenny couldn't help himself, having to get in one last dig at the political class that was destroying the country he loved. If some in the Washington Establishment had their way, the accounting profession would be nationalized, and every auditor would be working for the government.

"Thank you, Dr. Cramer, for your opinion on the deficiencies of the historical cost basis accounting model and for other enlightening comments," Congressman Walden said wryly. He concluded, "I believe that companies and investors regard conservative accountants like yourself, Dr. Cramer, and the historical cost information you provide as having declining utility." The congressman flashed a toothy false smile. "May we have the next witness, Lynn E. Turner, former chief accountant of the SEC and senior advisor and managing director in the forensic accounting practice of LECG."

The Amtrak train from Union Station in D.C. to 30th Street Station near the university in Philadelphia took just shy of two hours. Lenny exited the station from the Market Street entrance and hailed a cab. Normally he would walk the 15 minutes to campus for exercise, but his life was anything but normal lately. He felt pressed for time. He still had to arrange for one of his colleagues to cover his classes now that he was suspended but getting someone to teach his classes didn't eliminate coordinating the course, answering student emails, or grading mid-terms. He couldn't delegate that. Then there was the plagiarism charge. He was determined to clear his name with the Dean so that he could get the allegation removed from his record and be reinstated. What stressed him the most, though, was that he didn't seem to be any closer to discovering the identity of his attacker. Whoever had stalked him was still out there.

As Lenny stepped into his university office in Steinberg-Dietrich Hall, he put down his briefcase, turned around and hurried into the Accounting department office. He walked into the mail room to collect his mail.

"Hey, Lenny," Charles Ross said. "You're a hard man to track down. Just wondering, have you finished the draft of our stock buyback paper yet? We need to get that submitted soon if we're serious about being considered for the special issue on the impact of share repurchases on market prices."

Lenny turned toward Professor Ross. "Chuck, I finished it on Friday. It's in my middle desk drawer. The drawer's open—I never lock my desk. Here's the key to my office. Let yourself in and grab the draft. I'll stop by and get a copy from you later. I need to get my mail, pick up some supplies, and talk to the department chair for a second. I'll swing by your office in a few minutes, and we can discuss the draft. Go ahead and start reading it. Oh, and just leave my keys on the desk. I won't be long."

"Good. I have some free time now before my late afternoon class. By the way, did you call Douglas Skinner?"

"Yes, but I never caught him in." Douglas J. Skinner was one of the three co-editors of *The Journal of Accounting Research*, a top accounting academic journal. Lenny and Chuck were targeting JAR for publication and had hoped to get an idea from Skinner if their research sounded promising. Before he was elected president of the AAA, Lenny had served with Skinner on several American Accounting Association committees. There was a lot of politics in getting a paper published.

"See you in a few," Charles Ross said as he turned and left the department mailroom that doubled as a break room. Lenny collected his mail and went over to the communal coffee pot to get a cup of caffeine.

Mug in hand, Lenny waited outside his department head's office for about five minutes, sipping slowly while Chairman Stephen Penman continued talking on the phone. Lenny finally gave up, picked up some letterhead and other supplies, and headed back to his office. He made a mental note to call Penman later to talk about his meeting with the Dean. When Lenny arrived at his office, the door was wide open. His keys were on the desk where Chuck had laid them, but Charles Ross had never left the room. He was lying on the floor behind Lenny's desk, motionless. Without stopping to think, Lenny rushed over to Chuck, knelt, and picked up his colleague's right wrist to check for a pulse. Before he could feel the familiar thumping rhythm, he heard a loud hissing sound coming from under his desk.

Lenny jumped back, smashing into his desk chair. He scrambled to regain his balance. Between his legs he saw a large pale brown snake coiled, ready to attack. The hissing was rapid, cycling intermittently as the reptile made as much noise as possible with each intake and expulsion of its breath. Even the snake's skin pattern was menacing—three rows of thick black rings, bordered with yellow, intertwined to form a hellish chain across the body of the snout-nosed serpent.

Lenny inched his way backward until he was out of striking distance. He vaulted to his feet, ran out of the office, and slammed the door shut behind him. He was shaking all over.

For the next hour Lenny was in a daze. He wasn't even sure who had called 911. The paramedics were able to remove Charles Ross' body from Lenny's office by using open umbrellas to keep the snake at bay while they snatched the body from behind the desk. The snake was not cooperative in the least. Several times while the paramedics were dragging the body across the floor, the snake slithered from tile to tile, coiled, arched, and struck the umbrellas with its large fangs.

Charles was dead. The paramedics said he might have died of fright after being bitten by the snake. There were two small puncture wounds about three-quarters of an inch apart on his right arm.

Shortly after the EMTs had taken Charles' body, a herpetologist from the Philadelphia Zoo arrived to capture the three-and-one-half-foot snake. She explained to Lenny and the crowd gathered around his office that the snake was a Russell's Viper, indigenous to the Orient. She asked the crowd to stand back as she used professional snake tongs to snap at the snake until she grabbed it. Within minutes, the herpetologist had captured the viper and safely stuffed it into a snake sack for transport to the zoo.

Lenny knew he had to call Detective Calhoun. With Chuck Ross' death, the stakes had escalated. This disaster was all somehow linked to the mugging, Denig, and Dana. Not only was he genuinely worried for himself, but he was terrified that whoever was targeting him might hurt Rebecca.

The police investigator arrived about thirty minutes later. Detective Calhoun sketched out a scenario that confirmed Lenny's fears: "It's obvious someone broke into your office over the weekend and placed the snake in your middle desk drawer anticipating you would open it as part of your daily routine. Fortunately for you, and not so fortunately for Professor Ross, he opened the drawer first to get your research paper and was bitten. No doubt about it, Dr. Cramer, someone is trying to kill you. And they're willing to go to great lengths to do it. Exotic venomous snakes are not your typical murder weapon." The detective paused a full minute before continuing. "Dr. Cramer, you're a smart guy. This is serious stuff, and I'm not being dramatic. You got to be careful unless you want to end up like your colleague."

"Careful!" Lenny snapped. "How am I supposed to be careful? Oh, yeah, I understand," he said with thick sarcasm. "Right, like I'm not supposed to open any more drawers until you catch this maniac." Lenny started to shake again. "I'm sorry, detective. I feel like I've been dropped into the middle of a low-budget Hollywood thriller gone horribly wrong, except I have no clue who the bad guy is. Mugging, poisonous serpents, what's next? How do I make this madness stop? What can I do?"

"Well, for one thing, you're going to need to get a handle on your emotions. Ranting at me isn't helping. I'm not the bad guy. The Philadelphia Police Department is not the enemy. So, my advice to you is to sit down and list everyone who might want to kill you. Have you flunked any Ph.D. students recently? Are you involved in any fraud cases in which your courtroom testimony could put somebody behind bars? Do you use criminals as confidential informants for your forensic investigations? Think!"

"I don't have to think. It's Carson Denig. I know it," answered Lenny. "There's something about his operation that doesn't pass the 'sniff test.'"

"What about Dana Scott?" Detective Calhoun asked. "Didn't she go to Myanmar with you? She could be smuggling in embargoed goods like ivory or gems. That's gonna kick up a stink."

"It's not Dana," Lenny said. "Yes, she was on the Burmese tour, but she's not involved. I can assure you she's not behind this."

"Right, Lenny. That's what you told me before," Calhoun replied. He didn't sound convinced. "You could be wrong. And if it weren't for Professor Ross, you'd be dead. Women and snakes; snakes and women. Long history, Lenny, going all the way back to Eden. It's your life, Dr. Cramer. You've been given a second chance. Take care." Calhoun tipped his hat. "As soon as I find out anything, I'll let you know."

Later that evening, Lenny told Rebecca about the incident at the university. She was at the kitchen table working on her homework. Out of curiosity, she went over to the bookcase and found a description of the Russell's Viper in the family encyclopedia that her dad had purchased many years ago. Today everyone used the Internet, but she still preferred the books her dad had for so long. She read a passage to her father:

> *Daboia russelii*, commonly known as Russell's Viper, is an abundant, highly venomous, terrestrial snake of family Viperidae. It is found from India to Taiwan and Java, most often in open country. It is a major cause of snakebite deaths within its range. The dreaded viper grows to a maximum of about five feet and is marked with three rows of handsome, reddish-brown spots outlined in black and again in white or yellow. Due to its large fangs and the amount of venom expended at a bite, many toxicologists regard this savage creature as more dangerous than the common cobra. Snakebite symptoms begin with pain at the fang puncture site, followed by blistering and massive swelling. Victims often bleed from their gums uncontrollably before suc-

cumbing to death from septicemia, kidney, respiratory, or cardiac failure.

"Gross, Dad. It must have been horrible for poor Dr. Ross." Rebecca closed the volume and rushed over and hugged her father. Warm tears wet her cheeks.

Ten

Bagan is one of the richest archaeological sites in Asia. Jerusalem, Rome, Benares, none of them can boast the multitude of temples, and the lavishness of design and ornament that make marvelous this deserted Burmese capital on the Irrawaddy ... for eight miles along the river bank and extending to a depth of two miles inland, the whole space is thickly studded with pagodas of all sizes and shapes, the ground is so thickly covered with crumbling remnants of vanished shrines that according to the popular saying, you cannot move foot or hand without touching a sacred thing.

—Shway Yoe

Dana was proofing the letter which she had personally typed to Lenny Cramer:

Dear Lenny:

This letter is to formally confirm that you shall act as an accounting consultant for Jade & More. I would like you to resume your investigation the first week in February. I am enclosing a signed copy of the engagement letter you gave me back in September of last year. I apologize for not returning this much sooner. As I have mentioned before, there is a severe cash shortage and/or money is disappearing. Please help me.

I have informed Janet that you will be working on a new inventory system. She will assist you as needed.

171

Frank Harrison left two days ago, and he will be in Tucson
during the remainder of this week at the Tucson Gem Show. I
shall be in Thailand (Bangkok International Colored Gemstones
Association Congress) and later in the week in Naypyidaw (Aureum Hotel-Resort) at the Myanmar Jade Emporium. I will fly
back to Hong Kong for one day before returning to the U.S.

Warm regards,

Dana Scott
Jade & More

Dana signed the letter, put it in a white envelope marked personal,
sealed it, and dropped it into her Gucci purse. On the way to the
airport she would drop it off at Lenny's private office where he conducted his consulting practice. He was not there. She attached a
note to the envelope: "To my favorite gumshoe accountant" and
handed it to his receptionist.

On her flight from Philadelphia to Los Angeles en route to
Bangkok, she read several back issues of *National Jeweler*, the newspaper for the jewelry industry. The headline of the latest issue proclaimed, "Gemstone Prices Increase as Asians Scoop up Supply."
The gist of the article was that "the supply of reasonably-priced
gems was diminishing, mainly because Asian buyers flush with Chinese yuan were capitalizing on the falling U.S. dollar, and buying
up everything in sight."

Not good, Dana thought. That'll translate into a significant
increase in my cost of goods sold as the cost of my inventory
purchases go up.

She then skimmed an article about a handy rule of thumb for
determining a jeweler's daily cash-flow needs. After penciling out
some numbers on the back of her drink napkin, she was more
worried than ever. According to the author of the how-to article,
a successful retail jeweler's primary business goal centers on maintaining the proper cash balance needed for daily operations. This
target cash flow figure represents the optimal balance necessary to
meet the normal, anticipated expenditure requirements plus a reasonable cash safety stock. Dana computed her average daily cash
flow using the following formula:

	Monthly Cash					
Average daily	Expenditures	$60,000				
cash-flow needs =	30 days	=	30	=		$2,000

Assuming the suggested cash safety balance of six days cash, her total safety cash needs were $12,000. Add to that her average daily cash flow of $2,000 and she needed $14,000 cash on hand each day. She didn't have it. Her sales levels were good, so where was the cash going?

Dana gazed out the plane's window at the soft, white clouds. She knew the number one reason most small—and many large—businesses failed, was inadequate cash reserves. *Maybe I should go bankrupt*, Dana thought. She would be in the company of giants. Walt Disney had filed business bankruptcy in 1923 before he had created the cheerful, whistling rodent, Mickey Mouse. Big-three auto maker, General Motors, went bankrupt in 2009, and several of the airlines had declared bankruptcy. And even President Donald Trump's companies had filed for bankruptcy—not once but at least four times.

Dana knew that both personal bankruptcy and business liquidation for her jade business could be declared under Chapter 7 of the U.S. Bankruptcy Code. Chapter 7 is sometimes referred to as straight bankruptcy. Considering the extent of her cash flow problems, she didn't even consider the alternative—Chapter 11 bankruptcy—for Jade & More. She didn't have enough resources to weather a Chapter 11 financial reorganization which would allow her partnership with Frank to continue to function while they followed a debt repayment plan. What had Lenny told her? "Small businesses must avoid fraud like sea captains avoid icebergs."

During the morning of her first full day in Bangkok, Dana went to the Grand Palace Complex. Dana especially liked the temples, or *wats*, in Bangkok because of their colorful, multi-tiered roofs and carved gables.

The Temple of the Emerald Buddha inside the complex was breathtaking. Dana walked inside the main assembly hall of the chapel, or *bot*, and saw the Emerald Buddha. It was cut from a single piece of monolithic emerald and was 19 inches wide and 26 inches in height, according to the official guidebook. The Buddha was sitting high upon a golden throne flanked by other decorated Buddha images. Surrounding this throne were many offerings from kings, royal princes, and commoners.

The Emerald Buddha was dressed in winter clothes made of gold. Dana read in her guidebook that the King of Thailand dressed the Emerald Buddha three times a year in the appropriate clothes for summer, rainy, or winter season. According to legend, the Emerald Buddha was given to the Brahmin, Nagasena of Pataliputra, by God in 43 B.C., and Nagasena then magically placed seven relics of the Buddha into the statue.

Dana was impressed. More than 2,000 years old, she thought, and as stunning as ever. No wonder there has always been and continues to be high demand for precious gemstones, whether carved into royal art or fashioned into luxury jewelry. She knew, for instance, that during the last seven to eight months, the demand for emeralds had increased more than in the past six years. The continuing shortage in the supply of emeralds only made things worse.

Dana could only get within about 30 feet of the statue as it was perched atop a high pedestal decorated with Garuda, mythical half-man, half-bird forms. The color of the Emerald Buddha Deified was dull grayish-green and reminded Dana of celadon ceramic glazes. The surface glistened with polish which gave it a glassy appearance. Before she had even realized it, Dana began to estimate in her mind how many one carat emerald rings could be made from the statue. Abruptly, she stopped calculating. "That is so sacrilegious," she thought. "Besides, it's probably only jade, not emerald."

On the way back around the Grand Palace Complex, Dana stopped for a few minutes at the elegant Dusit Hall, a cruciform-shaped building with a tall golden spire. Dusit Maha Prasad or "audience hall" had a throne of mother-of-pearl surmounted by the usual nine-tiered white canopy—the mark of a duly crowned king. From there, Dana grabbed some lunch and headed back to her hotel, which was the conference site for the Gemstone Congress.

The Dusit Thani Hotel is a huge luxury hotel with 517 rooms and a lobby that reminded Dana of a railway station. Its name meant "town in heaven." During the afternoon she visited many of the booths where proprietors were selling colored stones. This place was ideal for purchasing many stones because of Thailand's most favored nation status and cheap labor force.

MFN or Most Favored Nation status is used by many developed countries such as the United States or Western Europe to help developing nations such as Thailand, Myanmar, Malaysia, or India improve their financial or economic condition through export trade. In effect, MFN provides for the duty-free importation of a wide range of products from certain countries which would otherwise be subject to trade tariffs. Under a framework of trade policies established by the World Trade Organization, WTO members are free to negotiate mutually beneficial trade agreements. The United States, Thailand, and Myanmar were early members of the WTO.

Since she was shipping the stones back to the U.S., Dana was careful to include the commercial invoice for each purchase, a shipping manifest or bill of lading for the package contents, and a U.S. Customs and Border Protection (CBP) Form 7501 describing the merchandise, quantity, gross weight in kilograms, estimated value, and country of origin for the stones. To avoid switches by unscrupulous freight and delivery services, she wrapped the gems in white paper which had her signature on various spots. She then sealed the paper with Scotch tape.

Some of the merchants smiled when she used her Geiger counter on the colored gems. One asked, "Do you think my stones came from Fukushima?" he joked, referring to the meltdown at the Fukushima Daiichi Nuclear power plant in 2011, following the 9.0 magnitude earthquake off the northeast coast of Japan and the resulting tsunami that devastated much of the Tohoku region.

Dana didn't break a smile. She knew that some gemstones were naturally radioactive, but who knew what people would do to improve the color of a stone.

There was nothing funny about the biggest Japanese nuclear disaster since Hiroshima and Nagasaki. The combination earthquake/tsunami had left 15,842 dead, 5,890 injured, and over 3,485 people missing across eighteen prefectures, with over 125,000 buildings damaged or destroyed. The estimated property damages ranged from U.S.$14.5 to $34.6 billion. After confirming the gemstones hadn't been irradiated, Dana placed the handheld radiation detector back into her bag.

In total, Dana purchased two heart-shaped emeralds, one heart-shaped ruby, two heart-shaped sapphires, three oval sapphires, two oval rubies, four round rubies, two imperial topazes, and a large amethyst. An auspicious day, she thought. *If I can do as well in Myanmar and Hong Kong, this trip will be very productive.* Dana felt as happy as a tornado in a mobile home park.

Due to a mix-up in flight schedules, Dana arrived in Yangon two days before the Myanmar Jade Emporium. This arrival worked to her advantage, giving her a couple of days to get to Naypyidaw, the site of the relocated gem show which had originated in Yangon. Dana had read that last year total sales at the show were $3.4 billion. The U.S. and European Union banned imports of several commodities in October 2009. Since the military generals get much of the revenue from the auctions, some gem dealers have tried to push for a boycott of the blood red rubies because they help support human rights abuses.

Travel by air to the official capital of Myanmar and host city for the Jade Emporium was out of the question. Although the Naypyidaw Airport was only 10 miles southeast of the capitol, she was told that it was now accessible through sporadic commercial flights, but only military generals from the Myanmar regime were able to get there by plane on a regular basis. Effectively, all others took the bus. Dana purchased a ticket for the four-hour bus ride for the first departure the next morning. That gave her one day in Yangon to explore. She had not come empty-handed.

Dana had brought mosquito coils and had purchased a carton of 555 Dunhill cigarettes and two bottles of Johnny Walker Red Label whiskey at the Bangkok duty-free counter. She exchanged one bottle for some Myanmar *kyats* with the taxi driver on her trip from the airport to Inya Lake Hotel. What she wished she had brought but hadn't was sufficient mineral water. She was worried her supply wouldn't be enough for the rest of her trip. She would have to purchase more bottles when she went out later.

That evening, Dana dined at the Karaweik Restaurant where she ate an excellent traditional Burmese meal. The combination restaurant-theatre was located on the eastern shoreline of Kandawgyi Lake and, from a distance, it looked like a large boat fashioned from two enormous golden ducks floating effortlessly on the water with a pagoda on their backs. Included with the dinner was a little cultural entertainment. While waiting for the Burmese dancing show to begin, Dana stepped outside to take some night photos of the Shwedagon Pagoda, officially called Shwedagon Zedi Daw, which she could see to the west. The golden dome at night was gorgeous as it seemed to rise from the far side of the lake. Later Burmese entertainers performed traditional dances on a huge stage with a large banner hung behind them proclaiming "Tourist Myanmar Welcomes You to The Golden Land."

The next morning Dana noticed a piece in a courtesy copy of the British daily, *The Guardian*, that had been slid under her door. Under the headline "Kachin Insurgents Come Under Attack," she read these paragraphs:

> The Myanmar army has launched a major offensive against the rebel Kachin Independence Army (KIA) in the far north of Myanmar. More than 10,000 government troops are engaged in the largest offensive ever against the KIA, which has been fighting martial rule intermittently since 1962 when a coup d'état led by Ne Win and a military junta launched the "Burmese Way to Socialism" campaign.
>
> The target of the offensive, which began on January 30, is the KIA's main stronghold in the southeastern Kachin State, adjacent to the China-Burmese border. Troops are advancing rapidly toward Laiza, headquarters of the KIA's political wing, the Kachin Independence Organization (KIO). The KIO has played a leading role in Myanmar's rebel movement. Sketchy reports indicate that 45 government troops are dead and about the same number of rebels have been killed. At least two helicopters are missing along with the crew members. There are scattered reports that the KIA has attacked government positions in other areas of Myanmar.

Though the news reminded Dana that travel in Myanmar was not without incident, she wasn't too worried. The Kachin area was a good 550 miles north of where she was headed.

The bus ride to Naypyidaw was uneventful. Once safely settled in the Aureum Palace Hotel, along the beautiful white stretches of sandy beaches, Dana worked on her plans for re-routing her planned gem purchases through a series of international shippers. She preferred the neutral term "re-routing" over the judgment-laden term "smuggling." True, U.S. Congress had passed the Tom Lantos Burmese JADE Act in 2008 which outlawed jade and ruby imports. As was popular recently, each new piece of legislation from Washington had to have a catchy name to go with it. The acronym JADE cleverly stood for Junta's Anti-Democratic Efforts. Congress had wanted to send a clear political message that it wouldn't tolerate continual human rights abuses by the ruling junta in Myanmar.

The only problem was that Myanmar jade and rubies were the best quality stones in the world. Ensuring a steady supply of high quality gems for American consumers was the essence of Jade & More's five-star customer service. "Smuggling" sounded so criminal. Re-routing was a much better term. Re-routing was harmless, much like when the navigator's voice from your GPS would indicate when you had missed your turn-off. Like a Global Positioning System, Dana was simply recalculating another path to allow her gemstones to reach the desired destination. Dana wondered if this type of justification might be like that of a corporate executive engaging in income smoothing manipulations?

The next day Dana spent her time previewing the jade on display at the Gem Emporium. Although she did plan to bid on some of the jade stones, she also wanted to visit the various showrooms. She especially wanted to buy some pigeon-blood rubies, which were unique to Myanmar. If she was unsuccessful in her bid for stones here in Naypyidaw, Dana planned to fly back to Hong Kong and purchase some jade for her shop there. The quality wouldn't be as good but getting the stones through customs would be much less hassle.

The next morning auctioneer U Win Pe began the official gem auction. He was a smiling, bespectacled, gray-haired Burmese man who had conducted every Emporium since 1964. He announced the first lot in fluent English and the wagering began. Each potential buyer began by writing his or her name and bid on a sheet of green paper, then folded it and placed it in a silver bowl. To the highest bidder went the rough ruby rock or jade boulder.

Frank Harrison wished he had a direct flight from Philadelphia to Tucson. It had been years since any major carrier flew non-stop from Philadelphia International Airport to the Tucson, Arizona home of the largest gem and mineral show in the U.S. This year's Tucson Gem Show in February promised to be once again the major event for colored stones buyers from around the world. His only consolation for having to make a layover was that he was flying first class. Since travel was a tax-deductible expense, Frank always booked his seat in the first-class section for his business trips.

Frank drove to the airport via Interstate 95. The direct link to the airport from the Interstate was constructed in the 1980s, and since then travel to the airport was much more convenient. To the right, Frank could see the Philadelphia Sports Complex and to the left the Food Distribution Center as he passed the Broad Street exit on the Interstate. Frank enjoyed going to ball games at both the Wells Fargo Center and the Phillies' Citizens Bank Park. Just this past weekend at Wells Fargo Center he had watched the 76ers beat the Celtics in basketball on Saturday, and the Flyers beat the Canadians in hockey on Sunday. "If only sports tickets were tax-deductible," Frank thought.

Frank's favorite place in the sports complex used to be John F. Kennedy Stadium. Although it had been torn down years ago to make room for the Spectrum II, later renamed the Wells Fargo Center, the Kennedy Stadium had hosted the annual Army-Navy football game for over a half-century, drawing crowds more than 100,000 people. As a child, Frank had often attended the games, and he was sad to see the venue for the annual rivalry between the two military colleges relocated across the street to Lincoln Financial Field.

As Frank approached the Schuylkill River, the dividing line between South and Southwest Philadelphia, the Philadelphia Naval Shipyard was clearly visible on this cold, clear morning. One of his favorite historical sites, Admiral Dewey's flagship, had been located there before becoming a museum piece at Penn's Landing. Also visible to Frank were the many oil refineries located along the Schuylkill River. The proximity of the Schuylkill River to the Delaware River made the location advantageous for oil refineries since oil barges could navigate the waters with relative ease.

Frank felt fortunate that he was able to find a place to park so close to the airport terminal. He used the camera on his cell phone to take a picture of the exact location of his car and walked briskly to the terminal. There was one hour and fifteen minutes until his flight. Plenty of time to compose an e-mail to Janet concerning some work to be done at the jade shop, he thought.

Frank walked up to the priority access airline counter to get his boarding pass. He had forgotten to check-in online earlier. He was greeted by a cheerful, sandy-haired, tall young man in his late twenties.

"Yes sir, what can I help you with today?"

"I'm traveling to Tucson," Frank replied as he pulled his e-ticket out of his coat pocket and presented it to the clerk.

"Do you have any luggage to check?"

"None." Frank always avoided checking baggage if possible. Not only was he concerned about the possibility of the luggage being lost, but he could not stand waiting for the luggage to be unloaded from the plane.

The clerk began to flex his fingers over his keyboard and looked at a monitor. "Would you prefer a window or aisle?"

"Aisle."

"One moment, sir."

Frank began tapping impatiently on the counter with his fingers. The airline clerk looked up and Frank could tell by his expression that something was amiss. "Mr. Harrison, I'm very sorry, but the first-class section of the plane is completely full."

"Can't you increase the number of rows?" a worried Frank inquired as the thought of a four-and-one-half-hour flight without a lot of leg room began to make him irritable.

"No, sir, first class is completely full on this flight and on your connecting flight." The clerk paused and added, "If you want I can check if there's any room in coach."

"Yes, please do that." Frank did not enjoy flying, and the thought of doing so without a lot of room for his long legs caused his annoyance to intensify.

"Coach is full also. It looks like your flight is oversold. Maybe someone will cancel or volunteer to take another flight. We're offering economy fare flyers a $200 flight credit plus re-booking on the next available flight. So far, we haven't had anyone willing to be bumped but there's still an hour before we start boarding. There's really nothing else I can do, Mr. Harrison. I have you on standby just in case. We'll call your name over the loud speaker if something opens up." The clerk gave Frank a sympathetic smile.

"Fine," Frank grumbled, obviously distraught. As a frequent flyer, he had learned from experience that yelling at the check-in clerk was pointless. And as a businessperson, he could understand that airlines accepted more reservations than available seats on the airplane to increase revenue per flight, but it was annoying nonetheless. His only hope was that the airline would increase the bump voucher to $500 to provide more incentive. People will do anything if the price is right. Frank gathered his carry-on luggage and headed toward his gate. Once seated at the proper gate, he began tapping out instructions to Janet on his tablet.

1. Discount the note receivable from Denig at our bank.

Frank began calculating. It was a $16,000, 6%, 120-day note so it had a maturity value of $16,320. Frank's concentration was temporarily broken by an attractive woman of about thirty who was sitting by herself. Frank started to straighten his tie and comb his hair. Before he could walk over to her, she was joined by another man who was obviously either her husband or her boyfriend. "Just my luck," Frank muttered to himself.

Frank resumed his calculations. "Let's see," he said softly with a sigh. "Maturity value $16,320, bank discount rate of 9%, bank will hold the note for the remaining forty days, so $16,320 times 9% times forty divided by 360 days in a business year equals $163.20."

Frank subtracted the $163.20 from the maturity value to come up with the proceeds equaling $16,156.80. Frank added to his memo to Janet:

1. Discount the note receivable from Denig at our bank. You should receive $16,156.80 in cash.
2. Make entry in books. Debit *cash* $16,156.80; credit *interest revenue* $156.80; credit *notes receivable discounted* $16,000.

Frank paused and smiled before deciding on adding the following:

> The *note receivable discounted* account is a contingent liability. That is, if Denig does not pay the maturity value of the note to the bank, then the jade shop must pay the bank.

Frank chuckled as he thought of the prospects of Denig reneging on the note. Pulling out his classic Hewlett-Packard 12c pocket financial calculator, Frank began calculating the cost of the bond he had purchased recently for the jade shop as a long-term investment. The broker had sold him a $10,000, 8%, five-year bond at 102 plus two months of accrued interest. Frank calculated the accrued interest by multiplying the $10,000 by 8% and then multiplying that total by the number of months of accrued interest (which is two) divided by the twelve months in a year. This process converted the annual interest to two months of interest. The accrued interest equaled $133.33. Since the bond sold at 102, that meant that it sold at 102% of its face value. The total cost plus accrued interest totaled $10,333.33.

3. Record purchase of long-term investment in bonds. Debit *long-term investment in bonds* $10,200; debit *interest receivable* $133.33; credit *cash* $10,333.33

Frank doubled checked the spelling on his email to Janet before pressing the send button. More than likely she would be able to post the entries before he even reached Tucson, although discounting the note would require a trip to the bank.

"Will passenger Frank Harrison please report to the ticket counter at gate 19."

Frank grabbed his carry-on bag and walked over to the airline counter. He was concerned the page could be regarding an emergency with his consulting business that required immediate attention. He hoped that it wasn't something which might affect his travel plans. "I'm Frank Harrison," he said to the young lady behind the counter. He looked worried. The sandy-haired clerk that had helped him earlier was busy issuing vouchers and rebooking passengers that had volunteered to give up their seats.

"Mr. Harrison, good news! A couple of our travelers have elected to reschedule their flights. We were able to seat you in the first-class section, but I'll need your stand-by ticket to make the switch."

"Terrific!" Frank gave her his ticket and received his new boarding pass. After thanking the clerk for her trouble, Frank breathed a sigh of relief, sat down, opened his briefcase, and began reading the latest issue of *Management Accounting Quarterly*. This trip is going to be great after all, he thought.

He read an article about financial reporting on the Internet. Professors Nitham Hindi and John Rich found that most websites of the 100 companies that they had surveyed contained an investor relations' section that included an annual report, links to financial statements, price information, the proxy statement, and the latest stock price. Having all the information available in one place made it much easier to research the financial condition of a company and evaluate its investment potential.

Carson Denig left Honolulu on Singapore Airlines. Soon he would be crossing the international dateline and he would lose a day. He always wondered if a person's birthday fell on the missed day, did that mean the person did not grow one year older? "Maybe that's the reason for the discrepancy in many people's ages," he chuckled.

Carson considered himself to be one of the toughest men alive. He had been a Navy SEAL—an acronym for Sea Air Land Team. This elite group of about 2,500 Navy personnel execute missions underwater, on beaches, and into harbors in enemy territory. In his first mission, Carson served as a member of Task Unit Whiskey that conducted underwater operations in Balboa Harbor, Panama to plant the C4 explosives that destroyed the naval assets of dictator and drug-trafficker Manuel Noriega. Operation Just Cause, the code name for the United States invasion of Panama, resulted in the removal of the Panamanian leader and general from power. Noriega was eventually captured and stood trial in the United States in the early 90s for eight counts of drug trafficking, racketeering, and money laundering.

Though Carson had left the SEALs in the late 90s, he had devoted himself to staying combat-fit. The daily training would come in handy for his next adventure—an exotic locale, big stakes with a big payoff, and risks kept to a minimum. Carson's regimen was an Olympic distance triathlon consisting of a 1.5km swim, 40km bike ride, and 10km run. At least once a month he would schedule a body-toning full Ironman consisting of a 2.4-mile swim, 112-mile ride, and a 26.2-mile marathon. His exercise program always reminded him of his SEAL training at the sand-colored compound in Coronado, California. Just down the bay from San Diego, Carson had undergone some demanding and punitive special operations training.

A five-mile swim against the Pacific Ocean currents, a 14-mile overland run and mountain-climbing exercises in full combat gear had been routine. He had become proficient with at least eleven different combat weapons and an expert at detonating a wide range of explosives such as limpet mines, cratering charges, and Bangalore torpedoes. In 24 weeks he had gone through parachute jump school at Fort Benning, Georgia, and had learned how to kill a sentry, abduct someone, and sink a ship.

Created in 1962 by President Kennedy, the SEAL force looked for physical and mental toughness. Carson remembered what his commanding office had said. "Our first criterion is a man's confidence in his ability to achieve and a tremendous determination to excel. You need an inner spark, a special kind of motivation to overcome all adversity, regardless of what is put in front of you." Carson would need this inner spark for his latest Rambo-type goal.

As a civilian, Carson Denig had quickly become a successful Philadelphia developer. Denig Construction, Inc. was one of his several corporations. He opened a folder and began reading the operating instructions for a new laser cutting machine his company had recently bought:

Carbon Dioxide Laser Machine

A revolutionary "sky-wars" breakthrough in our res-onator cavity provides a lightweight cutting torch. Weighing only 48 pounds, our continuous-wave laser cuts large metal structures. It is excellent for large metal beams.

Lasers have two important advantages over conven-tional tools. First, a laser beam does not get dull or change its size and shape because of wear. Second, its performance is not substantially affected by work piece hardness or machine ability.

The CO_2 laser produces an invisible beam of light whose wavelength is 10.7um and generates many kilo-watts of power. The CO_2 uses a precise mixture of three gases (carbon dioxide, helium, and nitrogen) for high power output operation.

The laser works by sending streams of energy through the chosen material, thereby causing sub-molecular particles to jump from level of activity to a lesser one (i.e., the material degenerates rapidly). Searing a path through 10 feet thick titanium at a rate of 20 feet per minute is quite possible. Obviously, careful control is necessary. The laser should only be used when con-nected tightly to a stable work bench, with the beam aimed into a large lead box. The beam is designed so that it will not penetrate lead.

The lead box also traps and thereby protects the oper-ator from any toxic metal fumes produced by the cutting process. Protective eyeglasses and gas masks are suggested for continuous use, however.

> Metal Engineering Company
> 8761 Pete Rose Way
> Cincinnati, Ohio 45209

Carson would certainly test the laser machine for performance and work piece hardness on this trip. Enough of that. Carson turned his attention to another closely-held corporation in his portfolio of companies that seemed problematic. Denright International had done quite well importing rubies and investing in publicly traded stocks of regional companies. The company had been incorporated in 2001 by himself, the then up-and-coming national politician Jim Bright and his wife, and Frank Harrison.

Carson had received 30 percent of the par value common stock; the politician and his wife, 45 percent; and Frank Harrison, 25 percent. Although the term *par value stock* has become somewhat obsolete, they had issued par value stock to each stockholder. No-par stock most often has a stated value and is non-assessable; that is, creditors could not hold the stockholders liable for any difference between the consideration given for the stock and its par value. The company had not repurchased any stock back from the stockholders so there was no treasury stock.

Carson considered three current problems facing Denright. First, recent tax law changes had made the corporate form more advantageous. There is still the advantage of corporate limited liability, but a corporation is still taxed twice—once at the corporate level and again at the stockholder level. Even with President Trump's lower individual tax rates and lower corporate rates, the flow-through entities such as partnerships and S corporations are still quite popular. A Subchapter S corporation is still a real corporation, but under the tax law there is no separate corporate tax. Since Carson did not wish the unlimited liability of a partnership, he was seriously considering the S election.

The second problem was less manageable. Some newspaper reporters were checking into the operations of the closely-held corporation. Carson had refused to return calls to about four different reporters last week. He pulled out a newspaper clipping from *The Wall Street Journal* and reread parts of it:

> House Speaker Bright's dealings with mysterious Denright, Inc. revive questions about his ethics and judgment. The closely-held corporation remains somewhat of a mystery. Its president, Carson Denig, would not return our phone calls, and a three-day stakeout at his apartment yielded no results. A next-door neighbor indicates that "I have never seen the gentleman, but he does get a lot of phone calls." The corporation lists its mailing address as a post office box in Philadelphia.
>
> Denright is responsible for much of Mr. Bright's financial success, but the treasurer, Frank Harrison, indicates that "I have never asked the speaker for a favor." Mr. Harrison is a well-known financial consultant in Philadelphia.
>
> While Denright does not have to disclose its dealings, instructions issued by the House Ethics Committee tell members to disclose the underlying holdings of such investment corporations. To date, Rep. Bright has not made any such disclosures.

The third problem was that Bright's wife had recently complained about the return on her investment in Denright. True, Denright had not declared any dividends, but the earnings-per-share figure for the corporation was exceptional. Earnings per share is the corporation's net income per share available to its common stockholders calculated as follows:

$$\text{Earnings per common share outstanding} = \frac{\text{Net income} - \text{Preferred dividends}}{\text{Weighted average number of common shares outstanding}}$$

Denright had no preferred stock, only common stock. Even though Bright and his wife had not received any cash dividends so far, the income from operations was being accumulated in the Retained Earnings account. In a corporation, net income increases an account called *Retained Earnings*, and dividends reduce this same account. *Maybe we can declare a stock dividend to stop her from complaining*, Carson mused.

Stock dividends present the illusion to the stockholder that he or she is receiving something of value, but, the corporation sacrifices no assets. The Retained Earnings account is reduced by the market value of the stock dividend, but Common Stock (at par) and Additional Paid-In Capital are increased by the same total amount to reflect the increased issuance of common stock. Thus, stockholders' equity is unaffected by a stock dividend, although its composition changes. Such a ploy just may be the solution to Mrs. Bright's complaints, Carson reasoned.

Since Carson couldn't make any further progress on the Denright problems, he returned the news clipping to his leather briefcase and withdrew a gold Cross pen and a yellow legal-sized writing pad. He drew a line down the center of the front page and across the top of the left side he wrote *Bangkok* and across the top of the right-side *Chiang Mai*. Under the caption *Bangkok* he began listing:

1. Steel/chain nets
2. Steel cables (4)
3. Rope (300 ft.)
4. Shotguns (2)
5. Rifle (1) plus scope
6. Shells
7. Hunting knives (2)
8. Machete
9. Chisel
10. Large suitcases (2)

Under the *Chiang Mai* caption he wrote:

1. Canteens (2)
2. Backpacks (2)
3. Snake bite kit
4. First aid kit

5. Mosquito repellent
6. Axe
7. Mess kit
8. Hammer
9. Cartons of cigarettes (15)
10. Hat, jeans, bush shirt
11. Iodine
12. Matches (waterproof)
13. Food and water
14. Sleeping tent
15. Sleeping bag
16. Waterproof coat

Then at the bottom of the page he wrote the word *have* and listed the following items:

1. Jeweler's loupe
2. Sneakers
3. Compass
4. Night binoculars
5. Lightweight bullet-proof vest
6. Laser cutting torch
7. Pocket knife
8. Calculator
9. Protective eyeglasses (2)
10. Gas masks (2)

He thought about but did not write down the word pistol. As a safety precaution he had packed his brown polymer pistol in his suitcase. It had a ceramic barrel insert and six springs—the only metallic parts. The remainder of the pistol was made of plastic. It would escape detection from most security detection machines, but Carson had decided not to carry it on his person.

The weapon was a non-metal assassination pistol issued in the early 1980s by the Soviet Union for KGB agents. Not until 1986 did the U.S. Government Office of Technology Assessment admit:

"From our investigations it appears that the materials technology does exist to produce non-metallic firearms

whose only metal components may be some small
springs."

Carson put his list back into his briefcase and pulled out a batch
of 8-by-10 photos. He looked slowly at each of the colored prints.
On the back of each was written north, south, east, or west. Ap-
proximate distances were written on a few them. Carson took a
felt pen and drew a horizontal line across the top of one of the
pictures between the Banana Bud and the *hti* on the Shwedagon
pagoda.

Carson knew that the Shwedagon or Golden Dagon pagoda was
the most celebrated object of worship in all the Indochinese
countries. The site of a depository of a relic of Buddha, legend in-
dicates religious activity at Shwedagon as early as 588 B.C.

When Carson's plane landed, the passport agent at Suvarnabhumi
International Airport in Bangkok was as thorough as usual. He
took Carson's passport and observed him closely. He compared
Carson with his photo—tall, bald, some black hair along the sides
of his head, and a small black mustache—not quite as pencil-thin
as the late Chicago insurance billionaire W. Clement Stone. The
agent consulted his computer console for about two minutes,
stamped Carson's blue passport, and handed it back to him.

Once Carson was waved through customs, he met Cimi Kiengsiri
in the airport lobby. They spent the remainder of the afternoon
purchasing the supplies needed in Bangkok. They began the drive
to Chiang Mai around 6:00 in the evening. Cimi drove steadily for
about seven hours, stopping only for gasoline. Carson was able to
sleep much of the way. He awoke at 1:20 p.m. when Cimi pulled
into the parking lot of a small hotel.

After a needed rest, Carson and Cimi purchased their remaining
supplies in Chiang Mai. The inside of Cimi's aging four-wheel-
drive Nissan was now full, as was the rack on top. Carson strapped
on his holster and inserted his plastic pistol. With their rifles and
shotguns within reach, Cimi began the drive up Route No. 108
toward Mae Sai. Carson again slept, waking only when Cimi came
to a stop at the end of the road. They saw Jake and another Shan
tribe member with three mules in the shade of an apple tree.

Jake's partner had red lips, almost like lipstick. Carson knew that many Burmese chewed a nut of the Areca palm as a mild intoxicant. This habit causes bright red lips.

They took about 45 minutes to unload the 4x4, pack the mules, and hide the Nissan off the road by covering it with bushes. Cimi took the distributor cap with him. Carson covered himself with mosquito repellent, and the four men began the trek north toward the Myanmar border. They reached Mae Sai around nightfall and slept in a grass hut. By sunrise the next morning the caravan had crossed the border into Myanmar—the golden land.

Carson agreed with a recent article in USA Today by Calum MacLeod entitled "Burma Seems Poised on Cusp of Growth." MacLeod wrote that "corruption and mismanagement are rife, while ATMs and decent roads are rarities, and large swaths of the country have suffered from civil war for decades."

Eleven

I recently heard a CPA remark that the only accounting principle which the Internal Revenue Service regards as "generally accepted" is "A bird in the hand is worth two in the bush." Although my friend overstates his case a bit—quite a bit—I cannot dismiss the thrust of his comment without some soul searching.

—Sheldon S. Cohen,
Former Commissioner of Internal Revenue

Lenny was feeling depressed. He was getting nowhere with the dean in trying to clear his name. It seemed that every attempt he made to reach Bob Hawkins was futile. Worse yet, the unfounded plagiarism charge had tarnished his reputation to such an extent, his consulting activities were falling off—especially among those who were Wharton alumni. With fewer clients, he should have had more time to spend ferreting out Dana's accounting problems, but he had been so preoccupied with trying to defend his reputation, that he had ignored the Jade & More engagement altogether.

Dana and Lenny had spent some time together around the Christmas holidays, but aside from the few moments they shared then, he had had virtually no contact with her for the past few months, except by phone. He had felt particularly guilty when Dana called him last week to tell him that she would be going to Myanmar and wanted a status report on how the investigation was going. He apologized to her for having nothing to report. He promised Dana that he would place a higher priority on trying to uncover her cash-flow problems while she was gone.

───────────

"Hey, Doc! Get a load of that guy!" exclaimed Woody, pointing to a teenager with many body piercings.

Lenny chuckled softly. He was sure that when the Founding Fathers had convened the Philadelphia Constitutional Convention in 1787, they had not imagined that protecting free speech would devolve into the right to self-decoration. "That's nothing. Do you see those scalp tats on that girl with the half-shaved head? Every available square inch is inked."

Woody and Lenny were "people-watching" on their way downtown to grab a bite to eat. For arranging the midnight audit of Denig's warehouse, Lenny was treating Woody to lunch. On their way to the restaurant, Lenny planned to stop off at the Jade & More shop. When Dana had called to let him know she was headed back to Myanmar, she had told him that she would leave with Janet a key for him in an envelope. This way Lenny could go in and work at his convenience. With Frank out of town too, Lenny felt that he could finally make some serious progress.

"So, Lenny," Woody said, interrupting Lenny's train of thought. "You're really thinking of leaving Penn for another school?"

"I really don't have much choice, Woody. Unless I can clear myself with the dean concerning my book, they have sufficient cause to fire me. Zero tolerance for plagiarism and all. The dean isn't cutting me any slack," said Lenny in resignation. "And Woody, get this. Yesterday, someone slipped a note under my door indicating that I was receiving Al Gore's award for Uplifting Research in Global Warming. *Uplifting*. That hurts, Woody. You know me. I would never steal somebody else's work."

Woody nodded. "Lenny, where are you looking to go?"

"If it wasn't for Rebecca being in school and having all her friends here, I might look out of state. But I don't think I'll leave the area, so I guess that means I'll talk to Villanova, Temple, and Drexel."

"Penn won't be the same if you leave," proclaimed Woody.

"Thanks," Lenny said as he smiled weakly.

The two grew silent as they approached Sansom Street. The thought of Lenny going to another university had left them both somber. They had been friends ever since Lenny had caught Woody napping in his faculty office with an unlit cigar wedged between his fingers. Lenny had opened the door in a rush to get his notes for class only to find the Penn Steinberg-Dietrich Hall building manager asleep behind his desk.

"You're welcome," Woody said as he opened his heavy eyes. If Lenny's noisy entrance had startled him, he never showed it.

"Welcome, for what?" Lenny responded.

"Well, for *not* only cleaning your office but for prepping your next class." Woody pointed to an opened folder on Lenny's desk. "Dr. Cramer do you think, only CPAs know how to cut, paste, and assemble?"

Lenny smiled at the clever yet polite definition of the acronym CPA. He had heard many other explanations as to what the initials stood for, most of which he couldn't repeat in public. He was curious to see what Woody might say next.

"Doc, I bet you're saying to yourself: What does a maintenance supervisor who grew up on the streets of southeast Philly know about accounting? Well, you might be surprised. I may not be able to tell a debit from a credit, but I do know this much. As my book-keeper mama used to say: *If you're suffering from depreciation, it can be an accrual world.*"

The puns were so bad, Lenny groaned aloud between chuckles.

Woody paused just long enough for the muffled laughter to stop. He stood up from Lenny's easy chair, fiddled with the controls under the seat, and then spun the chair to the right twice and to the left twice, in quick succession. Finally, he motioned for Lenny to sit. "Working just fine, Doc," he said. "I can check that off my To Do list. You did submit a facility request for a chair tune-up, right?"

Lenny smiled and shook his head. Woody's smooth performance was the best recovery from being caught sleeping on the job he had seen in years. He extended his hand to Woody. "Name's Lenny," he said. "What's your name, colleague?"

The chance meeting with Woody in Lenny's faculty office had been years ago. Lenny had been at Wharton now for quite some time. He had come to love where he worked, and the possibility of leaving was unsettling. The Penn campus felt comfortable to him, and he was used to the people there. The prospect of leaving made him uneasy over the uncertainty of it all. To a degree, Lenny felt that he was being tested. In less than two years his wife had died, and his career had been jeopardized. He could not help but feel that fate was dealing him a raw hand.

As Lenny and Woody approached the jade shop, Lenny found it increasingly harder to catch his breath. The cold winter day and the high winds that gusted between the large office buildings in downtown Philadelphia often made extended walking difficult during the winter. He was glad when they stepped into the jewelry store.

"Hey, they got some nice stuff in here," whispered Woody to Lenny as they both removed their gloves and unbuttoned the top buttons of their coats.

"Woody, it'll only take a minute to pick up the envelope from Janet," Lenny said. "Why don't you look around?" Lenny suggested as he left for the back of the store.

"Yeah, maybe I'll buy out the place," joked Woody.

In the back office, Lenny exchanged pleasantries with Janet and picked up the envelope from her that Dana had left for him. He then stepped into Dana's office to open the envelope and read the note inside.

Dear Lenny,

Enclosed you will find keys to the front door of the shop (#1 for the handset and #2 the deadbolt), the back office (#3), the desks (#4—same key fits all desks), and the file cabinets (#5 and #6). With Frank gone next week, you should have the opportunity to get a great deal done without having to sneak around so that he doesn't know you have been here.

You sounded a little down on the phone. I'm worried about you. Please cheer up. Things are bound to get better soon. I am confident that you will be able to get the plagiarism charge settled at school and put that concern behind you.

Take care,

Dana

Lenny put the keys in his trousers pocket and placed the envelope and note in his briefcase. He left the back office, waved good-bye to Janet, and joined Woody in the front of the shop.

"I hope I wasn't too long, Woody," Lenny said apologetically.

"Not a problem, Doc," Woody said, as he motioned for Lenny to come closer to the display case he had been inspecting. "There's something over here I want you to see."

"Ah hah! By your fixed gaze at the merchandise inside the glass, I surmise you are finally starting to appreciate the finer things in life such as jewelry. Is that it, Woody?" Lenny joked.

"Look at this," Woody whispered, pointing to a locked glass case at the end of a counter just in front of the display window. "Isn't that the same squirrel we saw at the warehouse that night?"

Lenny looked, and sure enough, the stone carving appeared to be that same hideous greenish-colored squirrel eating a nut. "You are right, it looks the same," replied Lenny softly.

"You can't forget anything that ugly," said Woody.

"I wonder how much it costs," said Lenny inquisitively.

"Doc, you're not seriously thinking of buying that thing, are you?"

"I'm just curious, Woody."

Lenny motioned to the sales clerk, who had just finished waiting on another customer. "Yes, sir," Phillip said, "what can I help you with?" Phillip looked at Woody and then at Lenny. He continued, "Another locket this time, Professor Cramer?"

"Good memory, Phillip," Lenny smiled. "I'm looking for something a little more exotic this time. I was wondering how much this wonderful squirrel in the case here costs."

Phillip unlocked the case and picked up the sculpture, along with the half-moon display box. He turned the box over and noted the stock number on the bottom. "One moment, sir," he said. "Allow me to check for you." Phillip walked over to a large black book which had the prices of all the merchandise in the store. After turning several pages, he returned to Lenny and Woody.

"That squirrel carving is made of some of the finest gem-quality jade known to humankind. It sells for only $6,500. I know it is expensive, but from what the proprietors of this establishment tell me, the jade it is made from is exquisite."

Woody began to protest. "$6,500! Why, that squirrel is—"

"Excuse me, Phillip," Lenny interrupted. "I forgot to introduce my co-worker, Woody." Lenny stepped forward slightly, crushing Woody's left sneaker with his wingtip. Woody growled. "Phillip, as Woody was about to say, it seems to me that $6,500 is a fair starting price for such a sculpture. But I want to think about it. Would you do me a favor? Would you hold the item for a couple of hours for me while I make up my mind? There's another animal-themed stone carving at one of your competitors that caught my eye as we were window shopping on Sansom Street this morning."

"Very well, Professor Cramer. Since you are a friend of Ms. Scott's I don't think it will be a problem," Phillip replied. After repackaging the jade squirrel into the display box, he moved it to a customer hold case near the cash register at the front of the store.

"Are you crazy?" Woody whispered.

"Come now, Woody," Lenny said, as he ushered Woody out of the jade shop as quickly as possible. "Thanks again, Phillip," Lenny called out behind him. "We'll be back shortly."

Once they were outside the shop, Woody stopped walking and said to Lenny, "Doc, have you gone nutso? Don't you remember that we saw those same squirrel figurines in Denig's warehouse marked as fakes? I helped you crowbar—"

"'Imitations,' Woody," Lenny interrupted. "Fine imitations, like cubic zirconia. Phillip would be so insulted you said 'fake.'" Lenny smiled. "Of course, I remember, Woody. The crates from Tijuana...."

"Then why in the world are you going to pay $6,500 for that phony jade," questioned Woody "And why are you grinning from ear to ear? You look like a kid who has been given the key to the Hershey chocolate factory."

"Woody, my friend, I think you've just help me solve Dana's cash flow riddle. So, that's why the cat-grin. I think I know how Dana is getting ripped off."

"Thanks for giving me credit ... but I'd be just as happy with 30 percent of your billings on the case," Woody teased. "Doc, I know this is elementary for someone with your brains, but can you explain to me what CZs have to do with how Dana is getting fleeced?"

"I don't have all the details worked out yet, Woody, but if my guess is correct, Carson Denig is selling imitation jade to Dana and the store is passing it off as authentic." Lenny paused for a moment, his gaze shifting upward as if he were thinking through a plan. "Step one is I'm going to have to look at the invoices to make sure. You know what they say; a fraud red flag is a terrible thing to waste."

"What about the Harrison guy? How does he fit into it?" asked Woody.

"I don't know, but he's involved in some way. I'm just thinking aloud here, but Frank Harrison may be getting a bribe from Denig on the profits he earns from selling imitation jade inventory to Dana," Lenny mused. "Woody, as soon as we've finished lunch, I'm going back to Jade & More to see what I can find out."

"I think I'll give you a hand," Woody suggested.

"Are you sure, Woody? Don't you have to go back to work?"

"Ah, they'll never know I'm gone," countered Woody. "Also, I haven't seen you this excited in a while. Besides, you need protection from yourself, or you'll end up buying that stupid squirrel."

Lenny laughed. He had to admit to himself that for the first time in many weeks he felt enthusiastic. This accidental discovery was the first positive breakthrough in trying to uncover Dana's cash flow difficulties. But sometimes chance discovery was part of forensic accounting and fraud detection. In fact, tips were the number one-way fraud was detected. He wasn't really interested in eating. It seemed like more of a distraction than it was worth. He preferred to go to work on Dana's books, but he had promised Woody lunch.

––––––––––––––

Just around the corner from the shop, Lenny and Woody found a bustling deli kiosk with relatively fast-moving lines. They ordered some sandwiches to go and ate them in Washington Square, over-looking the bronze statue of General Washington and the eternal flame lying at the base of the Tomb of the Unknown Revolutionary War Solider. Within a half an hour, they were back at Jade & More, seated around Dana's desk. The first thing Lenny did was look for the invoice on the squirrel. As he suspected, he found the documentation by going through the Carson Denig accounts payable file. But he was surprised to see that Dana, *not* Frank had been the one to accept the shipment from the freight company. She had initialed the bill of lading for the squirrel, logging in the purchase as having been received and inspected. This was disturbing. He mentioned his concern to Woody.

"Do you think that she thought it was the real deal," Woody asked "or do you think that she knowingly sells fakes to her customers?"

"I don't know, Woody. I'd like to give Dana the benefit of the doubt. Maybe this piece is a legitimate squirrel sculpture even though it came from Carson Denig."

"I'll bet you a beer it's bogus," Woody challenged.

"Bet's on. And I think I know how to find out if the piece is authentic jade," Lenny replied. He walked from the back office into the front of the store where he spoke to Phillip about buying the squirrel.

"Phillip, after thinking about what you said earlier about the quality of the sculptured jade, I've made up my mind. I've decided to buy the squirrel," Lenny proclaimed. "Is it possible for me to give you a deposit with my American Express card and be billed for the rest?"

"I don't think that will be a problem under the circumstances," replied Phillip. "You will have to fill out this deferred billing form indicating the terms of payment and your agreement to abide by those terms."

It took Lenny about ten minutes to fill out the form. Phillip packaged the squirrel, which weighed about five pounds, in its half-moon display carton, wrapping it carefully with tissue paper. While Phillip was doing this, Lenny went back to the office to let Woody know that he was going to go out for about thirty minutes. Woody, who had made himself comfortable in Dana's chair, said he might take a little nap while Lenny was gone.

Lenny thumbed through Dana's rolodex and found the address he was looking for. He collected the jade squirrel from Phillip and walked about halfway down the street to Irv's Jewels. Irv Moskowitz owned the shop. Dana had mentioned in an earlier conversation with Lenny that Irv was someone whose expertise concerning jade she trusted.

Inside the jewelry store, Lenny found a counter clerk and explained to her that he wanted to get an appraisal of the item he had just purchased. The clerk unwrapped the box to look at the squirrel and informed Lenny that given the size of the piece and type of stone, he would have to see the owner, who was the expert on jade.

Irv Moskowitz, having overhead the conversation, walked over, looked at the squirrel, and said to Lenny, "I hope you don't mind me saying this, sir, but if you were the one that bought this squirrel you have lousy taste. Make sure you keep that covered up when you leave; otherwise people are liable to think you bought that here."

"It belongs to a friend," Lenny replied with embarrassment.

Moskowitz put on his glasses and placed a bright light on the squirrel. He then rubbed his hand along the surface of the squirrel and began to shake his head. "This junk is one of the poorer examples of imitation jade I've seen. It's probably worth a little over $200."

"Are you certain?" asked Lenny.

"Well, it's a quick examination, so I may be off one way or the other by as much as $50."

"So, the maximum value of this squirrel would be no more than about $300?"

"If you were in a dark room and the buyer was snickered drunk, you might be able to get $300 for it," answered Moskowitz. "Do you mind my asking how much your friend paid for it?"

"$6,500."

"I will say a prayer for you tonight, sir, or for your friend," Irv said, "because you were taken. Do you mind my asking you where you bought this thing? I ask you because most jewelers on the Row do not like to see our image as honest businesspeople damaged by a few unscrupulous dealers," explained Moskowitz.

"It was purchased at Jade & More," replied Lenny.

"Oy gevalt! I know this Jade & More. They are good people," Moskowitz said in astonishment. "This dishonesty is something I will bring up with the proprietors, sir, because I am confident that they will refund your money."

"Many thanks for your services. How much do I owe you?" inquired Lenny.

"Sir, I think I speak for the rest of the proprietors on this street in saying that in good conscience I could not charge you for spotting such an obvious injustice. Nothing. You owe me nothing."

Lenny thanked Moskowitz and headed back to Jade & More. It was clear that anyone with any degree of expertise would recognize that the squirrel was not genuine. The only question in Lenny's mind now was whether Dana was trying to swindle people, and if so, how that could possibly create her cash-flow shortage? If she knew about the fakes, she should have excess cash from buying inventory low and selling it high. He decided that the only way to find out was to check the inventory list that Dana had completed a few weeks ago. The inventory list might give him the answers for which he was looking.

When Lenny returned to the office, Woody was sitting on a chair fast asleep. He woke up immediately when Lenny shut the door and put his unlit cigar back in his shirt pocket.

"Where have you been?" Woody asked.

"I told you before you started studying the backs of your eyelids that I would be out for a while. And while I was out, I just so happened to get the exquisite squirrel I bought appraised."

"You didn't, Lenny? You didn't purchase it, did you? I mean not really. Not six and half grand for that puke green whatnot?"

"I'll get my money back, don't worry," explained Lenny. "All part of a plan. Worst case I'll bill it through to the client, which could be interesting since I purchased it *from* the client."

"Lenny, you're rambling again," Woody commented. He leaned forward in the chair. "So, how much was it worth? The whatnot?"

"$300."

"Oh, yeah! You owe me two beers, my man. Was I right or what?" Woody did a little victory dance, raising his fists, Rocky Balboa style, as if he had just run up the 72 steps to the entrance of the Philadelphia Museum of Art. "So, what's next on this plan of yours, Doc?"

"One beer, Woody. I only bet one." Lenny held up his index finger. "Next on the plan … checking the inventory records. I want to see what items are not moving."

"Why is that?"

Lenny sighed as he walked over to a filing cabinet. "I have a theory. If some items are not selling on a regular basis, it may be because those items are imitations."

Lenny gave part of the inventory list to Woody and instructed him to place a tick mark beside every item on the list which was purchased six months ago or earlier. Altogether, they found 412 items included in inventory that were at least six months old. Of those, 383 were purchased from Carson Denig.

"It looks like Dana's business is being flooded by phony stuff from this Denig character," observed Woody.

"It's starting to look that way," Lenny said. "Woody, the next thing we need to do is to find the invoices on these items and see if Dana signed for each of them," Lenny instructed.

Lenny pulled out the Denig Gems accounts payable file and began comparing the number on the invoice against the invoice number which was on the inventory list. When he found a match, he would hand it to Woody who would, in turn, examine the signature on each invoice and mark off the item on the inventory list. After about an hour and a half they had located and reviewed all 383 vendor invoices.

"Well, Woody, what did you find?" Lenny asked.

"The dame's name is on each one," responded Woody.

"Oh, I see," Lenny stammered. "On the surface this is not looking good for Dana, but I'm sure there's a simple explanation," Lenny countered. "Woody, I'm just curious, but tell me how were you able to check them so quickly? You were scanning faster than I could sort the invoices to you."

"I'll have to admit, Doc, at first it took a little while to find her signature on the invoice," Woody explained. "But then I found a shortcut."

"A shortcut?"

"Yeah, let me show you." Woody grabbed about ten invoices and held them up to the light. "You see, you can look through all the invoices and see that the signature matches on each one."

"Let me see that," Lenny said. "You're right. These signatures are almost identical."

"See what I mean?" retorted Woody.

"Yes, Woody, but that's what's making me skeptical." Lenny scrutinized the stack of invoices a second time. "They are *too* similar. They look like they are traced." Lenny ran his fingertips over the signature on each page. "Here, feels this," Lenny said as he handed one of the invoices back to Woody. "Put your finger on the signature line and then run it over the writing on the rest of the page."

Woody did as instructed, waggling his head back and forth. "Yeah, I can tell a difference."

"That's got to be it, then!" Lenny said. "Frank has been forging Dana's name on these things. Here's the tip off. Did you know that forensic research shows that liars press harder when they write a lie?"

"Wait a second!" Woody said, as he signaled time out. "Doc, I may be wacky, but I'm thinking Frank forged your handwriting on that dude's case papers. He doesn't like you."

Lenny looked thoughtfully at Woody. "Hmm. I like it. That would explain everything. But let's make sure, first."

"How are you going to do that?" asked Woody.

"It shouldn't be difficult. We've just got to find something else with Dana's signature on it besides these invoices. Let's look around. There's got to be something here in the office." Lenny began opening the drawers in Dana's desk to find some type of document with her signature.

"Here's something," Woody said, as he pulled some papers from underneath the desk blotter.

"Let's see," Lenny said, taking the papers from Woody and comparing the signatures to those on the invoices. "No, these are the same," muttered Lenny as he handed the papers back to Woody. "Wait ... I just thought of something. I have that letter from Dana that we picked up this morning with the keys." Lenny removed the envelope and letter from his briefcase where he had placed them earlier. He compared the signatures, the one from Dana's instructions for the keys with that of one of the invoices. He seemed relieved. He turned to Woody and said, "Just as I hoped. These are not the same. The signatures are similar, but not identical. Frank Harrison must be forging Dana's signature on all types of company documents. No wonder she's in the dark about so many things."

"I don't mean to be too nosy, Doc," Woody wondered aloud, absorbed in his own search, "but what does a jade shop have to do with a helicopter and maintenance uniforms?"

"What are you talking about, Woody?" Lenny asked. "What's this with helicopters, uniforms, and a jewelry store? Now who's nutso?" he kidded.

"Those letters I gave you, so you could check the signatures, you remember, the ones from under the desk calendar thingie? Well, the second letter is about renting a helicopter," Woody explained. "I can't figure out what a chopper has to do with jade."

"Let me see them," Lenny insisted. He started to read the two letters, each on Jade & More letterhead.

> Mr. Cimi Kiengsiri
> 1087 Chaiyapoom Road
> Chiang Mai 50200, Thailand
>
> Dear Cimi:
>
> I thank you for the recent guided tour of the Myanmar border and setting up the meeting with the Shan tribe member nicknamed Jake. It was most helpful, and I will certainly have a need for your services in the future.
>
> During the first week of February, arrangements have been made for you to meet one of my associates, Carson Denig, and escort him to Mae Sai to meet Jake. On that trip to the Myanmar border, please deliver the enclosed letter to Jake.
>
> For your troubles, I am enclosing a US$100 bill. Thank you in advance. I shall be in Bangkok during the first week of February and plan to reach out to you then.
>
> Sincerely yours,
>
> Dana Scott, Jade & More
>
> DS: enclosure

Lenny was confused. There was nothing unusual about the first letter. It was innocuous enough—typical formal business correspondence. There weren't any references to helicopters or uniforms or jade. But the second letter was a shock.

Jake,

This letter confirms our prior agreement. Please proceed with the following:

1. Locate a medium or heavy-lift helicopter for use during the first week in February in Yangon. A Puma or Chinook is fine. But a CH-53, CH-54, Skycrane S-64, or Russian Mi-26 would be best. Ensure the aircraft is fueled and flight-ready.
2. Ascertain the diameter immediately below the Banana Bud. Determine what material this section is made of (i.e., iron, marble, etc.).
3. Acquire two maintenance uniforms.
4. Meet my associate, Carson Denig, on the Thai side of the Myanmar border during the first week of February. You know the spot.

Please confirm receipt of this letter. I shall be in Yangon during the same week at the Inya Lake Hotel before traveling to Naypyidaw for the annual gem fair.

Sincerely yours,

Dana Scott Jade & More

Lenny looked at Woody. "Tell me, Woody, where did you find these?" he asked as he held up the letters.

"Like I told you, I found the papers peeking out from underneath that large pad there on the desk."

"You mean under this thing?" Lenny asked as he lifted the blotter. There weren't any other loose papers under the giant desk pad but there were two objects he wouldn't have expected—a metal key and a sketch. The drawing he recognized immediately as the pagoda which he had seen while touring Yangon, Myanmar. He knew Dana was traveling in Myanmar this week from the note she had dropped off at his office along with the signed engagement letter, but Frank was in Arizona, right? That did not make any sense to Lenny. Something about this entire scenario was off. "Woody, what type of key do you think this is?" Lenny asked as he handed him the shiny brass key.

"It looks to me like one of those keys for a locker, like the type they have at the train or bus station or the airport."

Lenny looked at the key again. It had the number 289 imprinted on it. "There's only one way to find out, Woody. Let's go."

Of the three possible locker sites, the bus station was the closest to the jade shop. Lenny and Woody grabbed their coats and raced out of the office without a word to Janet, ignoring Phillip in the front of store altogether. The Philadelphia Greyhound Terminal on Filbert Street was a rather depressing place. It was well lit but was occupied by many street people and local drunks who sought refuge from the cold. Lenny walked over to the ticket agent.

"May I help you, sir?" the ticket agent inquired in a disinterested tone.

"Yes, could you tell me about your lockers," replied Lenny.

"Luggage lockers?" the agent asked without even looking up at Lenny.

"Yes, I was interested in whether you had a locker number 289."

"No. Next in line," the agent said as she ran the Emory board over her right pinkie.

"Wait a minute," Lenny said. "Are you saying, 'No locker number 289' or 'No, we don't have any luggage lockers available?'"

"No and no. Next in line." The clerk looked up to motion for the next customer to advance to the counter window.

"But you do have luggage lockers?" Lenny asked.

"No, not since the ATF raid right after 9/11. The Alcohol, Tobacco and Firearms guys found an abandoned suitcase in one of the lockers with enough explosives to level the building. If you ask me, I'm glad the lockers are gone because … because … a blast like that, and BOOM, there goes my job and then how'm I gonna pay the rent or get my hair done, or …" The clerk held up the back of her hands to flaunt her manicure. "… or get my nails done on a regularly basis because, you know, some religious fanatic terrorist decides he wants to go to a better place and take innocents with him. I like where I work, mister. I didn't cry when they ripped out the lockers."

Lenny wasn't sure what to say next. He and Woody were getting nowhere fast and he worried that if he said anything more it would trigger another round of rants from the laconic clerk. He wheeled around and motioned for Woody to join him. "We're going to the train station," he shouted to Woody.

"I'll bet you a beer that it's at the airport," Woody said, as Lenny approached.

"Why is that?"

"Whenever you look for something, it's always in the last place you look. Guaranteed."

"Woody, I'll take you up on your second beer bet of the day, double or nothing, only because we're practically at 30th Street Station, so it wouldn't make sense to bypass the train depot to go directly to the airport." Lenny smiled. "Besides, I agree with you on your look-last search strategy. Any time I look for a student's scantron in a stack, if I start at the top, it's near the bottom. If I start at the bottom, it's near the top. I call it Cramer's Principle. Never fails."

Located on Market Street between 28th and 30th Streets is the Philadelphia 30th Street train station, a magnificent structure and cultural landmark complete with sculptures, busts, and paintings. In addition to providing rail service to suburban Philadelphia, 30th Street Station is a stop for the Amtrak lines along the Northeast Corridor.

Lenny double-parked his car on the Market Street side of the station, left Woody to watch for parking enforcement officers, and walked into the busy train depot. He found the information window where an elderly man in his sixties directed Lenny to an area just beyond the sales/ticketing windows.

At the Amtrak Baggage Storage desk, a cheerful young lady in her twenties greeted Lenny. "May I help you, sir?" she asked.

"Yes, the gentleman at the information counter referred me here. I don't know if I'm in the right place or not. He said you provide temporary storage of luggage and personal items for train passengers."

"$3.00 per bag for 24-hour period. All baggage and /or personal items must be clearly marked with the traveler's name. You'll receive a claim ticket for each piece. To retrieve your luggage—"

Lenny held up the brass key, stamped 289. "Excuse me. I don't mean to interrupt, but I just wanted to know if this key is to any of your lockers," Lenny said.

The young lady took the key, examined it, and frowned. "I'm sorry, sir. As I was about to say luggage is stored in a secured baggage room. We don't use lockers. At least as long as I've been here, we haven't. Not self-service anyway or something that requires a key."

"And you've been here ...?"

"Two months," the clerk said. "I'm real steady. Haven't missed a day. Glad to have a job in this economy." The girl smiled and said, "Have you tried the bus station?"

Lenny took the mystery key from her and said, "Thank you for your trouble." He headed back to the car where Woody was waiting. "It looks like you won the bet, Woody. It's not at the train station."

"We better get going, Doc. A parking enforcement cop stopped about five minutes ago, and he said if we were still here when he returned, he would write a ticket."

There was an entrance ramp to the Schuylkill Expressway adjacent to 30th Street Station. Lenny turned onto it and headed to the airport. After a fifteen-minute drive, Lenny parked his car, and together he and Woody went into the airport. They walked over to the information desk where they asked to speak to someone concerning airport lockers. The locker expert was a middle-aged man wearing a white dress shirt and a black tie with a Transportation Security Administration name tag clipped onto his shirt.

"I understand you are interested in airport lockers," the TSA Baggage Screening officer said.

Lenny nodded and then Woody nodded. "Yes," they said, almost in unison.

"Would you mind coming with me." The TSA agent led them to a stuffy little office down in the Baggage Claim area, near the luggage carousel.

"Please sit," he said, as he motioned for Lenny and Woody to take a seat in the two side chairs, directly in front of his desk.

"May I ask what you were hoping to store in your locker? A bag perhaps?" Before Lenny or Woody could answer, the agent continued, "I notice you don't have any bags with you right now, so were you planning on renting the locker today and using it a later date?" He tapped on the keyboard of his desktop computer and swiveled his monitor around as if he were going to show them a locker availability calendar. The monitor's built-in web cam now pointed directly at Lenny. He heard a couple of simulated camera clicks and began to get nervous. Woody slid his foot over and nudged Lenny. The U.S. Department of Homeland Security logo screensaver disappeared, and a photo of Lenny appeared. The monitor flickered as face recognition software cycled through possible matches. Woody's picture then popped up next to Lenny's. The same search algorithm rapidly sequenced through a catalog of faces.

"Whoa. Whoa. Whoa." Lenny said. "There seems to be a colossal misunderstanding." He held up the mystery key. "We found this key and all we were trying to do was look for the locker which fits it. Nothing more. We are not terrorists. We are not trying to rent a locker to store a b—" Lenny stopped short. He had heard rumors about how unforgiving the TSA could be at the mention of the "b" word. He wasn't up for a body cavity search, and he suspected Woody wouldn't appreciate one either.

"You were saying…," the TSA agent said.

"So, there aren't any luggage lockers, right?"

The agent didn't say anything. The muscles on his face didn't move. He kept staring at the two of them.

Lenny gave a nervous laugh before continuing. "And because we inquired about lockers, and everyone is supposed to know that with heightened U.S. security post-9/11, major airports, such as Philadelphia International, no longer provide baggage storage, and because we look like two guys that would never hang out together, and because it's late and we look a little scruffy, you—"

"No match," the TSA representative said. "That could just mean you guys aren't in the system, but I'll cut you some slack, this time. Here," he said extending his hand. "Let me look at the key."

Lenny silently handed the key to him. He was afraid to say anything for fear of escalating the interrogation. When they had started on this little wild goose chase, he figured on some dead ends, but he had not figured on being 'sweated' because he was asking about bag storage.

"It's true, years ago we did have lockers, but as you so eloquently stated, for security reasons, we no longer do." The agent turned the key over, inspecting the side with the number. "289, hmmm" he said. "You know, back then, the keys were much smaller than this, maybe half the size." He handed the key back to Lenny.

Lenny slowly took the key, careful not to look overly stressed. His hands were shaking. No matter how hard he tried, he couldn't steady them. The unexpected adrenalin surge from the ordeal was too powerful.

"Relax. This little conversation we had today is SOP—Standard Operating Procedure. We're just trying to protect the country from those determined to destroy our freedom and way of life. Increased security is a burden we all share."

Recognizing that the airport was not the answer, Lenny and Woody quickly thanked the TSA agent and headed back to their car.

"Woody, that was intense," Lenny said.

"Brutal. I almost needed a diaper," Woody said. Lenny and Woody started laughing to relieve the stress, chuckling much longer and much louder than they usually did when Woody told one of his funny stories.

I-95 was practically deserted as they headed back to the city.

"You got any ideas, Woody? Where else in the city do you think there might be lockers of this type?"

"Maybe it's for one of those lockers in a health club," Woody suggested.

Lenny mulled the idea over in his mind for a moment. "Maybe not, Woody. Maybe it isn't for a locker at all. What made you think that it was for a locker in the first place?"

"It was just a feeling I had," Woody sighed.

"Let's go back to my office at Penn and take a better look at this key."

"Fine by me," replied Woody.

"There is, however, one good thing about this key not fitting a locker at the airport," stated Lenny casually.

"What's that?" Woody asked. "I can't think of anything good coming out of tonight."

"I won the bet," Lenny chuckled. "You owe me not one but two beers!"

"I remember … double or nothing," Woody said, joining in the laughter.

They had been on campus for a while before Lenny looked at his watch. It was now 11 p.m. Their efforts to re-examine the brass key and brainstorm the significance of the numbers 2, 8, and 9 stamped on metal were a bust. Woody did suggest the key could be for a storage cube at one of the many public self-storage units in the city or even a bowling locker, before fading off to sleep on the chair in Lenny's office. Woody had been snoring away peacefully for some time, before Lenny walked over to him and tapped him on the shoulder. "Woody, why don't you go home and call it a night?"

"Doc, what about you?" Woody asked between yawns.

"I'm going to leave soon. Don't worry about me."

"I still think you're crazy to be sticking your neck out for that Dana woman. She may be a head-turner, but if she's guilty, you're getting in way too deep."

"Woody, I appreciate your concern and for riding shotgun today on our wild goose chase, but I just don't think Dana is behind all this. Everything is *too* convenient. The signatures are too similar, and the letters you discovered were too easy to find. If she was trying to get away with something, I'm sure she would have been much cleverer in concealing it."

Woody walked over to the doorway, put on his coat, pulled his knit ski hat out of his pocket and placed it on his head. He looked at Lenny and said, "You may be right, but if she is being set up, wouldn't we have figured out what the key is for by now? No one's cleverer than you, 'ceptin' maybe me," Woody said with a straight face. "So, if us two very clever dudes have no clue what the key goes to after three failed attempts, my gut says the key is not a plant. It's Dana's key, all right." Woody knocked fists with Lenny and said, "I'll catch you later. You really need to get some sleep, yourself."

Lenny walked back to his desk and plopped onto his chair. The seat was still warm from Woody napping in it. Woody had been right about him needing sleep. They had been at this snipe hunt all day, and now his mind was thick, his thinking fuzzy, but he felt he couldn't stop now. Woody had brought up a good point. So far everything had been easy to follow to a certain extent. It was as if someone was leaving a perfect audit trail for him to follow, with the trail designed to lead directly to Dana. But, why did the trail stop now?

That didn't make sense... unless they had overlooked the obvious. And nothing was more obvious than a storage locker and they had followed that false lead to the current dead end. The logic was faultless. Key—lock—storage locker. But it was Woody's logic. Woody had been the one to suggest the bus, train, and plane stations. The only problem was that the trail hadn't been laid for Woody. This trail was for him and what was obvious to Woody wasn't necessarily obvious to someone with a forensics background. Forensic accountants are paper detectives. There had to be some paper trail for the key. Otherwise, the key wouldn't have been left on the desk for him to find. He couldn't help but snigger to himself as he contemplated the irony of it all—that the answer to the riddle was a simple key.

By now it was almost midnight. Lenny was frustrated enough with his lack of progress that he decided he needed to switch gears for a while and take a break from spinning his wheels. He turned his attention to his unopened mail. He retrieved from the corner of his desk, the little hand-held automatic letter opener that his wife Nola had given him as a stocking stuffer their last Christmas together. As he swiped the device over the tops of the envelopes, it generated a string-sized strip with each pass. The first envelope included an annual dues reminder for his CRFAC dues—his Certified Forensic Accountant certification. He was friends with Scott McHone, the owner of the American Board of Forensic Accounting.

The second envelope contained the familiar invitation to educators for a complimentary subscription to the *Wall Street Journal*, contingent on convincing at least ten students to sign up for the Journal-in-Education program. He liked the Journal, read it daily, but wasn't interested in requiring his students to subscribe just so he could get a freebie. The advertisement went into the shred pile. In the third envelope addressed to him, he was pleased to find a check made out to him for accounting services performed.

"That's it!" yelled Lenny in his office. He felt ridiculous for having missed it earlier. There is always a trail. Always! Basic Audit 101: For every check written there is an entry recorded in the check register that lists the check number, date, amount, payee, and a short description of what the check was for.

Lenny knew what to do. He put on his coat and grabbed his briefcase as he ran out the door. He hurried to his car, jumped in, and drove quickly to Jade & More. With so few people on the streets at that time of night, he was able to get to the shop in less than ten minutes.

Soon he was poring over Jade & More's three-checks-on-a page business checkbook, leafing through each side stub in the register in hopes of discovering what key number 289 was for. He skimmed the DATE row of the check stub, but his real focus was on the TO and FOR sections. The TO portion of the stub would tell him the name of the payee to whom the check was written; the FOR would indicate the purpose of the check. Like a lot of forensics work, reviewing the checkbook was tedious and time-consuming. But Lenny knew he was on to something.

About forty minutes through the audit slog he came up with a strong candidate. One week ago, there was a check made out to the Westin Hotel in Philadelphia. Key 289 could be a hotel room key. Lenny's excitement soon faded as he remembered that the newer Westin properties he had stayed in lately had all been built with keyless electronic locks and plastic smart cards for guests. That was the new norm for hotel security—individually encoded keys. His only hope lay in the fact that the Westin Philly had once been the Ritz Carlton Philadelphia, a luxury hotel from another era. Perhaps in the extensive 2007 remodel, Westin had kept the original Schlage mechanical locksets. It was worth a shot.

Lenny knew that most four- and five-star hotels, as a matter of policy to protect the privacy of their customers, do not divulge the name of a guest who has checked in or confirm the number of the room in which that person may be staying. To get the information he needed, he decided he would have to try a little social engineering. He dialed the hotel.

"Good evening, Westin Philadelphia," the hotel operator said. "This is Gina. How may I help you?"

"Yes, could you ring Dana Scott's room for me, please? I believe it's room 289."

"One moment, sir. I'll put you through." The line rang once and then went straight to background music.

Lenny hoped that by juxtaposing Dana's name with the key number and by asking to be connected to the room, he could confirm three things: that Dana was a registered guest, that she was in her room, and that the room number was, in fact, 289. But most of all he hoped the hotel operator would fall for his little confidence trick. Social engineering relied on people's trust and their instinct to follow social norms.

What Lenny had done was to create a believable pretext by acting with an air of authority and using an earnest tone on the phone. Such appeals to authority combined with knowledge of intimate details to which others would not be privy, pandered to human nature's reliance on class consciousness and social hierarchy. Lenny didn't use pre-texting often in his forensic investigations, but this time he felt justified. Circumstances warranted it. Hotel privacy policies were so overrated and tended to get in the way of legitimate needs.

Even major corporations had found social engineering through pre-texting a valuable tool. Before she stepped down as chairperson of Hewlett Packard, Patricia Dunn had hired a private investigator to use pre-texting to solicit telephone records of board members and journalists to find out who was leaking inside information. While Federal law did not prohibit fooling others to obtain private information, California law did. Dunn ended up apologizing to board members and shareholders alike for the HP spying scandal. Social engineering might get you what you want to know, but the technique had its downside.

It seemed like an eternity to Lenny before the operator came back on the line. "I'm sorry for the wait, sir," she said, "but our guest, Ms. Scott, left strict instructions not to be disturbed under any circumstances. Would you like to leave a message, instead?"

"No, thank you," replied Lenny. "You've been more helpful than you realize." Lenny locked up the Jade & More checkbook, immediately got his things together, and left the shop. The phone call to the hotel had confirmed one thing—Dana Scott was a registered guest. What he still didn't know was who and what was in Room 289. He was definitely going to find out.

The hotel was only a couple of minutes away by taxi. Lenny took a cab which circled Chestnut Park and dropped him off at the corner of 17th and Chestnut. He went directly to the elevator, ignoring the plush and elegant lobby. He pressed the button for the second floor, feeling embarrassed that he didn't just walk up the steps. Ordinarily, he could use the exercise, but he didn't want to draw unnecessary attention to himself this late at night.

For some reason he thought of the CPA joke, where do homeless accountants live? Of course, the answer was in a tax shelter. Students never laughed at the joke.

Room 289 was at the end of a long, poshly carpeted hallway. From the outside, it appeared that it might be a suite, rather than a standard guest room. He wasn't sure why Dana would need so much space. He wasn't even sure why Dana would have rented the room if she was in Myanmar as she he told him. There was only one way to find out. Ignoring the fact that it was well past midnight and that if he was wrong about this he would be apologizing to a very irritated guest who was a member of the elite 1% who could afford a corner suite in an expensive hotel, Lenny knocked on the door. There was no response. He knocked one more time, but again there was no response.

Lenny took the mysterious key out of his pocket and slowly placed it in the keyhole. It fit! He looked down the hall to make sure no one was coming, turned the key slowly, and then opened the door. The suite was huge. Inside there were two bedrooms and a large living room complete with wet bar. On the stone table in the living room, was a briefcase with Dana's name tag on it with a set of luggage on the floor beside it. The suite looked as if it had been unoccupied for a few days. Not a single item was out of place.

That was odd. Dana's things were here in Philadelphia when she was supposed to be at the Gem Emporium, half a world away.

Lenny wondered if Dana was really staying at the hotel or not. He called down to the front desk to try and find out.

"Front desk. May I help you?"

"Hello," Lenny said authoritatively. "Would you have housekeeping bring me some additional towels for Room 289? I just got back from my trip, and there are not enough towels in this room."

"I apologize for that sir. I'll have the towels brought up immediately. But, sir, are you sure you mean 289? I can see that is the number flashing on the front desk console but there must be some mistake. We—"

"There's no mistake. I returned earlier than expected and the sooner I get some towels the sooner I can get cleaned up," Lenny said sternly.

"Yes, sir. My apologies, sir. Housekeeping will have your towels in five minutes, sir."

Lenny walked around the suite. No clothes were hung in the closets. In the dresser drawers, there was nothing except a Gideon Bible and the Philadelphia area phone book. In the bathroom, there were no toiletries on the wash basin counter besides those provided for hotel guests. Whoever had checked in had never unpacked.

A knock on the door interrupted Lenny's silent investigations. He walked over and opened the door, where a young man in his late teens wearing a red uniform with brass buttons handed him four sets of towels.

"We're very sorry, sir, for the inconvenience, but we didn't expect you back until the end of next week."

"Well, I guess I surprised you by my early arrival," said Lenny as he gave the young man a ten-dollar tip.

"Thank you, sir," the housekeeping staff member said, bowing as he left.

Just as Lenny had suspected, no one had been in the room for a few days. The young man had confirmed it. He walked over to the luggage and opened it, but he found nothing but women's clothing, toiletries, and lingerie. Nothing suspicious there. Then he opened the briefcase. Inside, on top of a stack of files, was a one-way plane ticket to the Cayman Islands. The date on the e-ticket was for the day after Dana was to return from the Far East. He hadn't expected that. The Caymans were notorious as a haven for financial refugees seeking to hide assets and escape prosecution.

Lenny pushed the airline ticket aside and started to scan the file names on the tabs of the tops of the folders. The first two folders had background facts on the gem industry and travel tips for Thailand, Myanmar, and China. Typical stuff. But the third folder was different. The label on it read SHWEDAGON PAGODA. The contents made Lenny shudder. It was no mystery now what Dana was up to. Unless he could stop her, Dana was going to rob the pagoda of its beloved jewels.

Twelve

Despite its roller-coaster history, the Burmese people are convinced no lasting damage can befall the Shwedagon. Whenever the pagoda has been endangered, generosity has restored it to an even greater glory.

— "Insight Burma"

Lenny decided right then and there to go find her. Dana had been right. He usually did have trouble making decisions. It was an occupational hazard, his paralysis by analysis. He over-thought everything. Accountants did that. But not tonight. And not in this situation. He didn't need any more information. He had to go to Myanmar, and he had to try to convince Dana to abort her crazy plan.

He still couldn't believe she was truly involved with a scheme to rob a religious shrine. And if he did catch up with her, could he really stop her? She was so strong-willed. That's one of the things he liked about her. Of course, there was still a chance Frank was behind all this, setting Dana up to take the fall by leaving an incriminating trail of evidence that pointed to her.

Lenny's biggest problem now was time. Myanmar was a full travel day away and then there was the issue of visas. He didn't need one for the layover in Thailand, but he wouldn't be able to enter Myanmar without one. He could shorten the visa approval process by submitting the application directly to the Myanmar Embassy in Washington, DC, but that might still take a couple of days. That worked out to two, maybe, three days just to get approved to enter Myanmar. He wondered if he would be able to intercept Dana in time? He would have to act fast. He left the hotel in a rush for his university office.

Lenny looked at his watch. It was 6 a.m. by the time he got to campus. He had been up since six the previous morning, had spent the afternoon chasing down false leads on a mystery key that didn't seem to have any corresponding lock, and had worked all night examining canceled checks and the check register at Dana's office. He had spent the last few hours playing detective by breaking into Dana's hotel room at the Westin Philadelphia. Lenny caught a glimpse of himself in the small mirror he kept on the back of his office door. There was no doubt he had been awake all night. There were dark circles under his eyes. He was badly in need of a shave, and he looked ragged, with clothes wrinkled and hair unkempt.

Lenny called Oksana, the Ukrainian live-in housekeeper that had taken over the household chores after his wife passed away. He explained to her that he had to go to Myanmar via Thailand and that he would be gone for several days. "I know this is very sudden, Oksana. Please tell Rebecca when she gets home from school and tell her that I love her."

Next Lenny called the department coordinator and told her that he would be gone for several days. Since it was not unusual for him to spend the entire night working in his office when he was particularly interested in something he was working on, he kept a small suitcase at his university office packed with several shirts, two pairs of pants, and underwear. He added his black toiletry kit and his passport, closed, and locked his suitcase, turned out his office light, and locked his office door. He walked outside and caught a cab to the 30th Street Station.

Lenny took an Amtrak train to Washington, arriving at 1:15 p.m., feeling fortunate that he was able to get an hour of sleep on the way to Washington. He felt somewhat refreshed, but knew he was still close to running on empty. A cab ride took him to 2300 S Street NW. There he was very lucky. Even though it was past noon, the Myanmar Embassy promised to have his visa by tomorrow noon. The last time he applied for the visa it had taken 10 days.

To complete the new visa application, he had to attach evidence of his trip. He pulled out his iPad and booked a flight that shuttled up to New York and then flew to Bangkok through Hong Kong with a short hop to Yangon. Embassy personnel were kind enough to let Lenny e-print the screen of his tablet to provide proof of his itinerary. He was all set to fly out of Reagan National Airport, leaving at 1:25 p.m. tomorrow. He knew he was cutting it close, but if he picked up his approved visa from the Embassy before it closed for lunch at noon, he could make it to the airport and get through security in time.

Lenny couldn't do anymore in D.C., so he caught a train back to Philadelphia. That gave him some quality time to spend with Rebecca before he retired for the evening. Although he was completely exhausted, Lenny slept restlessly. He was worried. True, he had set his plan in motion, but he did not know what he was going to do once he got to Myanmar.

Lenny took Rebecca to her school on Tuesday morning and then took a shuttle flight to Reagan National. Lenny was waiting at the Myanmar Embassy at 11:10 a.m. As promised, Lenny received his visa before lunch, and then rushed back to Reagan National to catch the American Airlines' shuttle to JFK.

On the plane he read a story in *USA Today* entitled "Burma Hints at Freer Future." In the story, author Calum MacLeod wrote about Darko C., a guitarist of a local punk band Side Effect, popular in Yangon's Mr. Guitar Café. Darko said he was used to living with the occasional power outages that made rocking the Rangoon crowd a challenge, but at one time his band dare not sing about democracy heroine Aung San Suu Kyi. "Too dangerous. The censor board is vigilant," he had said. One bystander at the local nightclub confessed that "we don't expect our country will become fully democratic in the near future." Myanmar released 651 political prisoners in early 2012, hoping that the U.S. would lift their punitive sanctions. The Obama administration called the move a substantial step forward for democratic reform and eventually agreed to elevate diplomatic relations by 'exchanging ambassadors' with Myanmar in July 2012. Most U.S. sanctions were lifted on October 7, 2016, by Obama. But Europe and Canada slapped new sanctions on Myanmar in July 2018.

Lenny knew that all accountants had to be skeptical. As he told his students each semester, you must be a good detective to be a good accountant. Dana's beguiling charm aside, it was inexcusable that he had not followed his own advice. It had been unprofessional of him to accept her assertions at face value. He never did that with any of his other clients. He was trained to dig for the truth, to spot fraud and deception. As a forensic accountant, healthy skepticism was *de rigueur*. It reminded him of the book he was currently reading on his Nook e-Reader—*Liespotting* by Pamela Meyer. She claimed the average American can distinguish truth from falsehood only about 54 percent of the time—barely better than a blind guess. Chimpanzees have virtually the same success rate.

Lenny felt that he was better than a chimpanzee and that his professional experience counted for something. On average, Meyer had written, we encounter more than 200 lies per day. This tended to confirm what Lenny had previously read about students lying more than 50 percent of the time to their mothers. *To their own mothers.* He always wondered why university administrators allowed the students to provide input to the decisions to hire and fire professors through their end of the semester student evaluation questionnaires. Lenny had once asked his department chair for some "honesty dust" to toss around the classroom when he handed out those dysfunctional, internal control performance measures. That was what he needed now. He needed some honesty dust when he confronted Dana. Of course, all auditors could use this magical dust, but right now Lenny *really* need some.

After a 24-hour flight via Hong Kong, a sleepy and tired university professor landed in Bangkok. Lenny had been able to sleep only about two hours on the plane. He did watch the comedy Hangover 2, which takes place in Thailand, and two other movies. He fell asleep immediately in a comfortable chair in the Bangkok airport while waiting for his Thai flight to Yangon, and from there he would still have to make the 4-hour bus trek to Naypyidaw.

———————

"The next lot up for bid is number 546," the wizened old auctioneer shouted.

"Dana!"

Dana heard a familiar voice call her name at the same time she felt someone touch her on the elbow. She looked over her left shoulder and was startled. There was Lenny, standing just behind her in the Myanmar Gems Emporium auction hall, his hand resting on his suitcase. She could barely hear him over the din of the marketplace that was filled with international customers, mostly Chinese buyers. Westerners were very rare, considering U.S. sanctions resulting from the 2008 JADE act.

"What, uh, what are you doing here?" Dana asked.

"I need to talk to you now. Can we get away from this crowd?" Lenny asked quietly.

"Sure. I'm not really bidding on any of this jade, anyway. Lenny why are you here?"

"We'll talk outside."

Dana followed Lenny outside to some café tables away from the noise of the market. She noticed that his clothes were seriously wrinkled, and he looked quite tired.

Lenny parked his luggage next to one of the empty chairs and then sat down. He faced Dana with an angry, gunmetal stare. He didn't say anything right away and just kept staring into Dana's eyes.

Dana bent down and kissed Lenny on the cheek. "I am really glad to see you," she said. "Surprised … but glad." She sat down across from Lenny, giving him a quizzical look.

There was an uncomfortable silence for several seconds, before Lenny finally asked in a somber voice, "Dana, are you involved in a scheme to rob the jewels from the Shwedagon Pagoda?"

Dana looked stunned. "Are you kidding me? How would I do such a thing? *Why* would I do such a thing?"

In a soft voice, Lenny tried to explain. "While I was auditing your accounting records, I found copies of some letters underneath your desk blotter. You sent one letter to a person named Cimi. In the second, you arranged for a helicopter—"

Dana tenderly put her fingers on Lenny's lips. "Slow down, Lenny." She searched his eyes for a response. There wasn't one. "You're making this up, right? I don't know anything about helicopters. Why would I need a chopper? Are you writing a novel? Lenny, your imagination is starting to scare me."

"Look, Dana, I'm not making this up. Woody and I really did find the letters on your desk. And of all places on this planet you *are* here in Myanmar. It cannot be an accident that you are in this country during the same week mentioned in the letter. That's incredulously coincidental. I'm not that gullible," Lenny, exhaled loudly. "Dana, tell me this. How did you expect to get out of Burma? I mean Myanmar. The Burmese army would hunt you down, capturing you before you could cross over into Thailand."

"Read my lips, Lenny. I know nothing about such a crazy scheme. The best place to buy jade and rubies is here. Someone must have planted the letters on my desk to frame me. I'm not so dumb as to leave incriminating evidence lying around my office. Good heavens, Lenny, I don't even lock my drawers. Were the letters signed by me?"

"Yes, they were." Lenny observed Dana frown when she heard this. He thought about the tips Pamela Meyer had given in *Liespotting* for exposing liars by noticing facial cues but knew that a frown wasn't subtle enough. A frown could mean that Dana was uncomfortable with the disturbing news Lenny had given her or even his unexpected visit. "In fact," Lenny continued, "these letters are only a part of what's turned out to be a dangerous puzzle. Detective Calhoun thinks that you tried to kill me."

"Kill you? You merely got mugged."

"What about the room in the Westin Hotel?"

"Westin Hotel? What about the Westin Hotel, Lenny?"

"Now you're being coy. The room at the Westin Philadelphia with your three suitcases of clothes and a one-way ticket to the Caymans."

"I have no idea what you are talking about," insisted Dana. "An airline ticket to the Caymans? I'm sure I wouldn't forget about something like that." Dana's eyes started to glisten.

Lenny pulled a travel packet of tissues from his inside coat pocket and handed it to Dana. She pulled out a Kleenex and dabbed her eyes. Lenny reached over and gave her an unexpected hug. She had passed his test. The verbal grilling proved it. He was convinced that Dana was not behind any scheme to rob the Shwedagon Pagoda. He found Dana's mouth and kissed her fully. Dana did not resist.

"I missed you, Dana," he said, as he pulled away. "So much has happened since you left. It's been crazy-wild, starting with Chuck. Let me tell you the sad story. On Monday morning, a friend of mine, Dr. Charles Ross, was killed in my university office. Someone put a Russell's Viper in my desk, in the middle drawer, and Charles made the mistake of opening it. I found him dead in my office—the snake was still there, coiled, and ready to strike again. Dana, that snake was intended for me; Chuck was collateral damage."

"I'm sorry, Lenny," Dana said as she drew Lenny closer to her. "You said a Russell's Viper?" Dana asked. "I saw one up close during the Thailand trip, the one where I met you and Rebecca. It was so vicious, even in the cage. Those things will attack without any provocation. Frank was with me that day, too."

Suddenly, the color drained from her tanned cheeks. "Frank!" she screeched. "Frank Harrison knows how deadly the Russell's Viper is, and he would have the connections to obtain one. And Frank doesn't like you, Lenny."

Lenny just nodded. He then explained to Dana how he suspected that Frank was working with Carson Denig to steal from her. He mentioned the forged signatures he had found, the letters, the sketch of the Shwedagon Pagoda, and the plan to rob it. He finished with the mystery key and the discovery of the hotel room where he had found her briefcase, luggage, and the get-away plane ticket.

"The way I figure it," Lenny confided to Dana, "Frank must be framing you for the theft of the gems from the Shwedagon. I know he went to Tucson, but there is no guarantee that he's still there. I did speak to Janet before I left. She had no idea where Frank was staying in Tucson. When I called Frank's consulting firm, the office staff would not give me any information. For all we know, Frank left Tucson days ago and is already—"

Dana interrupted. "Lenny, when do you think the theft is going to occur?"

"My guess is tomorrow night." Lenny scratched his forehead. "The pieces are all starting to fall into place and make sense now. The letters Woody and I found in your office ... they indicated that you would meet Carson Denig on the Myanmar-Thailand border

this week. What if Frank isn't in this all by himself? Suppose Frank
and Carson Denig are working together on the heist. They know
you're here at the gem show scouting out stones. You have motive,
you have opportunity, and based on the letters, you have means to
pull off a covert operation to steal the jewels. You become their
scapegoat, conveniently distracting the authorities, making it easy
for them to disappear." Lenny paused a second before pounding
his fist into his hand. "Dana, this is serious. Myanmar prisons, especially the Insein compound in Yangon, are not part of the tourist
package. You'll never survive."

"Lenny, what should we do?" Dana looked worried.

"First, we probably should report what we know to the U.S. Embassy. Do you remember where it is? We were there on our last trip.
We met the Deputy Chief of Mission. What was her name? Elizabeth
or Elaine? Last name was Samson. Eleanor ... Samson. We'll talk
to her."

"The taxi driver should know where the embassy is." Dana pointed
to her left. The official taxi stand run by the military was vacant.
The government-owned taxis were newer Japanese models, but
with over 6,000 visitors to the gem show, the likelihood of finding
one was slim. A couple of rogue cabs lurked just across the street.
"This is not going to be any joy trip," she said. "Yangon is at least
four hours south. Most of the private taxis are illegal, and the cars
are around 30 years old, dirty and without air conditioning."

Dana and Lenny climbed into a Nissan truck after negotiating
the fare. The gray-haired Burmese driver had an angular face and
smoked a cheroot while changing gears and dodging packed buses,
old pickup trucks, and ancient, creaky autos. Along the
disintegrating sidewalks Lenny saw men wearing plaid sarongs,
punctuated every now and then by a blaze of saffron from the robes
of the many monks that wandered the streets.

By the time they reached Yangon they were drenched in sweat
from the humidity. The cab's open windows hadn't helped. Dust
swirled through the cab as it bounced over the road, the shocks
long since worn out. As they approached the city, Lenny was
saddened. He had forgotten how neglected and forlorn Yangon
looked. General Ne Win and his successor had managed to transform

one of the wealthiest nations in Southeast Asia into the most economically pathetic country in the region.

At one time Burma was the home of some of the early civilizations in Southeast Asia. But now the 26th largest country, with a population of 53 million, had one of the least developed economies in the world, and its health system was one of the worst with the average life span only 66 years. In comparison, the average life span in Japan is around 83.7, Thailand is 75, and the U.S. is 78.8.

The Nissan cab jerked to a stop just short of the barricades at 110 University Avenue in the Kamayut Township, in front of a rather austere looking, fortified multi-story complex that had replaced the crumbling, British colonial building that served as headquarters for U.S. diplomats until 2008. Lenny slipped the cabbie a $20 bill. Inside the U.S. Embassy they were confronted by an attractive receptionist and a military guard in full dress uniform, carrying an M-16 rifle—both Burmese. There was also a U.S. Marine guard stationed nearby.

"May we speak to Deputy Chief of Mission, Eleanor Samson?" Lenny asked rapidly.

With an exaggerated sigh, the receptionist turned and replied, "Do you have an appointment?"

"No, but it's extremely important that we talk to Ms. Samson at once. I'm Professor Leonard Cramer, and this is Ms. Dana Scott. We are both U.S. citizens. We have information about a potential major robbery here in Yangon."

"You probably should contact the police. Here, let me give you their address."

"But, Miss, this is a delicate, diplomatic matter. Is Ms. Samson in?" Lenny thrust his business card within inches of the receptionist's nose. His hands quivered. "Please give Eleanor my business card. Tell her it's urgent."

The receptionist said something in Burmese to the guard, took Lenny's card, and walked through a door on her left.

She came out shortly and said, "Ms. Samson is not here and the senior consular officer, Ambassador Thurston, is extremely busy right now. He has agreed to see you tomorrow at 10:30 a.m." The receptionist handed Lenny's card back to him.

Lenny didn't know what to say at this point. Dana was about to speak when in desperation Lenny exclaimed, "But by then it may be too late. Please tell Ambassador Thurston that we believe that an American citizen is going to storm the Shwedagon Pagoda tomorrow night by force and remove the jewels."

Without a word the petite lady snatched the business card back from Lenny, turned on her heels, and scampered into the Ambassador's executive office. Within 30 seconds a distinguished-looking man came striding out of the office, extended his right hand and said, "Dr. Cramer, I'm Brey Thurston. Please join me in my office."

Lenny shook the Ambassador's hand firmly and turned toward Dana. "Ambassador Thurston, this is Dana Scott. She is with me."

Thurston smiled at Dana and said, "Nice to meet you, Ms. Scott. Won't you come in also?" Dana and Lenny followed the newly confirmed ambassador to the Union of Burma into the modestly-decorated office, taking a seat on the modern but uncomfortable two-person couch that was part of the sitting area for informal chats and taking afternoon tea.

Lenny was the first to speak. "Mr. Thurston, it's a long story, but in a nutshell, we believe that a Carson Denig and Frank Harrison are planning an elaborate heist of the Shwedagon Pagoda jewels tomorrow night. Denig and Harrison are Americans."

"How?" Thurston asked incredulously. He quickly corrected himself, "I don't mean 'how are they Americans,' but 'how is that even possible'? The pagoda is well-guarded. The jewels are embedded in the structure itself."

"All we can tell you is that they have the help of a military-grade cargo helicopter."

"How do you know this?"

"Long story, short: A mugging, a Russell's Viper attack, an audit investigation, and some hidden letters," Lenny replied.

"Please explain, Professor Cramer. Give me the long story," Thurston said as he pushed the bridge of his glasses back into place.

Dana who had been quiet up to this point, interrupted, "I was the one who got Lenny into this mess. It's my fault he's here in Myanmar now."

"*Burma*," Thurston corrected Dana. "At a diplomatic level we have never endorsed the new country name forced on the Burmese people in 1989 by the National Unity Party, formerly the Burma Socialist Programme Party. I'm sorry for the interruption, Ms. Scott, but as the official representative of the United States of America—"

"Burma," Dana complied. "Anyway, as I was about to say, I own a jade shop in Philadelphia. While on tour in Thailand and Burma several months ago, I met Lenny and Rebecca, his daughter. We got to talking, and I asked Lenny, who is an accounting professor, to review my accounting records. The cash has been disappearing from my business. I wanted him to find out where it was going and stop the cash flow hemorrhage, or I'd have to close the doors to the shop."

Dana looked at Lenny and continued. "Since Lenny started auditing my company's accounting records, he has been mugged and almost killed by a Russell's Viper that was placed in his university office. Unfortunately, in fact, another faculty member who was in Lenny's office waiting for him for a meeting was bitten by the poisonous snake. Frank Harrison … he's my partner in Jade & More … well, apparently my partner has hatched a scheme to rob the Shwedagon Pagoda. Someone—maybe my partner or maybe another person, Carson Denig—placed some forged documents on my desk, which Lenny found during his investigation. We believe the letters were planted to try to frame me." Dana stopped and glanced over at Lenny.

Thurston looked up and asked, "Who is Carson Denig?"

Lenny held up his hand as if he were at a meeting, politely trying to ask permission to speak. "We really don't know," Lenny said. "I have tried to locate Carson Denig, with little success. Every time I called him, he wasn't available, and he has not returned the messages I left on his voicemail. I tracked down his home address, but I have been unable to reach him at his apartment.

"What I do know is that Carson Denig owns Denig Gems International which is one of Jade & More's precious gem and jade suppliers," Lenny continued. "But other than that, we don't know much. What we can say for certain is that Frank Harrison and Carson Denig have developed some type of accounting scam to defraud

Dana of her interest in the Jade & More partnership. We believe this attack on the Burmese religious shrine tomorrow night is all part of the same plot. I must have gotten too close to the truth in my investigation. Things have escalated. Dana's cash flow problems were just the tip of the iceberg. Ambassador Thurston, we need your help. What can we do?"

"This is a delicate matter," Thurston said. "There have been some anti-American activities in Rangoon over the past two weeks. The American School for U.S. expatriate children has been closed for safety reasons. We have advised Americans not to go outside at night. President Obama's visits in 2012 and 2014 may have encouraged a few clashes between ethnic rebels and the Myanmar army, forcing many villagers into refugee camps. The fighting is everywhere, especially in the mountainous northern areas that are rich in jade and timber. This attack would play right into the hands of these rebels."

Thurston stopped for a moment, lowering his voice. "You do know that the U.S. and many other countries still impose stiff sanctions against Burma. President Obama's personal visit with pro-democracy leader Aung San Suu Syi several years ago is seen as a minor thaw in U.S. and Burmese relations. While here, President Obama reiterated that Burmese leaders must end the violent campaigns against the eight ethnic minorities and break all military ties with North Korea. Professor Cramer and Ms. Scott, I hope both of you are staying someplace safe? The streets are dangerous for Americans. The renovated Strand Hotel is excellent. By chance, would you be staying there while in Yangon?"

"I was up in Naypyidaw for the Gems Emporium when Lenny paid me a surprise visit and convinced me to take a cab with him to the embassy," Dana said. "My things are still up there, but we'd be crazy to go back now. I was staying at the Inya Lake Hotel before I went to the capital and planned to spend a few nights on my return before flying out of Mingaladon. I'm sure we can get a room ... or two."

Thurston couldn't help noticing the look that passed between Dana and Lenny. "Inya Lake's even better," he said. "It's only a stone's throw from the embassy. Here's why I asked. I need to check with the State Department. Since we have some time, I would rather not contact the police yet." Thurston looked at his watch. "It's 2:30 p.m. now. Washington, D.C. is 11 hours behind us so it's only 3:00 in the morning in the States. I'll call you later tonight at the hotel or early in the morning." Thurston adjusted his glasses again, pushing them up on the bridge of his nose. "By the way, have you eaten at the floating Karaweik Restaurant on the eastern shore of the Royal Lakes? If you haven't, let me suggest that you go there for dinner. Very popular. When I learn anything, I'll contact you there or at your hotel."

"That would be great," Lenny said. "We appreciate you seeing us without an appointment. We know you are busy." Lenny suddenly felt tired and hungry. "I haven't had a good meal in two days—at least it seems that long. The thought of food is sounding good about now. Burmese cuisine would be a treat. Thank you for the suggestion. Just one more thing, Ambassador Thurston. Could we have your after-hours emergency telephone number, just in case? I'd ask for your mobile number, but I know cell service in Burma is iffy."

Thurston wrote his number on Embassy stationery and handed it to Lenny.

As Lenny and Dana were waiting for a taxi to take them to the hotel, Thurston sent two encrypted diplomatic cables. The first was addressed to the U.S. State Department in Washington, D.C.:

S: 162139X FEB 15 14:37:00
FM: U.S. AMBASSADOR THURSTON
TO: STATEDEPT WASHDC
CLASSIFICATION: SECRET//NOFORN
SUBJECT: REQUEST ADVICE—DIPLOMATIC IMPLICATIONS OF HEIST PLOT

Determine credibility of Dr. Lenny Cramer and Dana Scott, both from Philadelphia. Determine location of Carson Denig and Frank Harrison through passport control. Cramer and Scott reported a plot by Denig and Harrison to rob Shwedagon Pagoda by helicopter tomorrow night. Such an event would be a diplomatic disaster. Have all government agencies available report any suspicious helicopter flights. Please advise me of the proper actions to take.

A second embassy cablegram was sent to the U.S. ambassador in Bangkok, Thailand:

S: 162139Y FEB 15 14:43:00
FM: AMBASSADOR THURSTON
TO: U.S. EMBASSY BANKGOK, THAILAND
CLASSIFICATION: SECRET
SUBJECT: MILITARY INTERDICTION—SHWEDAGON PAGODA HEIST

Alert all military and political parties re potential plot by Americans Carson Denig and Frank Harrison to rob Shwedagon Pagoda in Yangon. Alert Thai Coast Guard re unscheduled helicopter flight from Thailand to Yangon area.

―――――――――――

At 14:46 hours a short text message originating from inside the U.S. Embassy in Myanmar, was sent to a satellite phone on the Thai-Burma border. "Accelerate project. Plot uncovered. Thailand notified, but Burmese authorities NOT alerted."

―――――――――――

Another aging Nissan cab took Lenny and Dana from the Inya Lakes Hotel to the Karaweik Restaurant. Even at dusk, the temperature was still about 79 degrees, and yet February was the most agreeable month to visit Myanmar.

Approaching the restaurant, Lenny first thought it looked like a large boat permanently moored on the Royal Lake. He could see the Shwedagon across the surface of the lake, along with the shimmering reflection of the pagoda in the water. As the cab moved closer to the restaurant, Lenny realized that the ornate concrete building formed a double bow depicting a water bird. Atop the gilded duck-shaped structure was a many-tiered pagoda.

Once inside, Dana remarked, "Lenny, look at the lacquer work on the walls. It's beautiful. And look how the artisans embellished it with a mosaic of marble, glass, and mother-of-pearl."

Lenny was too tired to share Dana's enthusiasm for the décor. The Burmese meal of rice, curry, and prawns was mediocre, more for tourists looking to get a taste of Yangon: quantity over quality.

Rather than traditional black Burmese tea with evaporated milk, they drank Chinese green tea. From their table, Lenny could see the towering Shwedagon through the dining hall window. Around 7:45 p.m. the floodlights on the pagoda came on, illuminating the rich yellows of the bejeweled *stupa*. After eating, Lenny and Dana walked along a porch near the restaurant and the lake.

"Look at the view of the golden dome on the Shwedagon. It's stunning," Dana said, as she moved a little closer to him. "Lenny, how do you think Frank is going to remove the jewels from the top of the *stupa* before security show up or the Burmese police arrive? It's 325 feet tall. That's taller than the Pennsylvania State Capitol in Philly," Dana said.

"I don't know. I wondered about that myself on my plane trip here. I believe the golden dome is made of concrete or steel so it's not going to go anywhere. Say, I got an idea. Why don't we go over there now and look a little closer? That might give us some clues. You mentioned security. I wonder who guards the shrine?"

Dana didn't know. She merely shrugged in response.

The only taxi they could find was another gypsy cab with an unlicensed hack driving an antique '77 Pontiac. The young driver, Padah, rambled on about the wonders of Myanmar, suggesting one tourist attraction after another. Both Dana and Lenny were silent during the bumpy and noisy ride to the southern stairway on Shwedagon Pagoda Road.

At the curbside entrance to the sacred landmark, Lenny gave Padah five dollars and then showed him a $50 bill.

"If you'll wait here for us to return, I'll give you the other half of this bill." Lenny tore it and handed half to the driver. "Do you understand?"

"How long I wait, sir?"

"Oh, about 30 to 40 minutes."

"No problem," replied the smiling brown-skinned cab driver as he pocketed the torn bill.

At the stairway Dana asked, "Do you remember the last time we were here? One of the students counted the steps up to the main platform. Do you remember the number?"

"Not really. It was 50 plus but felt more like 500. The stairs go straight up."

"One hundred and four, to be precise."

As they walked slowly up the stone stairway, they noticed that many of the stalls in the bazaar along both sides were closed or closing for the evening. Even the ever-present chanting of the monks and visiting pilgrims had subsided.

Dana pointed to two beams overhead. "Original Burmese teak beams," she said. "They are the only ones that survived the 1852 assault by the British during the Second Anglo-Burmese War."

About half-way up the steep stairs they crossed a concrete bridge. "At one time a protective moat crossed under this bridge," continued Dana.

At the top of the stairs were four guards. The human guard appeared to be asleep. The three other guards were mythological figures made of stone, the first, a pair of *chinthe* or leogryphs—half-lion and half-griffin—and the second a fierce green flesh-eating ogre.

The lone human guard jumped up. He pointed to his watch, then to Lenny and Dana's feet. He spoke rapidly in Burmese. Dana looked at her watch. "From what I think he is saying, we only have about 20 minutes. The pagoda closes at 10:00 p.m. and reopens again at 4:00 a.m. My guess is that any attack against the *stupa* will probably occur between midnight and 3:00 a.m.," Dana surmised. "Lenny, I'm just saying...."

She began to take off her shoes, and Lenny did the same. They walked on the inlaid marble slabs to the nearest of the eight sides of the gold-covered *stupa*. On each of the eight sides were eight smaller *stupa*s.

Dana and Lenny stood for a few minutes observing the main pagoda, and then began walking rapidly clockwise around the octagonal base. "Buddhists always walk clockwise around their monuments," Dana said. "It's religious custom."

"You've been studying your Fodor's Travel Guide," Lenny teased. "I'm impressed."

Dana pinched Lenny's side and then tickled him to get even.

They walked quickly around the fourteen-acre plaza encircling the dome, stopping briefly at the northwest corner to observe the

7 feet tall and 23-ton Maha Gandha Bell. Lenny remarked, "The British attempted to pilfer the cast bronze bell in 1825, but it fell to the bottom of the Yangon River when they were trying to get it to port. The resourceful Burmese were able to float the 6.6 feet diameter bell to the surface with bamboo poles."

Dana wasn't listening. She was thinking about what Lenny had said earlier in the day about ending up in a Yangon prison. She was worried. Suddenly she asked, "Suppose they try to get the gems tonight? We haven't heard from the Embassy yet."

"That's a possibility," he said. "Dana, why don't you let me take you back to the hotel, and I'll come back here and keep a lookout?"

"No, Lenny. You're *not* coming back by yourself. I'll stand guard with you. You're so tired you're likely to nod off and sleep through any action, if there is any."

"Dana, I can keep watch without dozing off. I don't think coming back with me is a good idea. Way too dangerous."

"Dangerous for whom? I have more at stake than you do. Remember, the letters have *my* signature on them, and who knows how many copies are floating around out there. Here's my plan. I'm going to leave you here, and I'll go back to the hotel and call Thurston. Cell phones are useless in Myanmar unless you buy a roaming SIM card, which I did not. Once I reach the Ambassador, I'll come back and join you for sentry duty." Dana gave a forced smile to indicate she was serious. "No arguments, Lenny," she said as she walked off.

On the ride back to the hotel, Dana asked Padah, "How do you get gasoline? I thought gasoline was effectively rationed because the official price of US$4.41 is so far below market that the queues at the gas pumps go on forever."

"They do, that, Miss," Padah agreed. He then laughed. "Only one thing runs smoothly in Myanmar—the black market. I can get gasoline on any side street for about US $6.50 per gallon. No shortage in the *zay*."

A Soviet-made Hind-A helicopter slowly rose at a 10-degree angle from the Mingaladon Airport to hover status. The olive-colored helicopter had two swatter missiles and 128 rockets in four pods. In the cramped quarters the former Burmese air-force pilot pushed the control stick between his legs forward, raised the collective pitch lever on his left further up, and gave more pedal to balance the increase in torque as he made the transition from hover to forward flight.

Through the protective glass of the military chopper, the khaki-uniformed pilot saw the floodlights on the golden dome suddenly black out as his aircraft reached balanced forward flight conditions. With many more moving parts, he knew the helicopter was much noisier than fixed-wing aircraft such as planes or ultralights. There were always trade-offs. For this mission agility was everything.

The pilot's flight pattern would take the aircraft just to the right of the *stupa*. The steady movement of the helicopter, lovingly nick-named the Krokodil by the Russians because of the fuselage shape and camouflage, gave him a detached feeling of power over the darkness and the danger ahead. He was glad the mission had been accelerated.

Lenny was sleeping in the back seat of the '77 Pontiac gypsy cab. Dana had offered to sit in the front passenger seat, so Lenny could stretch out. She dozed intermittently, waking to the constant snoring of the Burmese driver. At 12:40 p.m. Dana was startled when the floodlights on the golden dome went dark.

"Lenny, wake up," Dana whispered as she reached over the backseat and shook him.

Lenny opened his eyes slightly and groaned.

"The floodlights have gone out," she said

"What time is it?"

Dana switched on the rusted flashlight Padah had lent her and said, "Twenty to one."

Either the glare from the flashlight or the whispering awakened the driver. "What's up?" Padah blurted out.

"Do they normally turn off the floodlights at night, Padah?" Lenny asked.

"Nothing is certain in Myanmar, but the lights most often are left on," Padah replied. "The Shwedagon Paya is our number one visitor destination in Yangon. Our government will do everything in its power to keep it lit and the tourist dollars flowing."

Lenny was silent for a moment and then said, "I'm going to walk up to the platform and talk to the guard. Try to keep him awake now that the lights are off. Can you let me out, Padah?"

Padah opened his car door. The interior light didn't come on. He got out and opened the left rear door for Lenny since there were no inside door handles. Lenny pulled out his billfold, tore another $20 bill in half, and handed one piece to Padah. "Do not leave. You'll get the other half when I come back."

A big smile came to Padah's face. "I won't leave, Doctor! And I have lots of tape, if you wish to rip more bills." For Padah, tonight had been a gold mine. Dana had given him a carton of cigarettes for the trip back to the Inya Lake Hotel. At Yangon's Scott bazaar, a carton of cigarettes went for more than $41 at the official rate of exchange. Dana had promised to give the cabbie a bottle of Scotch when the night was over—worth at least $125 in the moribund economy. Most Burmese citizens subsist on an average annual income of US$4.20 per day, though official estimates were not considered reliable. Padha was on his way to clearing that in one evening.

Lenny went around the dirty Pontiac to get the flashlight from Dana, but she was already standing outside the front passenger seat with the car door closed. "I'm going with you." She had her binoculars.

Lenny knew it was useless to object, since she would come regardless of what he said. He took her hand and they both walked across Shwedagon Pagoda Road to the Southern Stairway. A nearly full moon lit the 104 steps ahead of them. All the shops were closed. The shrine was silent except for their footsteps on the surface of the stone staircase. The weak glow of the flashlight on the rough steps was eerie.

"Shhh-hh," Lenny said, as he put his hand on Dana's shoulder. They both stopped.

At first their labored breathing was the only thing they could hear. Then came the distinctive whapping sound of a helicopter far in the distance. There was a sour feeling in the bottom of Lenny's stomach. "Frank and Denig are going to hit tonight," he said. "Thurston should have taken this more seriously."

They both began walking faster up the wide, darkened stone walkway. The floodlights were still out. As the erratic whirring sound of the helicopter became louder and louder, they picked up their pace.

When they were about 20 steps from the top of the walkway the thump-thump-whoosh sound of the helicopter changed into a low stable whine. Somehow, both Dana and Lenny knew that the attack had begun. The helicopter was hovering somewhere near the Shwedagon Platform.

When Dana and Lenny reached the top of the walkway, the sound of the helicopter was deafening. To their surprise, there were no guards at the top of the walkway. They were all alone at the base of the shrine. Their fears had been justified. The pagoda would come under attack sooner rather than later.

The helicopter, running lights extinguished, was hovering above the towering *stupa*. Two ninja-like figures were dangling from rappelling ropes, working around the top of the darkened dome. Over the noise of the whirling blades, Lenny could hear another chilling sound. It sounded like a madman taking a chain saw to a slab of rock.

The dangling bodies were dressed in black, faces covered in inky paint, with lights on their safety helmets. They looked like West Virginian coal miners in the dark. Their faces were covered by low-profile gas masks.

Dana shouted over the noise into Lenny's ear, "Where are the guards or the police? There was at least one guard here this evening. We saw him, Lenny. He was here!"

Lenny shrugged. He had no idea where the guard was or what might have happened to him. He looked up again at the helicopter. He saw a third man open the utility hold in the helicopter and lower a net down. Without thinking Lenny went running down the main platform to the base of the pagoda. The down draft from the helicopter made it difficult for him to breathe. He began shouting, "Frank, we know that it's you. Don't do this!" The noise of the rotor wash was so loud that the three assailants, 325 feet overhead, would never have heard him, but the one stationed in the helicopter must have spotted Lenny running.

Once the net was in place, the man working the utility hatch of the chopper pointed an automatic rifle at Lenny and opened fire.

Lenny heard the bullets ricochet off a smaller *stupa* beside him. He ducked behind the nearest structures—a prayer pillar topped with a mythological *hinthe* bird and hanging bells. A fusillade of bullets struck the bells, producing a staccato-like ringing that echoed across the sacred grounds.

Lenny maintained his cover from behind the pillar. Unless he wanted to end up very dead, there was nothing he could do now. As he watched the fireworks above him, he began to see some monks moving silently from structure to structure, the rotor wash blowing their saffron-colored robes wildly. The shooter in the helicopter widened his range, firing sporadically at anything that moved.

Suddenly Dana darted behind one of the pillars, crouching behind Lenny. She shouted at him and handed him her field glasses. "Check out that lower figure there ... it looks like Frank."

At that moment the diamond bud at the very top of the pagoda crashed safely into the net. Lenny could see the cable supporting the net being retracted into the cargo bay of the helicopter. A second net was immediately lowered. The man that wasn't working the noisy saw repositioned himself, maneuvering into place to help the one doing the cutting. Together they successfully sliced off the second jewel-encrusted section of the towering dome—the flag-shaped vane (*nga myat na*) and the umbrella crown or *hti*. The dismembered portion of the treasure dropped silently into the net and was whisked up into the copter.

Lenny stood up behind the prayer pillar to get a better look through the binoculars. He looked intently at the two figures on the ropes and at the gunner in the cargo bay, but he was unable to positively identify any of the thieves.

About three minutes later, one of the Buddhist monks emerged from the shadows into the open walkway shaking both fists at the intruders desecrating the shrine. The man in the helicopter took aim and fired a barrage of hot lead. The protesting monk collapsed onto the marble floor, patches of his saffron robe slowly turning a dark red from his flowing blood.

The two robbers suspended above the dome didn't flinch but instead began to shoulder brace and push on the third section of the dome that had been weakened by the metal and concrete saw.

The Banana Bud fell into the net and was pulled up into the helicopter. The men dangling from the ropes, signaled to the crew above they were ready to be extracted and slowly twisted to observe the chaos below.

A Burmese soldier with an M-16 rifle snuck up behind Lenny and Dana. He motioned for them to take cover by moving deeper into the worship alcove of the prayer pillar. He stood up, aimed his rifle at the helicopter but before he could shoot, the darkened figure holding the machine used to cut the *stupa* into pieces, pointed his CO2 laser at the officer and a pin-like light split the darkness, severing the *hintha* bird topping the prayer column. The debris showered the soldier, as he ducked in fright.

As the two black-clad figures rode the retractable suspension cable up into the helicopter, the craft began moving toward the northeast. With the plundered cargo aboard, the helicopter was tail heavy, climbing slowly and unevenly at first, before it stabilized. The pilot expertly shifted from hover mode to forward flight as the craft soared toward the dark horizon. There was an occasional rifle shot from the ground as the whop, whop, whop of the helicopter blades became softer and softer. It was only minutes before Lenny and Dana could no longer hear the whirring clamor of the mechanical monster. The floodlights flickered back on.

The rape of the Shwedagon Pagoda was consummated—the golden spire had been forcefully denuded of most of its treasures. The towering golden dome was now flat on top.

Thirteen

Profit is only a pious name for legal plunder. Debt is like morphine. How do you suppose that millionaires get the property they possess if someone does not first lose it?
—J. A. Wayland

Burmese troops soon appeared en masse. A few primitive long-retired U.S. Air Force prop planes could be heard overhead, and mass confusion reigned. The old planes reminded Lenny of a Civil Air Patrol air show he had seen one year in Harrisburg, Pennsylvania. Padah, Dana, and Lenny were immediately taken into custody. Gunfire could be heard in the distance along with a thunderous explosion.

As the troops approached Dana and Lenny, Dana whispered to Lenny that they should keep quiet about the letters he had discovered in Philadelphia until they had had a chance to confer with Ambassador Thurston. Lenny agreed. Despite repeated questioning by military officials, the two of them refused to answer any questions during the interrogation that could possibly reveal foreknowledge of the attack on the Shwedagon Pagoda.

By now, Lenny was completely drained. He was beginning to feel the physical effects of lack of sleep, but the hard cot and the strong urine smell in the cell kept him awake ... or was it fright? He and Dana had been placed in separate jail cells after they were initially questioned, three hours earlier. Every now and then the guards would roust him, for additional questioning by military officials. He was beginning to imagine what would happen to him if, instead of being released, he and Dana were transferred to

Insein Prison. Just then Ambassador Thurston entered Lenny's bare cell.

"Am I glad to see you!" Lenny exclaimed.

"I can imagine," Thurston replied cordially. "Tell me," he said softly, as he bent his head down towards Lenny's, "have you said anything to these people about the things you confided in me in our previous conversation at the embassy?"

"Nothing," Lenny assured Ambassador Thurston. "Dana suggested that we not say a word until you arrived."

"Excellent," Thurston responded, his eyes widening. "Now I won't be too long, but when I return you just go along with whatever I say and hopefully you'll be out of here in no time. Do you understand?"

Lenny nodded in assent.

"Good," replied Thurston. "I shall not be long."

Thirty minutes later, two heavily armed guards appeared. They ordered Lenny to come with them. The guards took him to a much larger interrogation room than the one he and Dana had been in shortly after being arrested. He was relieved to see Thurston, Dana, and a man who appeared to be the commanding officer of the Myanmar military, considering all the medals he was wearing on his chest.

"Dr. Cramer," Thurston began, as Lenny was asked to sit down at the end of a long table next to Dana. "I have assured Senior General Than Kang that you are prepared to identify Frank Harrison as the man you saw at the pagoda, and that you are prepared to name him as the mastermind behind the entire operation."

Lenny really wasn't sure he had seen Frank during the attack on the pagoda, but he remembered what Thurston had told him about the importance of following his lead. "Yes, that is true," Lenny said as he cracked his fingers. "Frank Harrison ... the man at the pagoda ... mastermind," Lenny echoed limply.

He glanced over at Dana. He saw her let out a long sigh of relief at his answer.

Thurston turned to the Commander in Chief of the Myanmar Army. "With your permission, Senior General Kang, I will issue a national alert within the United States for the apprehension and capture of Frank Harrison. I will also notify Thai authorities about the possibility that Harrison may be in hiding in their country, so that they can alert their border patrols and customs agents. You have my promise to facilitate extradition to Myanmar once Harrison is in custody."

The general nodded in agreement.

"General, sir, unless you have any further reasons for detaining Ms. Scott and Dr. Cramer, I will escort them back to the Embassy," Thurston added.

"Release the suspects," General Kang ordered. The guards immediately removed the wrist restraints binding Lenny and Dana.

Thurston shook hands with the Senior General and motioned to Dana and Lenny to stand up. One of the guards returned Dana's and Lenny's personal effects, including their passports. The two of them left the military compound with Thurston, climbed into a waiting air-conditioned black Chevrolet diplomatic limousine, and headed to the Embassy.

"Luckily, there is a flight leaving Myanmar in ninety minutes," Thurston said sternly. "I have arranged for the two of you to be on the plane. I will have a member of my staff get your personal belongings and send them off next week. The important thing, for now, is for you two to get out of the country as soon as possible."

Lenny turned and looked at Dana, but she was just staring out the window. He turned back to Thurston and said, "Ambassador Thurston, I feel compelled to tell you that I am not totally sure it was Frank Harrison that I saw at the pagoda."

"Of course, you are sure," Dana interrupted. "Don't you remember my pointing him out to you?"

"I never got a real good look at him, Dana. It was dark, there was constant commotion, and the two men on the ropes were wearing gas masks and miners' safety helmets. The binoculars I was using didn't help."

"This confusion is precisely why you two must leave here immediately," said Thurston forcefully. "I don't want either of you to say another word about this entire incident until you are safely on American soil."

The trio continued to the Embassy and then to the airport in virtual silence. The return flight from Yangon to the States was uneventful. Once they got past the Myanmar to Guangzhou leg of the trip, Lenny slept most of the way from China to L.A. Dana was reserved, keeping to herself.

When the plane landed in Los Angeles, Dana told Lenny that she had some relatives she was going to visit in the Long Beach port area, and that she would see Lenny in Philadelphia in a couple of days. Lenny thought it was an unusual time for someone to visit relatives, but he was too tired and nervous to complain. He returned to Philadelphia early in the evening and went directly home to get a good night's sleep.

When Lenny awoke the next day, he just had enough time to say hello to Rebecca before she scooted off to school. He felt guilty that he had not spent more time with her lately and made a mental pledge to rectify the situation. He jumped out of bed, shaved, showered, and readied himself for what was likely to be another long couple of days.

After arriving at Wharton, Lenny called his dean to make an appointment, so he could hopefully straighten out the plagiarism charges with the help of the new information he had about Frank Harrison being a confirmed forger. Lenny then tracked down Woody and related to him the facts of what had taken place while he was in Myanmar. Woody was uncustomary speechless and just shook his head in disbelief.

Lenny checked his calendar to confirm that he had a luncheon to attend in Cherry Hill, New Jersey, the next day. He really did not want to go, but it was sponsored by a group of CPAs in southern New Jersey, and the luncheon was a good opportunity for him to pick up some consulting work. With all that had happened, business had been slow lately, and he could use the supplemental income.

Woody stopped by the office later in the day to see if Lenny wanted to collect on his winning beer bet after work. Lenny laughed and told Woody he'd take a rain check … that there were some loose ends he needed to tie up first before he could cash in on the celebratory brew he was due. About an hour later his office phone rang.

"Doc, this is Woody. I thought you would want to know that the FBI arrested that Frank Harrison guy today. I saw it on a news crawler on the bottom of the screen in the break room. There was also coverage on all the 24-hour cable news stations."

"Where'd they pick him up?"

"At the Philly airport. He had just got off a plane from Arizona."

"Arizona was just his alibi, Woody. A front. He *did* go to Arizona, but as soon as he got there he flew to Thailand and from Thailand crossed the border illegally into Myanmar as part of the assault team. I'm relieved they caught him," Lenny exhaled deeply. "As the sole eye witness, now I feel a little safer. At least I can sleep a little sounder with Frank off the street."

"Oddly, the news anchor didn't say what Harrison was arrested for, Doc. In fact, I've been checking the newspapers on the Internet since you filled me in this morning, and none of them even mention the robbing of the pagoda."

"I'm not surprised, Lenny. Both governments are trying to keep it as quiet as possible because of the potential for political turmoil. If the Burmese people were to find out that U.S. citizens were involved in the destruction of their holy site, it could cause an anti-American backlash in Myanmar and a possible terrorist retaliation here in the states."

Lenny chatted with Woody a little longer, before getting back to the stack of term papers he had to grade. Soon he took off for home to spend a quiet evening with Rebecca.

Although Cherry Hill is officially in New Jersey, it is within thirty minutes of downtown Philadelphia and is a suburb of the City of Brotherly Love. Cherry Hill is a township of around 70,000 people with many large single-family homes in clean, well-kept residential neighborhoods. The towns in Camden County are home to several fine restaurants, the 600-acre Garden State Park, and many high-tech service industries which serve mostly suburban clients. Lenny found Cherry Hill quaint and peaceful, but he preferred a bustling city life to the boring predictability of the suburbs.

As a former president of the American Accounting Association, Lenny was seated at the head table of the monthly meeting of the Southwest Jersey chapter of the New Jersey Society of CPAs. He had been asked to present a certificate of lifetime achievement to Charles T. Wengston for his work in establishing a drug and alcohol rehabilitation program for accountants. He was about to unfold his napkin to place it on his lap when a short, blond-haired man of slight build sat down beside him. Lenny refolded the napkin, set in on the table next to the luncheon place setting, and extended his hand to the man. "Hello, I'm Lenny Cramer. Glad you could join me. It was starting to get lonely up here." Lenny looked up and down the head table to indicate he was the only one who had taken his place so far.

"Pleased to meet you. My name is Charles Wengston."

"Charles *T.* Wengston. Yes, I read your bio last night. I must congratulate you on your work on alcohol and drug abuse. Your story's intriguing. What got you interested in it?"

Charles smiled "That's very kind of you, Lenny, but most the credit goes to the foundation volunteers. They're the real heroes … the ones turning the tide on substance abuse. But to answer your question, my interest in alcoholism really began back when I was an undergraduate at Pfeiffer University and a friend of mine was killed when he was binge drinking and drove his roadster into a tree."

Lenny's ears perked up when Charles mentioned Pfeiffer. "So, you went to Pfeiffer University," Lenny reaffirmed. "A friend of mine went there too. She is about the same age as you, but I doubt you would know her. She was in an entirely different field."

"Who might she be?" Charles asked. "It's a small liberal arts university in Misenheimer, North Carolina. Chances are I may have known her or heard of her."

"Dana Scott."

"Oh, sure, I remember Dana. She was the top accounting student my senior year. She was captain of the tennis team and had an accounting assistantship. We called her 'The Legend.' I remember how she scored in the high nineties on an Advanced Accounting exam while the next highest grade in the class was in the seventies. I haven't seen her in years. What accounting firm is she working with now?"

Lenny was stunned. "Are we talking about the same Dana Scott? About 35 years old. Attractive. Well built."

"That's the one. Like myself, she was from New Jersey. We had quite a large contingent from New Jersey there at Pfeiffer. We were known as the Garden State Go-getters. I know ... kind of corny ... but what can you expect from a bunch of overachievers?"

"She was an accounting student?" asked Lenny in disbelief.

"The best in the school," replied Charles.

"Will you excuse me, please?" Lenny asked as he stood up and headed for the door. He couldn't believe how sly Dana had been. She had been lying to him from the beginning, claiming not to know her debits from her credits, or the difference between an asset and liability. He thought back to his mugging, the Russell's Viper, and P.P.D. Detective Calhoun's repeated warnings to be wary of Dana. A chill went down his spine as he walked to the men's room.

Lenny decided to go back to his faculty office after the presentation. On the drive from Cherry Hill, he had this nagging feeling that he had been snookered like an amateur. It wasn't Dana that had been set up after all—it was him. He was the target of the fraud. He gathered together the two papers he had that contained what he knew to be Dana's signature and those documents he assumed Frank had counterfeited by forging Dana's signature. He also located the three MBA cases that supposedly had been prepared by Robert Hawkins. He telephoned Detective Calhoun to share his newfound suspicions of Dana and to give him a quick synopsis of the ransacking of the Shwedagon shrine.

"Lenny, you get those documents to me right away," Calhoun said forcefully. "We'll run some handwriting tests on those signatures and analyze them immediately."

Lenny didn't waste any time, arriving at the police station thirty minutes later. He handed over the documents to Calhoun who told him that it would probably take anywhere from two to five hours to process them. Lenny decided to camp out in the squad room and wait for the results. In the meantime, he reported to Calhoun in detail what had happened during the pillaging of the pagoda.

"Lenny before you got here, I checked with a friend of mine at the FBI," Calhoun said. "He told me that, as of right now, the only evidence they have against Frank Harrison are the two witness statements given by you and Dana Scott to Ambassador Thurston that you saw Harrison at the pagoda on the night of the assault. Frank says he has a solid alibi. He claims he was in Arizona during the entire incident."

"Detective Calhoun, I have to confess that I can't say for sure that I ever saw Frank Harrison during the raid. Dana said she thought she saw him, but I never got a clear view of him. Just before I met with Superior General Kang for the formal interrogation, Ambassador Thurston pulled me aside and told me to go along with what he said for Dana and me to be released as soon as possible."

"That's a worry, Lenny. You're one of two eye witnesses that put Frank at the scene. Maybe the FBI can shed some light. When I talked to my *fibbie* friend, he told me that as part of their investigation, they want access to the documents you brought in today. In fact, I wouldn't be surprised if they are probably trying to contact you now," added Calhoun.

Just then Calhoun's desk phone rang. The forgery analysis of the signatures was complete. The expedited review had taken only two and a half hours. Calhoun went to get the results and told Lenny to stay put.

Lenny didn't have plans to go anywhere until he had some answers. Ordinarily, he would have found a police station fascinating. People of all occupations coming and going constantly. Computer terminals with access to criminal databases all over the world sitting on most of the desks within his line of vision. But Lenny was not in the mood for mindful observation, instead, he kept thinking about the signatures. What if what he believed were Dana's autographs were, in fact, bogus and what he thought were Frank's forgeries were really Dana's handwriting. He wasn't sure what was real anymore. Had Dana made a fool of him? And if so, did that mean he had fallen for a con artist and thief? Was he guilty of unintentionally helping her destroy the Shwedagon Pagoda?

Calhoun walked briskly back into the room holding the documents that Lenny had brought him earlier. He sat down next to Lenny and showed him the letter that Dana had written to him before she left for Thailand—the one in which she had enclosed the keys to the office.

"This document we know contains Dana Scott's genuine signature," said Calhoun. He then pulled out a P.O. for goods that Jade & More had purchased from Denig Gems. "Now this purchase order to Carson Denig contains a signature that is very similar, but just slightly different from the one on the letter to you. Whoever signed the P.O. applied more pressure as they wrote on the paper, which can be detected by the thickness of the strokes. Here, you can see it easier in this enlarged copy of the two signatures."

Lenny looked at the magnified versions of the writing. The differences were clear. Lenny felt relieved. "I knew that she couldn't be involved. Why did I even suspect her?"

"Wait a second," cautioned Calhoun. "Let me show you this third letter—the one to the Shan tribe member requesting assistance in securing a helicopter. While the signatures, again are not identical, I think you can see that when they are magnified, the signature on the third letter is much closer to the first letter that Dana wrote to you, Dr. Cramer, than to the signature on the purchase order to Carson Denig."

Lenny examined the digital enlargements of the signatures. Clearly, the signature on the letter requesting a helicopter was the same as the one on the letter to him. He looked at Calhoun with resignation. "Oh wow, I feel so stupid. I guess this means that Dana was involved."

"I truly am sorry, Dr. Cramer," Calhoun said. "I know this must be difficult for you. Dana is an attractive woman, and I know you had more than a client relationship going with her. Regretfully, I have one more piece of evidence I need to share with you. During the analysis of the documents you provided, we were able to lift several sets of fingerprints. We found your fingerprints and one other set on all three documents. We feel fairly certain that the other prints belong to Dana Scott."

Lenny looked around the station awkwardly. He regretted not listening to Calhoun earlier or paying heed to Woody's warnings. He looked back at Calhoun and asked, "What happens now?"

"Before I came back here from the lab to show you the evidence, I issued an APB for Dana Scott's arrest. We hope to pick her up shortly."

Lenny chuckled weakly, "I guess that an APB in your profession does not stand for Accounting Principles Board, as it does in my profession."

Calhoun smiled. "Not quite. It stands for All Points Bulletin. Depending on which jurisdiction you're in, you may also hear the newer acronym BOLO which stands for Be On The Look-out." He paused briefly and then continued, "Dr. Cramer, I will let you know of anything that develops from our attempt to locate Ms. Scott. For now, you should go home. Once we arrest her, we will probably ask you back to make a statement. Don't go far. Oh, and one more thing. As for helping you with your plagiarism charge, I wish I had some news for you, but we cannot tell from the photocopy of Mr. Hawkins's cases whether it's your handwriting or not. But my people will continue to work on it."

Lenny shook hands with Calhoun and headed out into the cold February air. Somehow, Lenny noticed neither the cold air nor the fine sleet which started to fall. His mind was completely numb.

———————

"I won't be long, Rebecca. You just wait here in the lobby for me."

"I'll just play online Scrabble against McKinna on my phone," Rebecca answered. "Dad, I know you've already said 'no,' but can't I go in?"

"No, I want you to just wait here, and then we'll go out to dinner," promised Lenny.

Lenny walked to the visitation area of the minimum-security facility where Dana was being held until her trial. It was three weeks to the day since her arrest. As Calhoun had suspected, it was confirmed that her fingerprints were on all three documents Lenny had provided to the police. She had plea-bargained to get a reduced sentence in exchange for testifying against Carson Denig. Lenny really wasn't sure he wanted to see Dana, but he had so many unanswered questions and he needed closure.

The prison guard brought Dana to the visiting area. She looked tired and pale to Lenny. She smiled weakly as she sat across the table from him. The guard waited off to the side at a point where Dana and Lenny could easily be observed.

"Hello, Lenny. You look good."

"Hi, Dana." Lenny searched her eyes. Neither spoke for the next few seconds.

"How is Rebecca doing?" she finally said.

"Rebecca is fine. Thanks for asking." There was another awkward silence. Lenny decided it was time to pursue his main purpose for being there. "Thank you for agreeing to talk to me."

"I feel I owe you an explanation," Dana said softly. "It all snowballed so quickly."

"Dana, why did you do it? Why did you get involved in this?"

Dana sighed loudly before responding. "It all started when I stumbled across the scam that Frank Harrison and Carson Denig were pulling on me. A couple of months before I met you, I found the purchase order where Frank forged my signature and saw that he and Carson Denig were stealing money from me by arranging, without my knowledge, for Jade & More to buy inferior merchandise from Carson Denig at top-of-the-line prices. I then confronted Carson Denig with my findings. I wanted to know if Frank was in this rip-off all by himself, or if he was colluding with Denig."

"What did Denig do?"

"He laughed and then he told me about this elaborate plan he had to steal the treasures from the Shwedagon Pagoda—not just the 76-carat apex diamond at the tip of the *stupa*, but everything, all the studded gems in the gilded pagoda ... all 5,451 diamonds, all 1,383 rubies, all the sapphires, all the topaz—all of it! Millions of dollars in gems. I guess I let greed get the best of me. The plan was, with Carson Denig's help, to let Frank continue to think that he was stealing money from me by bilking Jade & More. Then, as payback, we were going to pin the blame for the pagoda heist on Frank."

"So, Frank wasn't involved with the pagoda robbery at all?" queried Lenny.

"No."

"Wow, Dana! I know Frank is no angel, but you and Denig are shameless," Lenny said in disgust. "I'm sure by now you've probably heard that your plan didn't work out after all because the helicopter carrying the top of the pagoda crashed."

Dana winced.

Lenny's indignation wasn't helping him get to all the answers he was looking for, so he decided to back off. He wanted to move on to other things that he was more interested in, but he wasn't sure how to approach the subject. He decided to be direct. "Dana, I need to ask you about the mugging and the snake."

"I was wondering when you were going to get to that. You must believe me, Lenny, when I tell you this. I had nothing to do with either one. Frank was responsible for the mugging. He told Carson that you were getting close to uncovering his inventory fraud. To appease Frank, Carson had one of his henchmen ambush you on the way to your meeting with Denig at the hotel. Frank wanted to send you a message to discourage you from digging too deeply into Jade & More's accounting records. I'm being honest with you, Lenny. I didn't know anything about it until after it occurred."

"And the snake?"

"I swear to you, I was in Thailand when that happened. I knew nothing about it. Lenny, that was all Carson's idea. He was concerned that you might interrupt the pagoda operation. He knew that you were resourceful and not afraid to blow the whistle. He didn't want to take any more chances. Carson gave me his word he would not do anything to you personally, that he had other ways to ensure you would not disrupt our plan, but after I left for Myanmar, he must have figured I wouldn't be able to stop him."

"You knew that I was framed for plagiarism, didn't you? In fact, you knew early on."

Dana glanced at the guard and then turned back to face Lenny. She ran her hand through her hair, grabbed a clump, and twisted the lock into knots. "Yes, I did Lenny," she said. "Carson told me before I went to Thailand for the Bangkok Gem Congress what Frank had done to you. I'm really sorry. I hope you will be reinstated. I knew the ordeal was causing you financial difficulties, but I thought that a suspension was better than the physical harm Frank originally had in mind."

"Oh, so you were looking out for me," Lenny said sarcastically. "Thanks for conspiring with Frank to serve up the lesser of two evils." He made a mental note to begin the process of filing a lawsuit against Frank for character defamation when things settled. "There's one other thing I am curious about, Dana—why me? Why did you need me to be involved?"

"In order to place suspicion on Frank, we needed an outside party to discover that Frank was a scoundrel. We needed a professional, someone with a trusted reputation who could determine that Frank was stealing money from me. An accountant was the obvious choice. Neither Carson nor I ever expected you to find the documents and the key hidden under my desk mat before I could retrieve them and escape to the Caymans. We figured that the police would find the planted clues. With your forensic assistance, the police should have had enough evidence to arrest Frank."

"It almost happened that way—Frank taking the fall. But I wonder, wouldn't the inventory paperwork have placed some suspicion on Carson Denig?" Lenny inquired.

"Think about it, Lenny. What do the invoices from Denig Gems really show? That he sold phony jade carvings at inflated prices to a willing customer. At worst he would be accused of merchandise fraud, but that would only happen if I pressed charges. The purchase order/ inventory trail leads nowhere. If Carson had stuck with the plan, Frank wouldn't ever be able to siphon the profits out of my business again, and my cash flow problems would be over permanently. I should be sitting on the beaches in the Caymans right now. But Carson screwed up. After the snake killed your colleague and the attack on the pagoda left at least one Burmese monk dead, the authorities want Carson for much more than passing off imitation jade."

"Where is he?"

"I really don't know," Dana answered.

You don't know, or you don't want to know, Lenny almost said but it was time to leave. His curiosity was satisfied. He stood up and looked at Dana. "I appreciate you leveling with me. I know you didn't have to say anything. Things must be rather difficult for you now."

"Lenny," Dana said softly as her eyes began to moisten. "I want you to know one thing. I never deceived you about my feelings for you. That was real. I hope that someday you will find it in your heart to forgive me."

Lenny thought about the mugging, the loss of a valued colleague, the time wasted traipsing all over the city during the investigation, and the trek all the way to Myanmar and back. He thought about the attack on the pagoda, the bullets smashing into the prayer pillar, and his fear of being jailed in a Burmese prison. He thought about Dana's betrayal. All these thoughts ran through his head and he responded unemotionally, "Good-bye, Dana, I'm just glad you didn't get me killed."

Sad but relieved, Lenny walked out of the visiting area. Rebecca was happy to see him but could tell he was miserable. "Dad, I have an idea."

"What's that?"

"Why don't we plan on taking a trip overseas in the spring? Maybe to Southeast Asia."

Lenny turned to his daughter and could see from the smile on her face that she was joking. That was all it took for both to burst into laughter. Lenny put his arm around Rebecca and squeezed her as they walked outside.

When Lenny got back to the house after visiting Dana in jail, for some reason he felt he should try one last time to reach Denig. He dialed Carson Denig's number. No one was there. After listening to the familiar voicemail greeting, Lenny left a brief message with his name and phone number, and asked Carson to call him. He was not optimistic; Carson had never returned his calls before.

The next day Lenny's dean called him and announced, "Good news, Lenny. Robert Hawkins is dropping his charge of plagiarism against you. Your suspension is lifted; you are officially reinstated in the School of Business. Before you go, Lenny, let me offer you some advice: Please be more careful in the future. Do not give back student papers."

Three days later an anonymous envelope addressed to Professor Lenny Cramer arrived at Lenny's university office. Inside was a clipping from a Bangkok newspaper:

> On Friday, government and religious officials cele-
> brated the return and refitting of three of the stolen
> sections back onto the Shwedagon Pagoda. More than

200,000 people watched and cheered as the military helicopters and workers repaired the damage done by three foreigners to this sacred shrine.

A government official said that the all three of the sections that had been stolen from the pagoda were found in Northern Myanmar undamaged. The many diamonds, rubies and other precious stones were still intact, including the 76-carat apex diamond. Apparently, the helicopter involved in the pagoda attack crashed in the jungles of Myanmar, after lowering the stolen pieces of the shrine into a deep ravine.

The official indicated that three badly burned bodies were found in the helicopter wreckage. One body was believed to be that of Carson Denig, an American ruby dealer affiliated with Denright, Inc. Denig was also a Philadelphia developer who had close connections to U.S. House Speaker Bright. Rep. Bright told reporters at a press conference that "All of my investments are held in a blind trust. I have never met, nor do I have any knowledge of Carson Denig."

A senior Burmese spiritual leader stated that "Buddha has protected the Golden Pagoda once again. Neither man nor nature can take the legend from us." The Shwedagon pagoda now rises once again to 326 feet above its base just as it did before the daring midnight attack on the holy shrine last week. According to legend, the 2,500-year-old glittering golden pagoda has been rebuilt many times after being damaged by earthquakes.

On Friday morning, Lenny received an unexpected call at the office. "Hello," he said.

"Dr. Cramer, you've been trying to get in touch with me. My name is Carson Denig. I'm returning your call."

Lenny was dumbfounded. "Denig? I thought you were dead. They found your body in the ... Wait a minute. There were four people in the helicopter. The newspaper only reported three dead and that you were one of them. How'd they get it wrong?"

"They didn't. And it is best that I remain dead. This way, once Dana testifies against me, she will probably get a lighter sentence and earlier parole. I suggest you immediately forget this conversation. Understood?"

"How do I know you are Carson Denig?" Lenny asked.

"Suppose I told you that I could have easily killed you with the laser while you were hiding behind the prayer pillar. Remember the soldier who ducked beside you and Dana?"

Lenny swallowed hard. Seconds passed before he regained his composure and asked, "Denig, was it worth destroying a religious shrine, killing an accounting professor, and slaughtering an innocent monk?"

"That's why I'm returning your call. I want to be very clear, I had nothing to do with the Russell's Viper. That was all Frank's doing. So, if you wish to avenge your friend's death, look to Frank and not me."

"I'm curious, Mr. Denig. How much were the stolen gems worth? I'm sure you've been able to find buyers for them."

Carson cackled. "I should have known better. If the Emerald Buddha in Bangkok is really made from jade, shouldn't I have expected similar fakes on the Shwedagon Pagoda?"

"What do you mean?" Lenny exclaimed.

"There were *no* jewels on the precious pagoda. If I were a cynic, I'd say the same is true of the original Buddha hairs over which the shrine is built. It's all a hoax!"

"What happened to them?"

"Who knows? There was a minor earthquake in 1970, and the pagoda was clad in bamboo scaffolding while it was being refurbished. The socialist government could have easily replaced the real jewels with fakes at that time."

"The very top of the *stupa*, the Diamond Bud section, it has a 76-carat diamond in the center of it. Surely that did not just disappear?" Lenny questioned.

"Here me out, Lenny. I did a little research on that. The English Dresden is a 76.5-carat pear-shaped diamond that apparently is in India now. Remember, the British were in Burma and occupied the pagoda for two years after the First Anglo-Burmese War in 1824.

Then in 1852 the British took and pillaged the pagoda for 77 years until 1929. The English Dresden was discovered in 1957."

"So, you think the British were involved," repeated Lenny.

Carson continued, "The Sierra Leone diamond was cut from a 75-carat crystal found in Sierra Leone in 1959. It was eventually cut into a 32.12-carat pear-shaped gem. Then there's the Nepal Pink, a 72-carat, old Indian-cut, rose-pink colored diamond seen in Nepal in 1959. The present ownership is unknown. Of course, General Ne Win took control of Burma in 1958. He had a 40-year window of opportunity to swap out the stones from 1958 until 1998 when his influence began to wane."

"Okay, what you're saying is, it's possible that the gems have been gone for many years." Lenny thought about that for a moment. "Nah, I'm not sure I buy your story, but what do I know? I'm not the one with the jewels. Denig, just curious. How did you escape?"

"Luck. We lowered the pagoda into a ravine, and I went down to check on the gems. A Myanmar military helicopter spotted our chopper and started chasing it. Apparently, the copter crashed, and my three assistants died. I immediately began to dig out the stones. What a major disappointment! Most of them were zircons, garnets, quartz, glass, and junk. I swear on all that's holy, someone else robbed the Shwedagon Pagoda, Lenny Cramer. It could have been the British. It could have been General Ne Win and his military junta thugs. But I can tell you this for sure, it wasn't me. Honest to God."

"Ok, Denig. Not that I believe you, but what are you going to do now?"

"Assume a new identity. I'll survive. SEALs always do. By the way, Lenny, if you haven't figured it out by now, you should know that Dana has grown very fond of you and Rebecca. A word of advice, Dr. Cramer: Do not try to find me. You'll only make things worse for Dana." The line went dead.

Lenny respected Denig's frankness but abhorred everything else about the man. And though he had every reason in the world to hate Dana for betraying his trust so completely, he couldn't bring himself to make her life even more miserable. He had been made a fool before and revenge would not plug the hole in his heart or help him explain to Rebecca how some people are not trustworthy. Life was not always black and white. Lenny knew that no matter how much he was hurt, cruelty and vengeance had no place in his world, or the world he envisioned for his daughter.

Myanmar, the exotic, the golden land, had been transformative, in one respect: Making tough decisions was now beginning to be second nature for him. No more indecisive wavering. He had become eminently resolute. And he did not equivocate on this important decision.

Lenny would *not* try to locate Carson Denig.

———————

Adequate documents and records are parts of internal control. They include invoices, receipts, checks, and the accounting journals. All documents should be pre-numbered to ensure that no document is missing. Pre-numbered sales invoices discourage theft by cashiers or the sales staff. The total cash collected should be checked against the cash shown as collected on the sales invoices. If sales invoices are not pre-numbered, the cashier could destroy the receipt and steal the cash.

—Alan Campbell and Michael Flores

Other Novels by Larry Crumbley

- Ultimate Rip-Off: A Taxing Tale, 5th edition, 2012, Carolina Academic Press, 919-489-7486; Fax 919-493-5668, $28.00.
- Trap Doors and Trojan Horses: An Auditing Action Adventure, Carolina Academic Press, 919-489-7486; Fax 919-493-5668.
- Costly Reflections in a Midas Mirror, 4th edition, 2019, (cost/managerial accounting), Carolina Academic Press, 919-489-7486; Fax 919-493-5668, $25.00.
- The Big R: A Forensic Accounting Action Adventure, 3rd, 2014, Carolina Academic Press, 919-489-7486; Fax 919-493-5668. $29.00.
- Dangerous Hoops: A Forensic Marketing Action Adventure, Baton Rouge: LSU Press, 2011.
- The Bottom Line is Betrayal: An International Business Action Adventure (general business), 7th, 2014, $27.00.
- Deadly Art Puzzle: An Advanced Accounting Action Adventure, 2nd forthcoming, Carolina Academic Press.

Fortune, June 29, 1991, quoted Crumbley: "to be a good accountant, you have to be a good detective," and called his latest novel an "instructional thriller." Crumbley appeared on the front cover of the December 1988 issue of *Management Accounting* as a bespectacled Mickey Spillane. Kathy Williams, author of *The Case of the Purloined Pagoda* said to "move over Arthur Hailey." *WG&L Accounting News* compared Crumbley to Indiana Jones. The sometime fedora-donned Crumbley in trench coat could be the John D. MacDonald in the accounting arena with thirteen academic novels under his belt.

David Albrecht said the Golden Spire "is entertaining, and as satisfying as many Hollywood movies. This is not a dull, dry book. It deals with a fraud investigation. Of course, there's the original fraud. Then there's the framing of the fraud investigator, the framing of the fraud originator (by another bad guy), and how the fraud investigator figures it all out. And, it is competently written. The plot has twists and turns, most of which I was unable to see coming."